FRANK MCKINNEY'S
MAVERICK
APPROACH TO
REAL ESTATE
SUCCESS

FRANK McKINNEY'S
MAVERICK
APPROACH TO
REAL ESTATE
SUCCESS

How You Can Go
from a $50,000 Fixer-Upper
to a $100 Million Mansion

Frank McKinney
with Victoria St. George

WILEY

John Wiley & Sons, Inc.

Published by John Wiley & Sons, Inc., Hoboken, New Jersey.
Published simultaneously in Canada.

For general information on our other products and services or for technical support, please contact our Customer Care Department within the United States at (800) 762-2974, outside the United States at (317) 572-3993 or fax (317) 572-4002.

Wiley also publishes its books in a variety of electronic formats. Some content that appears in print may not be available in electronic books. For more information about Wiley products, visit our web site at www.wiley.com.

Library of Congress Cataloging-in-Publication Data:

McKinney, Frank, 1963–
    Frank McKinney's Maverick Approach to Real Estate Success : How You Can Go from a $50,000 Fixer-Upper to a $100 Million Mansion/ Frank McKinney with Victoria St. George.
        p. cm.
    ISBN-13: 978-0-471-73715-5 (pbk.)
    ISBN-10: 0-471-73715-1 (pbk.)
        1. Real estate investment—United States. I. Title. II. Title: Maverick approach to real estate success.
    HD255.M373 2005
    332.63'243—dc22

                                                    2005026193

Printed in the United States of America.

10 9 8 7 6 5 4 3 2 1

*To the many desperately homeless people throughout the world
whom we have been blessed with touching
via our Caring House Project Foundation.
You will never know the profound impact you have had
on my purpose for writing this book and for living.*

CONTENTS

ACKNOWLEDGMENTS

My best seller, *Make It BIG! 49 Secrets for Building a Life of Extreme Success*, represents more of a philosophical approach to succeeding in the business of life.

The anticipated success of that book was acknowledged by recognizing those who were influential in shaping my life, as well as what followed between the pages of *Make It BIG!*, beginning with certain grade school teachers, on through to those responsible for the publishing of the material contained in *Make It BIG!*

Frank McKinney's Maverick Approach to Real Estate Success—How You Can Go from a $50,000 Fixer-Upper to a $100 Million Mansion is all about real estate. On May 19, 1986, we began with the renovation of our first $50,000 starter home. Now, as of the time of this printing, we are designing and creating from the ground up the world's most opulent spec home with an asking price well above $125 million.

In the space allotted I am honored to take the time to acknowledge those who have helped me create markets over the past 20 years. Some of you are no longer with me, others no longer with us. It is important to note that all of this began a little more than four years after I graduated from my fourth high school in four years with a cumulative 1.8 GPA. So rest assured that there are many who contributed to the past 20 years. What you are about to read was not supposed to happen.

This book is a celebration of 20 years of making real estate markets where they never existed before, and I wish to express my gratitude to all the people who contributed to our success. Since this book is already too long by thousands of words, I am forced to keep my acknowledgments on the short side—a difficult task with 20 years to reflect and draw upon. There are many who contributed to our achievements, far more than will be acknowledged. For those omitted, you know who you are and what role you played. Forgive me for not mentioning you, and thank you for your patience and trust.

I feel compelled to start with those who influenced me to get into real estate in the first place. I want to begin by thanking my late father, Frank E. McKinney Jr., who passed away in a plane crash on 9/11; not the 9/11 you know, but the McKinney family's 9/11—September 11, 1992. My dad had a tough outer shell that concealed a sensitive and loving soul. He was a driven man, a very successful bank executive and three-time Olympic medalist (gold, silver, and bronze) in swimming. Growing up as a troubled teenager, I don't remember much from my father's many lectures and heated discussions about my behavior, but I do remember him telling me that 97 percent of my character was perfect; it was the other 3 percent that continued to be my downfall. In helping me identify what that 3 percent was (and we all have it, by the way), he helped guide me toward real estate without ever mentioning the words.

When I moved to Florida in 1982, wanting to leave my troubled years behind and become a responsible young man, I thought I might want to be a banker like my father. We were polar opposites, but nonetheless I would share this idea with him from time to time before I left home. I am now about the age he was when he started to subliminally discourage me from following in his footsteps, and I find it hard to comprehend how unselfish he was. After all, he had followed his father's footsteps; I was Frank III; it would have been completely normal for a father to encourage his son to stay in the family business. But he didn't. He'd say, "Mickey, there's no money in banking and too much structure. You're better off creating something where you can express yourself without the conservatism required of a banker." With only a few words on many occasions, he encouraged me to seek my highest calling outside of the norm, and that's what I have done. Thanks, Dad.

My mom always believed that God and a contingent of guardian angels who worked in shifts around the clock were watching over her son. She used to call me the "miracle child" when I began to succeed in real estate. These were not miracles, only God answering the prayers from one of only a few living saints that I know—my mom. Neither she nor my father was disappointed that I didn't pursue college. They let me find my own way without road-mapping my formative years. It was my mom's early belief in me, and her patience with certain phases that we encounter as we grow, that allowed me to find my highest calling in real estate so early.

My wife, Nilsa, and I have been together almost the entire time I've been in real estate, and her parents, Laura and Ernesto Colon, and Nilsa's brother, Erik, and his wife, Nicole, have been there for nearly my entire career. They're family. We've spent many nights around the holiday dinner table laughing at the pranks (think wisdom teeth) that could only take place between family members who love each other.

While my entire family (four sisters and a brother) has been involved in my real estate career, my brother, Bob, has played an important role in helping navigate all the challenges and successes of those years. Bob is 10 years younger and has been a part of all my creations. Before he was a teenager, he would visit from Indiana and sit at the early $50,000 open houses with me. We'd toss the football in the front yard while we waited for potential buyers. Bob is now a very successful real estate developer and broker in Indiana, and he has lent significant input to the creation of our nine-figure spec home. Thanks, "Chook," for never letting me lose the little boy inside. (Now everybody will call him "Chook." What are older brothers for?)

Speaking of older brothers, I am the oldest of six children, and my thanks would not be complete without acknowledging my four sisters, Martie (who made $50,000 on her first real estate deal), Marlen (whose equity in her home has tripled), Madeleine (I wish I had her demeanor), and Heather, my little sister, who is just now buying her first house. Thanks, sisters, for helping me when I was starting out.

I want to thank all of the lead handymen and subsequent general contractors who have worked with me or my companies. I haven't heard from many of these men in years, but it was they who taught me the nuts and bolts of building. Rueben (Bud) Bishop, who was my first handyman, Bennie Moreno, Ron Sofield, Mark Schwartz, Roger Jacques, Jim Kleen, Dave Farrow, John Kilheeney, Greg Linder, Bob Berry, and John DiDonna—I haven't forgotten about any of you. I know I was (or am) difficult to work for sometimes, but the Frank McKinney Way was not designed to come easy, and I want you to be proud of our results.

I've had many great employees who do their jobs far better than I ever could. Some have moved on; others are still with me. The support of Mark Bernardi, my personal assistant, has allowed me to write this book, make many speaking appearances, and still have plenty of time for my true passion—real estate. Lori Tanner, our internal operations manager, not only keeps all of our books straight but is responsible for keeping the Frank McKinney Way in the forefront of our clients' minds long after our mansions have sold. I also want to thank Ray Ferrera, our project manager. While he is no longer with us (but I will get him back), he held the longest tenure of employment at Frank McKinney & Company and helped grow this company into what it is today.

Still others have helped shape the character behind the career; they might not have been directly involved, but they certainly provided guidance. Rich DeVos is one of a few living heroes of mine—if only I can retain what I have witnessed in him and live my life more like his. Donald Trump has been kind enough to endorse my books and mention me in his. Donald has influenced much about my career, and I want to thank him for providing such meaningful and lasting influence. My very good friend Peter Blum has become kind of a surrogate father for me. He sets a wonderful life example for me to try to follow. I enjoy our lunches together. There also are a few fictional characters who I want to thank for their influence on my career, those being Robin Hood and Willy Wonka.

Many of the clients who have purchased our estate homes over the years have turned into great friends. Some I can mention only by first name out of respect for their privacy, like Dan, Malcolm, Alfred, Peter (two Peters), Cynthia, Jack, Janet, Daniel, Charles, Victoria, and Tom. Others have provided a kind of mentorship where I was fortunate to learn the inner workings of a successful person's mind. Many of these men and women helped me make each project better than the last. They include George and Sandy Valassis, Tom Melone, Jeff Levitetz, John Ferber, and Joe Edelman, to name a few. Even those who haven't purchased but provided valuable feedback, I thank you for taking the time.

Many real estate brokers and other professionals who have worked in our marketplaces have helped build our success almost from the beginning. Brokers such as Jack DeNiro, Randy Ely, Clark French, Cathy Jorgens, and their associates provided valuable early input. Our current brokerage, Premier Estate Properties, has been making markets with us for the past five years. Joe, Gerry, Pat and Laura Liguori, and Carmen D'Angelo are the best. They do things the right way, the Frank McKinney Way, and I'm delighted that they will be selling our nine-figure home, among our other offerings.

I don't like the negativity and sensationalism that permeates the airwaves and print media. Often I avoid this useless drain in favor of my own reality. However, I want to thank all the members of the media who have sprinkled my story around the world over the years. Not all features were glowing, but I'd like to think most provided the viewer, listener, or reader with entertainment, curiosity, and a call to action in their lives and perhaps in the lives of others.

Cooperation between government and private enterprise must take place for free enterprise to work. In the case of construction, whether it's on the ocean or inland, this relationship is critical. There are so many individuals from the cities where we have had the privilege of working, yet I only have room to thank Mary McCarty, Tom Lynch, Jay Alperin, David Schmidt, Jeff Perlman, Alberta McCarthy, Lula Butler, George Diaz, Jerry Sanzone, Susan Ruby, Brian Shutt, Bill Benjamin, Basil Diamond, Tom Gerrard, Kelly Gotleib, Tom Thorton, Tom Coffman, Tony Mauro, Greg Dunham, Trela White, Dick Schofield, Karen Hancsak, Jan Moore, Lisa Peterson, Mark Hull, and all the others from the building departments of the various coastal municipalities. You helped guide many of our projects through to success, both for us and for the cities in which they were created.

If it weren't for the vision and foresight of our bankers and those who provide our financing there would have been no year two in my career, let alone 20. I've had a 24-year relationship with Bank of

America, and special thanks go to Joe Silk, Maxie Washington, Victoria Rixon, Jim Gallagher, Bruce Allen, Scott Shealy, Sam Fisher, Chris Willis, Chris Gialanella, Bryan Joyner, Dorothy Payne, Lauren Chaney, Lynn Parker, and many others, for working so far outside of the box that we decided a few years ago to throw it away completely! Now that is hard for bankers to do, so to all those at Bank of America I thank you for your trust and confidence in me.

I've had a 16-year relationship with some of the greatest, most competent lawyers in the country. I enjoy a closeness with Scott Elk, our transactional and real estate lawyer, and I look forward to seeing him because it means we're either buying an opportunity or selling one. Scott's partners, Eric Christu and Devon Coughlin, protect us, defend us, and if necessary represent our role as plaintiff, and they do so with great success. I also want to thank another partner at the firm, our estate planning attorney, Adam Bankier, for taking care of things so well that when I go to the big mansion in the sky, all of my loved ones and our charity will be well cared for. I want to thank all of the junior partners, associates, paralegals, bookkeepers, and secretaries at Elk, Bankier, Christu & Bakst.

A quick thank-you to Northwood University and to its president, Dr. David Fry, and the provost of the Palm Beach campus, Dr. John Haynie. They supported my first book, *Make It BIG!*, appointed me to a seat on the board of governors, and bestowed me with an honorary doctorate degree. It was nice to finally be able share with my family my college degree, especially this one, as it took nearly 20 years to obtain! I enjoy my interaction with my fellow board of governors as well as the young men and women on the three Northwood campuses. Northwood is the absolute best business school in the country, where students can go to learn the importance of free enterprise, then implement the privilege upon graduation. You may not have heard of Northwood, but remember, there were perhaps few who had heard of Harvard after its first 25 years of existence.

During a time when my understanding of the passage in the Bible, "To whom much is given, much will be asked," was becoming clearer I decided that, in addition to sharing our blessings from the sales of our estate homes, I was going to direct all proceeds earned outside of real estate from my appearances, book royalties, and related offerings to our Caring House Project Foundation (caringhouse-projectfoundation.org). I founded the Caring House Project Foundation (CHPF) in 1998, and it earned 501(c3) status in early 2002. The CHPF's mission statement reads: "The Caring House Project Foundation's primary objective is to provide housing, food, and medical support for the desperately homeless around the world, particularly in South America, Indonesia, the Caribbean, and in the United States of America." In 2004 and 2005 the CHPF provided shelter for 1,824 desperately homeless people, and more than 95 percent of all monies donated went directly to those who needed assistance.

As the CHPF grew, it became clear that Nilsa and I could not run the foundation without competent guidance and support. Where would we be without our board of directors, the men and women who see to it that thousands of lives are touched through the angelic hearts of those who give to the CHPF? I would like to thank board members Pam Cahoon, Paola Fernandez Rana, Marti Forman, Gint Raciunas, Ezra Kreig, Dennis Moran, Mike Magi, Gladys Whigham, Commissioner Addie Green, Sheila Smith, Nilsa McKinney, Robert McKinney, and Scott Elk for understanding the joy that comes from sharing one's blessings by serving. While not a board member, Marlene Green is the foundation's part-time director of development and marketing, and her expertise has brought us beyond our previous limitations. I also wish to acknowledge all who have donated to the Caring House Project Foundation, including you who purchased this book. I want all of you to feel good when you lay your head on the pillow tonight, because through your generosity you have brightened the life of one of God's children.

I have been fortunate to be invited to appear and speak for many great organizations all over the country, and a few hosts have been extremely generous in their direct support of the CHPF. I want to thank Robyn Thompson (the queen of rehabs), who has been responsible for more than $200,000 in donations to CHPF, Angel Aloma, Jeff and Sophia Kaller, Jane Wilcox, David Dweck, Michael Masterson, Justin Ford, Juan and Sharon Restrepo, Mike Kiel, Dwan Bent-Twyford, Amy Witt, Bill Twyford, Wendy Patton, Jan Shoonbridge, Sherman Ragland, Diana Rainoff, Cameron Dunlap, Bonnie Stelzer, Bob Burns, Mike Litman (responsible for more than

$100,000 in donations), John Assaraf, Alex Gajano, Stephen and Alicia Pierce, and many more.

In 2005 I participated in the Badwater Ultramarathon to raise awareness and money for the CHPF. The invitation-only Badwater Ultramarathon is recognized globally as the single toughest foot race in the world. It starts in the Death Valley desert in July at the lowest point in the Western Hemisphere (elevation 282 feet below sea level) and finishes 135 miles later, high on Mt. Whitney (elevation 8,500 feet above sea level). Badwater tests the athlete's stamina and will against a brutal stretch of scorching hot highway—a hellish environment of more than 130 degrees, with pavement temperatures as high as 200 degrees. There are no aid stations, and all 80 racers must provide their own support and crew. If it weren't for my crew—Jay Batchen, my primary pacer, Nilsa, who was on the course the entire time, Mary Kashurba, who paced and aided with medical, Joe Kashurba, her sixteen-year-old son, who was just amazing and served as our videographer, Mike Magi, who paced and made my supplement drinks, and Mark Bernardi, who drove and prepared drinks—I never would have made it. I want to thank Marshall Ulrich; while Marshall was not on our crew, he lays down Marshall Law when it comes to the triple crown of adventure racing. Nobody has accomplished more. His insight helped get me to the finish line. A special thanks goes to my coach, Lisa Smith-Batchen, who sacrificed much over the months leading up to the race in order to see me to the start line, and who talked me through some of my lowest points during the race over the satellite phone.

I'm not sure my success over the last few years would have been as significant if it wasn't for Mike Hamilton, my first editor at John Wiley & Sons, Inc., who took a chance on my first book, *Make It BIG! 49 Secrets for Living a Life of Extreme Success*. This book helped establish us as more of a brand name in ultra-high-end real estate. Now the thanks go to Laurie Harting, my new editor at Wiley. Laurie helped me realize why I love real estate so much and why it is important that I share my knowledge with you. Of course when you graduate high school with a 1.8 GPA (grade point average) a great ghostwriter is a must. Victoria St. George of Just Write plowed through more than 1,000 pages of material to help me create this work. Without her writing and editing expertise this book would have been hundreds of pages longer than even the longest Harry Potter book! I also want to thank my personal publicist for this book, Jessica Jonap, and our public relations firm Pierson Grant, Jane Grant, and Maria Pierson for helping spread the good news with so much passion.

Finally, my thanks and eternal gratitude go to my very reason for living—my wife, Nilsa, and my daughter, Laura (aka "Ppeekk," pronounced "Peekey"). I disagree with the statement "behind every successful man is a strong woman"; in my case it should read "beside," not behind. Nilsa and I have been together since August 5, 1987. We were married on September 3, 1990. (Notice what has happened to my real estate career since those dates?) While I may be the public face, Nilsa is the strength. Our estate homes are beautiful because of her interior design talent. She can run the companies without me (and often does). Let this be a good lesson to anyone who wants to succeed in real estate, or in any other career for that matter: Your spouse will be a significant contributor to your success or otherwise. I've been fortunate to have had Nilsa along for nearly the entire 20-year ride. Honey, I hope you've enjoyed the circus. I'm certainly blessed to have such a loving and caring wife.

I close my acknowledgments with my little girl, Laura. I have a framed picture on my desk of Peek reading *Make It BIG!* when she was six years old. She is now seven and wants to know what I am going to say about her in my second book, as she was quick to find the references to her in the first. My hope is that one day she will look back on her father's career and life and be proud of who he was and what he did for those less fortunate.

I cherish the times we go to the houses I have built, and she walks through with me and tweaks everything to make sure it shows well. Not long ago she noticed a sick fish in one of our elaborate fish tanks. We brought this to the attention of the fish person who, upon diagnosis, told us we were fortunate to have discovered the illness early, as all the fish would have died if the sick fish hadn't received treatment. Now, as we are designing our nine-figure spec home, Peek and I will walk the proposed oceanfront site with a blank piece of paper and she will proceed to describe the layout of the house and what rooms and amenities belong where. After our tour we will go and get a Slurpee from 7-Eleven, like always.

I walk my daughter to school every day. Since she was four years old in pre-kindergarten and for the past four years, rain or shine, we have walked together, hand in hand, for the most important 15 minutes of my day. We have yet to drive even once. We always pick up a rock or shell during our walk. We have a large collection of these keepsakes (more than 500), and one day we'll make something special out of those rocks and shells. These times are so precious because she is precious. She fills my heart with the warmth only a parent can know. I love you, Ppeekk.

INTRODUCTION
Twenty Minutes
Equals Twenty Years

I magine you're one of about 50 fortunate people who have come to the beautiful Gold Coast of Florida for a rare weekend gathering called "Frank McKinney's Succeeding in the Business of Life Experience." You're going to learn from someone who has earned a reputation as the "maverick" king of high-end, speculative real estate. He was dubbed "the real estate rock czar" by the *Wall Street Journal*, and his latest ultra-luxurious masterpiece was on the market for $50 million. You've been told that you'll receive personal success coaching from the man who has defined new levels of splendor when it comes to the creation of multimillion-dollar, custom-built oceanfront mansions. You're expecting to spend three days in the lap of luxury, learning real estate secrets that will help you, too, make millions.

You drive from the Palm Beach Airport down South Ocean Boulevard (State Road A1A) toward the beach communities of Palm Beach, Manalapan, Boca Raton, and Delray Beach, following the map you've been given, and arrive at—what? Instead of an opulent oceanfront mega-mansion behind imposing gates and surrounded by lush trees and flowering vegetation, you see a small, modest, one-bedroom house in a mediocre section of town, with card tables set up in a tiny front yard. It's about 96 degrees and 96 percent humidity—a typical Florida spring day—and as soon as you step out of your car, you're drowned in sweat. You're thinking, "Where am I? And what in the world have I gotten myself into? This house can't be more than 800 square feet!"

The real estate king is nowhere in sight, but there's a gentleman wearing a polo shirt with Frank McKinney & Company embroidered on the breast pocket. He waves you over and checks off your name on a list. "Welcome!" he says. "Please have a seat in the bus parked at the end of the street. We'll be leaving shortly."

"Where's Frank? Where's the $50 million house?" you ask.

The man smiles. "Frank will join us later. Hop on the bus—it's air-conditioned and you'll be more comfortable."

At that point, you'll do almost anything to get cool. You take another look at the house in front of you. It's modest, sure, but it's well built and attractive and looks as if it's been cared for by the owners. But why were you told to meet here? Certainly this house could have no relation to the Real Estate Rock Czar. You're full of unanswered questions as you walk down the block and climb onto the bus. Most of the seats are already full of people chatting with each other. From the buzz it seems that no one else has any more idea of the plan than you do. You sit next to a gentleman and start getting acquainted. He, too, is wondering what in the world is going on.

In the next 10 minutes five more people, all of them sweaty and confused, board the bus and take the remaining seats. Then the driver of the bus gets on, followed by the man in the polo shirt. "We're ready to leave now," he says. "For those who don't know me, I'm Robert McKinney, Frank's younger brother. I've been working with him for the last 20 years on a number of his projects, and he's asked me to lead the first part of this experience.

"You're here to discover what it takes to become as successful as Frank has been in real estate. You may have heard Frank speak about his secrets of building a life of extreme success. You probably read his first best seller, *Make It BIG!*, and you want to have a world-class real estate tycoon as your role model and mentor. Well, you're about to enter a time capsule. We'll be driving by many of the houses and markets Frank has created. It will take us approximately 20 minutes to drive from Frank's first $50,000 fixer-upper to his $50 million mansion. *Each minute of our trip represents a year of Frank's 20-year career in real estate.* Think about that as we ride along."

The bus pulls out as Robert points down the street. "The house where we started our tour was the first residence Frank constructed as part of his Caring House Project Foundation. He built it for Buster, a homeless man whom Frank met while feeding the homeless from the back of a truck in Delray Beach. As you know, your fee for this weekend was a donation to the Caring House Project Foundation, most of which will go to build critically needed housing in one of the world's poorest countries—Haiti. It takes only $4,000 to build a concrete home there for a family of eight who never have lived in a house before."

As you are driven through the streets of Palm Beach County, Robert acts as tour guide, describing several homes in neighborhoods that range from middle class upward. "There's the very first house Frank bought for $36,000 in 1986. It was falling down and the neighborhood was really bad—drug dealers, drive-by shootings. Frank saved $30,000 working as a tennis pro to buy that house and renovate it. He sold it after six months for $50,000, making a $7,000 profit. That was his first big real estate deal." Bob grins. "By the way, the same man who bought that house from Frank 20 years ago still lives there. The neighborhood's come up quite a bit—comparable houses in the same block are now selling for over $150,000."

The bus enters a slightly better neighborhood. "This is Bankers Row," Robert says. "Frank bought and renovated five houses along this street, making profits of $20,000 to $40,000 or more on each. See that house with the fountain? That's where Frank and Nilsa were married. They bought it for $75,000 in 1989. It has a guest house and wonderful architectural details throughout, including an original 1920s fountain in the front courtyard. That house recently sold for $1.7 million."

The bus turns toward the ocean, and Robert points out a lovely, uniquely styled home on the water. "That's Driftwood Dunes, the first piece of oceanfront real estate Frank ever bought. He'd been buying, renovating, building, and selling less expensive real estate for six years, doing well on every deal and building up his net worth. He bought the oceanfront property for $775,000. To cover the purchase price and the capital needed to rebuild the house according to his vision, Frank had to sell everything, including his own home, his car, and even some of his clothes. He and Nilsa lived in a studio apartment for four years so he could put every dime into the renovations. He sold Driftwood Dunes in

1994 for $1.9 million. Since then, Frank has invested only in the finest direct oceanfront properties in Palm Beach County."

This is more like it! You settle back in your seat as the bus travels down A1A, the only road along this stretch of Florida's Atlantic coast. You crane your neck to see one magnificent mansion after another as Robert ticks them off: "That's Chateau d'Amoureaux, a 12,000-square-foot oceanfront estate done in the style of a French chateau. Frank renovated it extensively and sold it for almost $6 million in 1996. There's La Marceaux, the first oceanfront property Frank designed and built from the ground up, also in the French style. It's 23,000 square feet and has a two-story-high living room, a 3,000-square-foot master suite, room for six cars in the garage, its own private beach, and a replica of the Oval Office. That sold for $12 million in 1998. There's the piece of oceanfront land that Frank sold for $27 million. He was going to build two houses on it but the land deal was too good to pass up. By the way, most of the estates that Frank renovated or built have more than doubled or even tripled in value since he initially sold them. We'll see two of his latest estates tomorrow. We just closed on both of them, for $7 million and $17 million, respectively. They were on the market for less than 90 days."

"What's the average time on the market for these kind of properties?" someone asks.

"Fifteen *months*," Robert answers. If you weren't impressed before, you're impressed now. Selling two multimillion-dollar properties in less than two months? How could Frank do it?

The bus pulls through security gates into a driveway that looks as you had always pictured it would: tall palm trees arching overhead, lush green foliage interspersed with colorful flowers along the roadside, a slight mist in the air that lowers the temperature a couple of degrees immediately. Down a slight incline to the right you see a full-sized tennis court surrounded by greenery. The bus parks next to the 12-car garage and you get out. The massive wooden front door is open and you look through it into the two-story living room with its floor-to-ceiling windows and magnificent view of a vast stretch of white sand Florida beach. To your left is a two-story guest house next to a hand-built rock wall. Cascading over the rocks is a waterfall that drops directly into a beautiful swimming pool. Every inch of the property around the pool, guest house, and house is landscaped with exotic foliage flowers and plants that provide the perfect setting for this magnificent estate.

As the group walks toward the front door, you ask Bob McKinney, "How much is this place worth?"

"Actually, Frank created and sold this estate in 2000 for $30 million," Bob replies. "He bought it back in 2004 and sold it again with an asking price of $50 million. Values have gone up that much in the last few years. But remember where we started? Twenty years ago Frank bought his first house for $36,000 and sold it for a $7,000 profit. That was a $50,000 house at the time. Now Frank's houses sell for $50 million and he's planning one that will sell for more than $125 million. But it's taken 20 years of taking risks and a lot of hard work for him to get to this high level. Now, we have iced tea and lemonade set up around the pool—please help yourself."

The journey these 50 people took is the same one I hope you will take with me through the course of this book. It's a journey I've been proud and humbled to take; it has provided a good life for my family, created beautiful homes for people to live in, and helped me build housing for homeless people in the United States and some of the poorest countries in the world. It's allowed me to become an artist and to stretch myself every single day. And in recent years, it's given me the privilege of sharing my journey with others so they can achieve success in real estate and, more important, in the business of life.

My first best seller, *Make It BIG! 49 Secrets for Building a Life of Extreme Success*, described the habits, traits, beliefs, and philosophies that have made me who I am today. (You can see more at www.frank-mckinney.com.) Over the past 20 years, I have spoken to people in hundreds of companies, business organizations, real estate investment clubs, nonprofit groups, schools, and social organizations. All of them questioned me intensely on the specifics of my career. How did I locate properties? How did I find financing? How did I buy? How did I sell? How did I risk? How did I succeed while still doing it my way? As I answered their questions, I began to realize that I had never done what the pros say is important when it comes to real estate. Instead, I'd done it my own way, and that difference helped me succeed at the highest possible level. I decided it was time to describe my own unique approach to real estate—not just the techniques but also the psychology, because I've found that what's inside your head (and the minds of your buyers and sellers) has just as much impact on your success as what's on the bottom line of a contract or closing statement. This book is the summary of my 20 years of real estate—the highs and the lows of the journey from $50,000 fixer-uppers to $100 million oceanfront estates.

If you're reading this book, I assume that you are interested in real estate as a potential investment vehicle. Like people who attend my Experiences and speeches, you're ready to hop onto the real estate bandwagon; or perhaps you've already bought one or more properties and would like to move up. Perhaps you've made some money, perhaps you've lost some, or perhaps you've been too fearful and intimidated by the complexities of real estate to do much more than open the newspaper on the weekends and dream. If so, relax—what you'll learn from this book is designed to help anyone find profitable deals that lead to a greater net worth and financial abundance.

My goals for you on this journey are threefold. First, I'd like to encourage you to take the leap into investing in real estate. Exercise that risk threshold! Real estate has been my profession for more than 20 years (I am 42 now) and it has given me a wonderful career while supporting my family. As you'll read in later chapters, real estate creates consistent wealth for more people than any other investment. I believe it also can be more satisfying than almost any other investment opportunity. After all, you can't put your hands on a stock portfolio or other intangible investment the way you can on a piece of real estate you're building, renovating, buying, or selling. And you have greater control over the value of your real estate than you ever do with stocks, bonds or other investments.

Second, I'd like you to be realistic about what it will take for you to succeed in real estate investing. While you can make very good money in any one transaction, building true success will take time, money, energy, and focus. Over the course of my career I've sold homes at many different price points to buyers ranging from first-time home owners in up-and-coming neighborhoods to billionaires looking for the absolute best in oceanfront property. I've spent 20 years in the trenches, honing my skills and intuitions, and enjoyed every minute of the journey, but it's hard work. When I sell an estate today, yes, I do have a multimillion-dollar payday, but that's a reflection of hundreds of deals with much smaller profits and thousands of hours of research, design, and physical, mental, and emotional investment. I wrote this book so you could shorten your learning curve by benefiting from my years making markets where none had existed before, but you'll still have to put in the time, energy, and effort to succeed. So if you're looking for the latest get rich quick scheme, buy another book and good luck to you. If you want to learn how to build your net worth through creating value in real estate, then keep reading.

Third, you must be willing to be a Maverick. In my real estate career I've never done things the expected way, because I found that the way it's usually done was either inefficient or ineffective. Instead, I've taken the road of high risk, high visibility, and high reward. People have told me I'd never succeed, and I've loved proving them wrong by changing the mind of fate itself. The title of Maverick is one I wear with pride, because to me it means finding and taking your own road, going against conventional wisdom, and doing what *really* works. Today I'm considered a visionary, an innovator, an artist whose canvases are the sun-drenched beaches of Florida's Atlantic coast. But I'm still a Maverick, and I hope to be until the day I die. This book is designed to teach you, too, to go against the grain and discover the Maverick way of creating your own real estate fortune. The principles I use are simple, clear, and directly applicable for any kind of real estate property from $50,000 and up. They've been proven to work with one home or one hundred. I have shared these precepts with beginning investors who are now well on their way to creating wealth through real estate. And I believe you will find the Maverick approach can be your key to wealth as well.

The 20 years I've spent in real estate have taught me a lot—not just about what it takes to build wealth and to be successful, but also about how much it means to any family when they walk into a house they can call their own. It's also taught me the value of sharing your blessings with others. This book is part of my commitment to share with others the blessings of my life by helping people step into a brighter future, whether it be with a new home, or a new or better career as a real estate investor. My hope for you is that by reading this book, following its precepts, and using them as a jumping-off point as you build your net worth by investing in real estate, you, too, will become a Maverick success and can share your blessings as well.

One of our first $50,000 fixer-uppers, circa 1986.

1

From $50,000 to $100 Million: Why the Maverick Approach Works

I still remember writing the check for my very first real estate deal in 1986. It was for $36,000, representing $30,000 that I had saved as a tennis pro and the balance that I had borrowed from my tennis students and a few friends. I had spent six months studying the niche I had decided to focus on: distressed single-family homes in Palm Beach County, Florida. I had gotten my real estate license and put a lot of time into choosing exactly the kind of properties I would focus on in my new career. I had a burning desire to get into what I believed could be my ticket to success. Strange that my ticket would be a decrepit, foreclosed, graffiti-covered wreck in a bad part of town! But in that $36,000 foreclosure were the seeds of the multimillion-dollar deals that form the basis of my professional life today.

If you've ever seen me or read my first book, you know my approach to life is considered somewhat unorthodox. I guess I've always been a bit of a rebel. I left my family's home in Indianapolis, Indiana, at age 18 to make my own way in Florida. I never attended college. At age 19 I developed a successful business as a tennis pro, grossing more than $100,000 a year, and then set my sights on a more lucrative career in real estate. I wanted to do things my own way, to make my own mistakes, and create my own successes. And I did all three, building a reputation as a Maverick while I built my net worth. (Remember those words, "net worth," as they are key to the Maverick approach.) I rarely took no for an answer; I would find creative ways to make deals, complete renovations, or build new multi-million-dollar oceanfront estate homes. I developed ongoing relationships with banks, brokers, and investors. Because I saw value where no one else did, I was able to acquire properties at great prices and then to sell them at profits of 20, 30, 50, even 100 percent. I focused intensely on marketing and selling the homes I had renovated, targeting first-time buyers who didn't know how to move from renting to owning. For six years I cut my teeth on $50,000 to $100,000 deals and learned enough to build a personal net worth of more than $1 million. More important, I learned enough to make the leap to the far greater values and risks represented by Palm Beach County oceanfront property.

While I thought things would be different with million-dollar (and later multimillion-dollar) properties, I discovered that every lesson from my early foreclosure deals could still be applied. The payoffs (and the risks) of my projects have gotten bigger over the past 20 years, but everything I learned from those first few properties continues to be a part of my Maverick approach to real estate. I still focus on my particular market, know it inside out, and then raise the expectations of buyers by providing them with more value per dollar than they ever could imagine. I still have to buy at the right price. I still make my money the day I buy, not the day I sell. I still have to renovate or build intelligently, targeting improvements to fit the tastes and pocketbooks of potential buyers. I still focus a good part of my efforts on the marketing and sale of the property, making sure that every part of the experience entices the client to make the emotional decision to buy. (And if you think selling homes to first-time buyers is difficult, try marketing multimillion-dollar properties, when only 50,000 people in the world can afford your masterpieces and only a handful of them are actual buyers!) I still approach every deal, showing, interaction with banks, brokers, clients, and employees as a Maverick, going past the boundaries of what others consider possible or profitable.

Let me give you another way of looking at my approach to real estate. Imagine that on successive days, four envelopes arrive in your mailbox. On day one you open the first envelope and discover the deed to a piece of property worth $50,000—pretty good, you think. The next day you open the second envelope and find the deed to a property worth $500,000. Much better! Eagerly you anticipate day three. You receive the deed to a property worth $5 million! You sit by your mailbox on day four waiting for the mailman. When the envelope arrives your eyes widen and your breath stops—it contains the deed for a palatial estate worth $100 million!

In astonishment you look at the outside of the envelopes—no return addresses, no indication of the senders. Then you notice a fundamental fact: *Each envelope was delivered because it had just one first-class stamp in the corner.* The exact same kind of stamp brought you properties worth $50,000, $500,000, $5 million, and $100 million. The Maverick approach to real estate success is like that first-class stamp. No matter what the value of the property, this approach will allow you to locate, negotiate/buy, renovate, and market/sell everything from a $50,000 house to a $100 million mansion.

WHY REAL ESTATE?

Over the past several years, and as far as I can predict into the future, real estate has been hot and getting hotter. Ninety percent of the eligible U.S. population owns a home and/or an investment property, or wants to. That's more than 150 million people! Throughout good times and bad, enormous fortunes have been created with this tangible commodity, and its lure will never go away. Since 1968 The National Association of Realtors® (NAR) has tracked statistics on home sales in the United States. You can go to their web site, www.realtor.org, to read quarterly reports on home prices in 136 metro areas across the country. They track existing home sales (which include figures for single-family, townhouses, condominiums, and co-ops), new home sales, percentage increases or decreases in sales numbers, median home price, average home price, and much more.

As of the writing of this book in late 2005, here's one snapshot of the current marketplace.

- Median home prices rose 15.1 percent in the previous year.
- Annual home sales were projected to be around seven million units for the current year.
- Sixty-six metro areas experienced double-digit increases in home values in one year. Only six areas had a decrease in home values.
- Low mortgage rates and a wider variety of mortgage products are allowing more people to buy their first homes and/or buy real estate for its investment potential. A San Francisco research firm that tracks loan statistics states that the number of mortgages for investment properties increased 43 percent from 2001 to 2004.
- The U.S. Census Bureau states that the number of houses in the United States valued above $1 million almost doubled between 2000 and 2004. A report in *USA Today* stated that sales of luxury homes priced over $10 million increased 56 percent in 2004.
- According to the U.S. Department of Housing and Urban Development, in the 30 years between 1972 and 2002, the median home price in the United States appreciated at an average annual rate of 6.1 percent. During the same period, the cost of living increased an average of 4.2 percent per year. For more than 30 years, the price of housing has appreciated faster than inflation.
- Real estate is the most stable investment choice in most years and financial conditions. In 2000 and 2001, while millions of people saw their stock portfolios shrink in value and then stagnate, they also watched the value of their homes appreciate significantly.

Real estate today can feel like the stock market of the late 1990s, with the same frenzy, the same "gotta get in" mentality, the same lack of evaluation of the deal because no matter what you pay for a property, things will keep going up and you'll make a profit, right?

Wrong. The Maverick approach doesn't advocate jumping on board simply for the ride; neither does it suggest jumping ship when hot markets start to cool off. One of the advantages of investing in real estate for more than 20 years is that I have participated in booms and busts, buyers' and sellers' markets, and periods of bidding wars for foreclosures to times when no one came to the courthouse steps to bother to bid. From this perspective, I still believe that real estate is one of the best investment vehicles available, but you have to be smart, systematic, organized, and take considered, selective risks.

I believe that, when done correctly, real estate investing is a powerful and valuable approach to building wealth. Why?

- *You have greater control over the value of the asset.* Unlike a stock, where the value can be decreased by the actions or inactions of the company, real estate value is determined by the property, what you do with it, and the surrounding market.

- *There is tangible value in real estate.* Like most other people, I bought Internet stocks in the late 1990s and then watched their value go from hundreds of dollars per share to maybe $2 or $3. However, unless there are a series of major disasters in succession, your real estate is likely to hold its value—as long as you purchased it at the right price. Yes, the market and economy will affect the value of your property, but you're not likely to see your investment lose half its worth overnight.

- *Because there is tangible value in real estate, banks are willing to loan you money to purchase it.* You can buy investment property for as little as 10 percent to 20 percent down, and mortgage interest rates are relatively low. Compare that to stocks, where you can sometimes use the brokerage's money (margin) to purchase shares, but if the value of the stock drops, you must immediately put in more cash to cover the difference.

- *The time frame in real estate investment is longer, allowing you to make better decisions.* Yes, you need to be ready to take advantage of a great deal when it's offered to you, but unlike a stock or commodity, the price of the property is unlikely to go up or down within the next 15 minutes or an hour.

■ *Owning real estate will increase your net worth over time, far more than stocks or bonds.* As soon as you purchase a property, your net worth begins to increase by the total value of that piece of real estate plus appreciation, less mortgage principal pay down. Even if you put only $20,000 down on a $100,000 house, you now own a $100,000 asset. Sure, you have mortgage debt equal to the balance of the purchase price, but if you bought the property right and improve it, as I describe, your net worth will grow with each passing day.

■ *When done correctly, the money you invest in improving your property will provide disproportionately high returns.* In what other investment can you spend $2,000 to $4,000 on cosmetic repairs and increase the value of your asset by $10,000 or more?

The Maverick approach to real estate will help you maximize these benefits while increasing your net worth dramatically. By adopting its precepts and applying its first-class stamp mentality to your real estate transactions, even if you start small—with one foreclosure and/or fixer-upper, for instance—you quickly can move up to bigger and more profitable projects with confidence.

Here's what the Maverick approach offers the real estate investor:

■ It focuses on the most common type of real estate investing: single-family homes. In this category you'll always have the most buyers and sellers and the greatest opportunities for profit. It's where most people will be comfortable investing because they've already bought their own residence (or they will).

■ Anyone can earn enough buying and selling single-family homes to make real estate their profession, should they choose to. You can do this even if you have another job (as I did when I first got started). And even if you're still a renter, the principles in the Maverick approach are basic enough for you to learn and practice with ease.

- You can use this approach in your own area, city, or community. You don't have to search the entire country to find deals; in fact, I strongly suggest you don't (see Chapter 5). As long as you take the time to get to know your own marketplace and understand what buyers and sellers really want, you can become successful in any area of the country.

- The lessons that enable me to buy and sell multimillion-dollar homes are the same that I learned with $50,000 foreclosures. Once you understand these principles, you can make a lot of money at every level of investment. You can start with a foreclosure you purchase for $1,000, or with a $50,000 fixer-upper, or perhaps with a $150,000 condo, or jump right in and buy that $1 million opportunity.

- The Maverick approach doesn't require buying and selling hundreds of properties. My success primarily has been built by owning one property at a time and increasing its value. However, the Maverick approach works with 1 property or 100.

- Because it stresses adaptability, the Maverick approach works in up and down markets. For example, when high-end real estate took a pause after the dot-com bust, I had anticipated the change in the market and adapted my property acquisitions accordingly. (I went from selling a $30 million mansion to creating and selling homes for $7 to $20 million.) When you know your market, you can anticipate trends and succeed despite the odds—something a maverick loves to do!

- The Maverick approach is constantly updated because real estate is what I do every day. My multimillion-dollar projects provide my livelihood, but I'm still in touch with entry-level projects (the kind many readers will start with) because I build transitional shelter for the homeless and construct homes in Haiti, Honduras, Nicaragua, and Indonesia as part of my Caring House Project Foundation. Every week I'm signing off on a $5,000 solid gold faucet for the master bath in my latest $100 million creation while I'm choosing the best quality at the most reasonable price point for 20 toilets to be shipped to Haiti. The advice in this book has been tested in every economic bracket, market, and situation you might encounter.

WHY DABBLING WON'T WORK

I am continually surprised by how many people are interested in real estate. I probably shouldn't be—low mortgage rates and home equity lines of credit, paired with double-digit increases in home values, have made real estate an attractive investment vehicle for people who want something better than their lousy mutual funds or almost-no-interest CDs. But what usually happens? The average investor picks up a couple of books on real estate. He reads about flipping or "nothing down" strategies. He sees infomercials about creating massive wealth while only working weekends. He watches testimonials from ordinary people who have become millionaires in their spare time. Maybe he buys a tape program or even attends a seminar or two where he meets like-minded people eager to get in the real estate game before it's too late. But that investor keeps procrastinating, finding all kinds of reasons he can't or won't get into real estate at this time.

Recently I was asked to speak for a friend's real estate boot camp. There were more than 1,000 people at the event, and I was the final speaker of the weekend. I usually start by telling the audience that I don't have any big-ticket product to sell them (that usually brings a round of applause), and any proceeds from my talk or book sales go directly to help build housing for poor people in the countries I mentioned previously. Then I ask, "How many people are here specifically for real estate?" At this boot camp, probably 990 people raised their hands. (The other 10 were husbands or wives there to support their spouses.) "How many of you have done fewer than five deals?" Around 500 people said yes to that. "And how many have done one deal, or are looking to do their first one?" At least 400 people put their hands in the air. Nearly half the people in the room had never done more than one deal!

In my 20 years in real estate, I've had hundreds, perhaps thousands of people ask me for my secrets to success. But few of them actually put in the work of finding, making, and closing deals. The ones who do often let their first failure (i.e., a deal in which they lost money) stop them from trying again. But whatever goals you may have for your real estate investments, nothing will happen until you take action. I see so many people driving the interstate in Florida, spending hours each day commuting to work that they don't like or find fulfilling or feel pays them enough. Don't let yourself be caught in that trap. If you choose to take the risk, the Maverick approach can be your gateway to more freedom, financial abundance, and satisfaction. It may not be the easy path, but I guarantee you will feel your efforts are more worthwhile, simply because you are finally taking control of your own financial future.

I have a lot of admiration for people like Robyn Thompson, the self-described Rehab Queen. She financed her first real estate transaction—a condo purchase—with money she earned waiting tables at Denny's. For the past 7 years Robyn has bought, rehabbed, and sold more than 235 properties. She also teaches other people to find bargain houses and condos in Connecticut and Orlando. Robyn loved my first book and has asked me to speak at several of her boot camps. Robyn once confessed to me that she wanted to make the jump to higher value homes, but she was afraid. We talked about how important it was to exercise your risk threshold when it came to investing as well as every other area of life. Shortly afterward, Robyn called to tell me she had just bought her first $2 million property in Florida. She had done her research, found a great deal, and was excited about the prospects of applying everything she already knew to renovate and sell her new acquisition.

Robyn has a massive amount of expertise and drive; she just needed the confidence to apply it to a new market. That's why the Maverick approach is so valuable. Success is never about what we know how to do; it's about what we do with what we know. It's also about stepping out of your comfort zone and taking intelligent risks that you believe will present a greater possibility for profit than loss. But you have to take action. You can't do a million-dollar deal until you know your market, accumulate your resources, build your alliances, do your research, and then buy your first investment property.

However, don't feel you have to succeed based on my criteria or compare yourself to Robyn Thompson, your next-door neighbor who brags about the killing he made last year, or anyone else. I believe that when it comes to real estate, I'm successful when I can answer yes to the following three questions: (1) Did I make the profit I had projected? (2) Did I make a market where none had existed before? (3) Did I learn something of value that will help me do better on my next deal?

To succeed with the Maverick approach you must be ready to put in the time and work needed. In my years of investing and, more recently, teaching others how to invest, I've found that the person, not the system, makes all the difference. The Maverick approach can lead you to a successful career investing in real estate, if you're willing to expand your idea of what's possible. But you've got to apply the Maverick first-class stamp to your own investment properties. Once you do, your success and net worth will grow much faster than you ever thought possible.

PART ONE

ARE YOU READY FOR THE MAVERICK APPROACH?

I n my company we create a specific plan, what I call a vision statement, for every single project/job/acquisition. Before I acquire the property, there is already a plan in place for each stage of its development and eventual sale. In the same way, you need to have your own plan in place before you adopt the Maverick approach to investing in real estate.

That plan starts inside you. The Maverick approach isn't just a list of strategies or a checklist of actions that will get you from point A to point B. To go from $50,000 fixer-uppers to $100 million mansions requires a mental game plan that will allow you to take calculated risks, look for value where no one else can see it, and understand the psychology of buyers, sellers, bankers, brokers, and, most important, yourself. You must be willing to step into the shoes of true Mavericks, who go against the expected ways of investing and enjoy taking their own road to success.

To walk the path of the Maverick, you must do three things:

1. Get rid of your old ways of thinking. Maybe you've already invested once or twice in real estate, or you're just getting into the market. Maybe you're looking to invest $5,000, $50,000, or $500,000. Maybe you've read 20 books on real estate and have taken another 10 seminars, or maybe this is the first

book you've picked up on the subject and you're skimming it to see if it's worth your time. Whatever your current level of knowledge or interest, you must start by setting aside everything you think you know about real estate investing and be willing to adopt the principles and strategies described in this book. If you take out your big eraser, come to this fresh, and apply everything you learn even once, I believe you'll see good results.

2. Be selective in listening to the advice/information swirling around you. It seems there are hundreds of different ways of getting into the real estate game, and you might find it difficult to focus only on the Maverick approach. In addition, you will undoubtedly encounter bankers, brokers, and other real estate professionals who will want you to do things the ordinary, conventional way, and they'll tell you that your strategies will never work. However, a Maverick has to train others to adopt his or her views, not the other way around. Feel free to listen to them for any information that will help you understand your market while ignoring their antiquated suggestions about how things must be done. Then you can enjoy proving them wrong and watching them change their ways to accommodate you when your deals result in successes they couldn't have imagined.

3. Focus on and follow your plan. When I'm invited to be a featured speaker at different venues, I see many beginning investors who have tried flipping, lease-optioning, buying-and-holding, landlording, and nothing-downing—all in two years or less. I tell them, "Look, many real estate strategies have their good points, but you have to *stick* with something. If you have 13 real estate books on your shelf, throw 12 of them away and put all your efforts into number 13. Focusing your efforts is the only way you can succeed in the long run."

I believe that following the Maverick approach will help you achieve great success as a real estate investor, but only if you commit to learning its precepts and applying them in a disciplined way through time. If you're willing to do that, keep reading. If not, put this book on your shelf with all the others—maybe some day you'll be ready to invest your time and energy into creating a more abundant financial future. Don't worry: I will be ready when you are. However, I hope you'll decide that time is now and you're ready to adopt the Maverick approach to real estate success.

As your final preparation, let me share with you what I believe are 10 truths about real estate investing—the foundation of success upon which every true Maverick can build a career and a significant net worth.

THE MAVERICK'S 10 TRUTHS ABOUT REAL ESTATE

1. *You must have patience.* Real estate is not a get-rich-quick scheme. It takes time to build your net worth. Some people can make money "flipping" properties, buying and selling them within a few days or weeks, but in most cases, the time line for a real estate deal is months or years. If you want investments you can buy and sell quickly, choose something like stocks or bonds.

2. *You must have access to some capital.* The "no money down" approach is a guaranteed way into too much debt. I used a combination of savings and private investors for my first purchase, and I rolled my profits into other purchases. Most banks will loan you anywhere from 70 percent to 80 percent of the value of the property, but you must find ways to come up with the rest. We talk more about financing and money in Chapter 7.

3. *You must take risks.* This is not an approach for the faint of heart. There were many times I wasn't sure where my next meal was coming from because all my capital was tied up in properties. I was flying so close to the sun that my face was blistering! Some deals I literally put everything I owned on the line because that's what was needed. Other times I've

walked away from negotiations because I knew the terms weren't right. You must be willing to constantly raise your risk threshold in order to go from the small deals to the blockbusters.

4. *You must learn everything about your market so that ultimately you can shape it, or even make one that never existed before.* I studied the foreclosure market for six months—going to foreclosure sales, reading the paper, visiting the courthouse, and talking to other people—before I wrote that first $36,000 check. As part of the Maverick approach you'll learn to decide on the type of property, the area, even the neighborhood where you want to invest. Then you'll investigate, research, walk the streets, meet the people, look up the county records, and so on, until you can quickly and accurately determine whether a property meets your investment criteria.

5. *You must build alliances.* You can do everything by yourself, but why? I have a very lean organization, but the people I choose to work with are vital to my success. I have had a relationship with the same bank (Bank of America) for the entire 20 years I have been investing. I use the same realtors when I can. I employ many of the same contractors and workmen on each project, because I know they're the best at what they do.

6. *You must set high standards.* When I first started renovating foreclosures, a few times I did things like painting over woodwork that should have been scraped first, or hanging drywall without checking for termite damage underneath, but it always came back to haunt me. I decided right then that everything I did had to meet my own expectations for a great job. I prided myself on giving the best value for the money on my smaller homes, and I was able to get more for them because I took care of the details. Today the oceanfront mansions I create are works of art, with every single element crafted from the finest materials. I require that all my partners in the creation of these homes—banks, brokers, workmen, landscapers, designers—adhere to the highest standards

of workmanship and behavior. But that high standard starts with me. And if you adopt the Maverick approach, you must set your own standards higher than anyone else would do for you.

7. *You must be able to make decisions quickly but not emotionally.* While there always will be another property, the great deals can appear and disappear in a heartbeat. You must have the confidence to make decisions quickly when called upon to do so. You also must be able to separate your emotions from the deal. I've seen far too many people get emotionally hooked by the terms of a deal or by their vision for a piece of property (I've also come close to being stuck in that trap myself). Then they pay too much or accept terms that are not in their favor. Similarly, I've seen people trapped by fear because they're overextended or they've been carrying a property for longer than they'd planned, and their emotions cause them to take far less than the investment is worth. When it comes to investing, you must leave your emotions out of the equation and make your decision based on analysis and the true gut instinct that you will hone to perfection.

8. *You must be willing to work hard.* Embarking on the Maverick approach will take a lot of effort on your part, especially in the beginning when you are on the steep side of the learning curve. You must put in the time, effort, and research to learn your market, find properties, build your alliances, get your financing, and develop your skills as a salesperson, renovator, builder, financial analyst, and more—often while you're working at another job and/or raising a family. In business, there's a saying: "When you first begin any venture, you expend ten units of effort for one unit of reward. As you persist, this proportion reverses, and eventually you'll be able to expend one unit of effort and reap ten units of reward." Now, I'm not at that point myself yet, but over the years I've learned how much effort I must expend and where to focus my attention in order to produce the greatest results. You will, too—as long as you work hard from the start.

9. *You must be consistent and humble.* If you think you're going to make a 100 percent return on your first investment, you'll quickly discover how wrong you are. Small, consistent profits are the best way to build a massive net worth. If you try to hit only home runs, you'll end up striking out and losing more deals than you win. The market is a great teacher, but you control whether you learn its lessons quickly or slowly and how expensive those lessons are. If you approach real estate investing with a "beginner's mind," as the Zen masters say, and with a willingness to ask for what you want while being realistic about what you will receive, then you're more likely to have consistent, moderate successes instead of big, flashy failures.

10. *You must find ways to enjoy yourself along the road to success.* I didn't start investing in real estate saying, "Wow, won't it be great when I can build those multimillion-dollar houses on the oceanfront!" Even at the beginning of my career I enjoyed every property, deal, renovation, and sale. I celebrated each time I went to the bank to deposit the sales check and write another for my next property. You must find enjoyment in every stage of the Maverick approach. Otherwise, you'll end up after 20 years with a lot of money (perhaps), but you'll have lost the one thing money can't buy—time.

You may be surprised to see that the first part of this book isn't about choosing properties and doing deals but instead is all about what you must do before you ever sign your first sales contract or make your first down payment. That's because a Maverick doesn't believe in the "ready-fire-aim" school of investing. No matter what's happening in your market, the wrong deal is still the wrong deal, and you'd better be very clear about what the right deal will look like so you'll recognize it when it comes along. Preparation and planning are the foundation of the Maverick approach, not only because they will help you recognize and make the best deals but also because they will help you change your thinking to that of a Maverick. It's a lot easier to go against conventional wisdom when you've done the research and laid the groundwork to give you confidence that your plan will succeed.

In the next four chapters I share with you key strategies in the following areas:

- *Building your personal foundation.* These attitudes, understandings, strategies, and plans will help you begin successfully while others dabble and fail.

- *Thinking people, not property.* Have you ever known a house or piece of land to buy or sell itself? Every deal you will do is with another person who has wants, needs, and desires. Learning to listen to the people you deal with and determine what they truly want (which is rarely represented by a specific dollar figure) will get you the best possible outcome from each deal.

- *Creating relationships before you need them.* How many of us wait until we need a loan to find out the name of the loan officer at the bank? Bad idea. Build your relationships long before you need them and those people are more likely to be there when you do.

- *Shaping your marketplace.* Yes, you need to know as much as you can about properties in your particular area/county/ neighborhood/street. But your goal isn't just to know your market but to make it. Where some people believe that success comes from doing what everyone else is doing, a Maverick succeeds by raising the bar, doing the unexpected, and creating a market rather than trying to fit their properties into the current mold. Knowing how and when to stretch the boundaries in your marketplace is essential to the Maverick approach.

Get ready: It's time for you to take your first step toward the Maverick approach to real estate success!

Our $100-million-plus ocean-to-Intracoastal estate home.

2

Make the Decision NOW to Put in the Time and Effort to Succeed

I never went to college and graduated from high school with a 1.8 GPA, but I feel that over the past 20 years I have earned a Ph.D. in succeeding in the business of life, a master's in real estate entrepreneurship, and a "double major" in the school of hard work. For many years I worked harder, not smarter; I've never shied away from putting my hands, back, and strength into a job. When I first came to Florida, I worked digging sand traps on golf courses. I was the only blond guy on a crew of very hard-working Haitians, and I learned a lot from them. (I also learned that I didn't want to spend my life digging ditches, although I earned the nickname The White Haitian due to my strong work ethic.) After a while I started my first business as a traveling tennis pro. I was working 10 hours a day in the blazing Florida sun, teaching tennis at high-end condo complexes and new waterfront single-family residential communities. I did that long enough to amass some capital and make some great connections— people who introduced me to real estate investing and loaned me part of the money for my first property. For six months I studied real estate while teaching tennis during the day.

When I bought my first property, I did almost all the unskilled renovations myself even though I was still putting food on the table with my tennis business. I was involved with every single aspect of real estate investing—locating, negotiating, finding financing, buying, renovating, building, decorating, furnishing, marketing, and selling my little houses. Eventually I brought in other people to do much of the construction work, but I still visited every property daily to supervise and help whenever needed. (To this day I continue to visit our properties nearly every day we are working on them.) I ran open houses on weekends; I offered seminars for first-time home buyers to teach them how to qualify for mortgages (and use the money to buy one of my houses, of course). I even walked the neighborhoods with flyers to draw people to my seminars and open houses. Those experiences gave me a foundation that nothing else could have. They gave me the freedom to experiment with every aspect of the business to see how I could do it better, faster, or different from the common way. More important, they taught me the value of commitment and dedication. I had to decide that I was willing to put in the time and effort it would take to achieve the levels of success I desired. The name Frank McKinney would not equal Real Estate Rock Czar or King of Ready-Made Dream Homes if it hadn't been for the long days spent renovating rundown properties and countless consecutive weekends of open houses and showings over the past 20 years.

You, too, have to decide to put your time and effort into the Maverick approach. It starts with your personal foundation—the attitudes, understandings, strategies, and plans that will help you plunge in successfully while others dabble and fail. It's like flying lessons. Before you climb into the cockpit, you have to spend a lot of time mastering flight manuals, understanding the mechanics of flight and the particular aspects of the airplane you wish to fly, going over the plane's control panel and the meaning of each of the indicators. Only when you are confident with book knowledge will you be allowed into the plane with an experienced pilot next to you. In the same way, to apply the Maverick approach you have to learn your business from the ground up. I'll be happy to act as your flight instructor and show you how to get started, but you have to bring the commitment and effort that will make the lessons worthwhile.

THE FRANK McKINNEY WAY

In my company, we have what we call the Frank McKinney Way, a credo that forms the basis of every project. It is a commitment to the highest levels of quality and attention to detail that will create an exceptional experience for potential buyers from the first showing to the handing over of the house keys after closing and beyond. The Frank McKinney Way is essentially a distillation of every transaction, property, and lesson I've learned over the past 20 years. It is a culture, a way of living that has produced our current level of success. It is also the end product of applying the Maverick approach day in, day out, to life as well as work.

Let me give you an example in action. The Frank McKinney Way begins even before we close on the purchase of a property. As soon as we get access, our cleaning crews take out any dead vegetation and garbage. Anything left untidy or in disrepair by the previous owner is fixed and/or removed. I myself walk the property line to make sure it is clearly defined and any excess foliage is clipped back, so that potential buyers can see the extent of the lot. Each square foot will provide the buyer with additional value, and vegetation overgrowth gives the perception that the lot may be smaller than it is. This is absolutely essential when it comes to the kind of property I deal with, where every front foot of oceanfront land sells for between $80,000 and $120,000. Therefore, I want to make sure the property line is unobstructed and the grounds are immaculate.

As soon as we purchase, and before we begin negotiations with our real estate brokers to represent the property, we immediately put up simple signs proclaiming FOR SALE 561.555.1234 FRANK McKINNEY & COMPANY. Every day I check the appearance of the property from the road to make sure it looks clean before and during construction. We also have brochure boxes on the road and on the oceanfront side, just in case someone is walking on the beach, sees the house, and is interested in it. (One of our recent properties had a dock on the Intracoastal Waterway. We put a brochure box on the dock in case somebody was going by on their yacht.) For the brochure display we usually enlarge and laminate the four-page, full-color brochure, put it in a nice frame that also includes a clear, enclosed brochure holder, and then mount the whole thing with a FRANK MCKINNEY & COMPANY sign underneath. The entire display is lit from below so people can see the marketing materials at any time, day or night. Whenever I do a property walkthrough (at least once a week), I check those displays. I carry a bottle of glass cleaner and a cloth, and I clean off any salt spray or dirt that may have accumulated on the laminated brochure, the FRANK MCKINNEY & COMPANY sign, and the brochure holder. I also check the brochures to see if they're fresh, faded by sun, or warped by moisture or salt spray. I take out any damaged ones and make sure there's a supply of clean, fresh brochures in each box.

During construction we hire a full-time laborer to make sure at the end of every day each room is swept clean and there are no nails, sawdust, or any debris left anywhere in or around the house. Other laborers organize and store all building materials daily, and a third group makes sure all of the Port-O-Let temporary toilets are spotless. Why go to so much trouble? We want to make sure that if a potential buyer walks up to the house or vacant land on the very first day we own it, the property is in good enough condition that we would feel confident showing the buyer around. I've had people make offers on houses I haven't even started renovating, simply because we took care of the details right from the start. Every single day I own a property we are working to make sure a potential buyer will have the full-on Frank McKinney experience, and I've trained several people to hold the same high standards for our properties.

Over 20 years of building, designing, renovating, and marketing properties at all price ranges, the level of perception I've developed is acute. When I walk through, I'm always looking for what's not exactly perfect yet. I'm rarely satisfied because I know there's always something that could be better. That doesn't mean I'm not happy with our properties; I'm happy with our results, and I want to see how we can make our process easier, smoother, and simpler, and create even more magnificent productions. My drive for perfection was the drive that created the Maverick approach. Because I am never satisfied with the way things are done, I'm always looking for new methods for accomplishing greater results. Of course I would prefer achieving these results with less effort, but I also know that in many cases more effort makes the difference between good, great, and the Frank McKinney Way—magnificent.

Today the Frank McKinney Way starts with the people in my organization who have learned to live it and make it second nature. To create your own version of the Frank McKinney Way, you must be willing never to settle for less than the best. Not from others necessarily, as you will undoubtedly run into (and probably have to work with) many people whose credo is to get by rather than to do their best. But the only way you can ask them to raise their standards is to elevate yours. You must demand the best from yourself. You must be the one who sets the example, puts in the work, and holds the responsibility for making sure your deals, properties, and relationships are of the highest quality. By doing so, you will discover that the benefits of the Maverick approach will spread far beyond real estate investing and enhance your life in ways you can only imagine.

BEGIN WITH YOUR VISION AND PASSION

The Frank McKinney Way begins each new project not with a mission statement, but with a vision and passion statement—a written document that captures the drive to reach higher and do better every day, not just to exceed expectations but to explode our own ideas of what can be accomplished. On the next page is the vision and passion statement for two estates that I sold in late 2004 for $7 million and $17 million. Every single person in my organization had copies of this when we were working on these properties. The statement was included in each person's binder for the property and referred to on an almost daily basis. Statements such as these are part of the planning and development process for any project we undertake. While we also have objective plans (more on those later), everything starts with a vision and passion statement.

Someone once said that money may get us to the job, but passion is what gets us through the day. I encourage you to create your own vision and passion statement for your real estate investing career. What excites you about it? What inner resources will it require? What must you bring to the table to create success? What benefits will you

---

Our Vision and Passion Statement
Oceanfront Estate Homes
860 South Ocean Boulevard & 4555 Coquina Road

From commencement of design until the sale of these magnificent projects our team shall endeavor to apply our collective resources (human, financial, time & spiritual) to create estate homes that are unparalleled in their reflection of vision, quality, detail and marketability.

It is understood to create an exciting new marketplace, as we will be doing with 860 & 4555, our team shall approach the projects with the utmost pride, cutting-edge creativity, military-like efficiency, diligence and good old-fashioned hard work. The projects will present us with situations that are sure to challenge us beyond our current capacity. This is good. As long as we accept the challenge as a chance to exceed our known limitations, 860 and 4555 shall make us stronger individuals, all part of the best team in the business. While we are fortunate to have the ability to create such masterpieces, owning the homes shall be the true privilege of two very fortunate buyers.

We shall approach each day on the job, each walk-thru, showing, decision, phone call or meeting with this passion statement in the forefront of our minds. When 860 and 4555 are finished and sold we will look back and say, "Passion statement fulfilled." Let's make it happen!

---

obtain—financial and personal? What obstacles must you overcome, and how will you beat the odds? When you look back on this project/career, what will you say about yourself? Who are you? Are you a real estate investor? An entrepreneur? An artist whose canvas is the sun-drenched pristine beaches of Florida's Atlantic coast? (That's my own professional identity. What's yours?) Your statement should include any feelings, emotions, lessons, people, financial outcomes, and personal and professional results that you consider important.

One of the great advantages of a clear vision and passion statement is its ability to help you decide whether something is worth your time and effort. In your real estate career, there will be many opportunities. (Open the newspaper or call a broker, and you'll find out quickly how many opportunities there are on any given day.) Eventually you'll get to the point that others will bring you many very tempting opportunities that promise great returns. However, tempting opportunities also can be traps if they (1) take you away from your core focus before you're ready, or (2) require you to enter an area of the business you aren't passionate about. I fell into this trap a few years ago when I agreed to build a custom mansion for someone. They wanted to have a Frank McKinney house, but they also wanted to make all the design decisions. Essentially I ended up as the general contractor on the project and not feeling a part of the result the client wanted. Yes, I made a profit on the deal, but I was miserable. I learned that I'm not excited about building someone else's vision—I want to create projects that will reflect my own commitment to continually stretch the boundaries of luxury and beauty in oceanfront estates. With a strong, clear vision and passion statement you, too, can set yourself up for both satisfaction and success in your real estate career.

CREATE YOUR PLAN FOR SUCCESS

Once you have vision and passion, you need to design your pathway for reaching the vision while feeling the passion. This requires a plan with specific objectives. Every year, around December 31, I go on a retreat and spend a couple of days contemplating my accomplishments of the past year and designing my plan for the year to come. This is some of the most important time and effort I put in each year. The only way to know if you have succeeded is to create specific objectives against which to measure your efforts. With specific objectives, you are creating your own tailor-made plan for success.

Each year I have my own personal objectives for business, family, charitable work, health, finances, and spiritual growth. We also create a company-wide annual objective plan. We use these objectives as our guide throughout the year. We check our progress on these objectives weekly, do a formal, company-wide review quarterly and a year-end assessment each December. I believe the more frequently you check in, the more likely you are to achieve your goals, because you can see when you're off track and then make corrections before you go too far in the wrong direction.

Setting clear objectives allows you to focus on what you need to do each day, week, and month. Clear objectives make your vision and passion concrete. They also keep you from being overwhelmed. Most entrepreneurs (and I include real estate investors in that group) are besieged by tasks, opportunities, and demands. It's easy to become stressed when you know you have 30 tasks to complete by the end of the day. It can be very difficult to prioritize and do the 20 percent that will give you 80 percent of the results you desire. Instead of focusing on tasks, stop for a moment and ask, "Am I fulfilling the objectives for this project? Is this fulfilling my objectives for the year?" Objective plans can help you focus on the 20 percent while you either leverage, postpone, delegate, or eliminate the other 80 percent.

Objective plans greatly benefit anyone with whom you work. Most staff discussions can be shortened or eliminated when you bring the focus back to your common objective plan. When I meet with my team, I tell them, "You're going to have a lot of things you do every day, but if you focus on and accomplish the 10 objectives reflected in our annual objective plan, we'll have a great year. Nothing else matters." In the hustle and bustle of every day, you can expect the fertilizer to hit the rotating cooling device on a regular basis. But with a focus on a small number of objectives, you can control the spatter and keep making progress toward your overall goal.

On the next page is an example of the objective plan and year-end review for Frank McKinney & Company for 2004. "860," "4555," and "701" refer to properties we were developing that year.

Notice our first objective for the year: "Do your initiatives, decisions, and actions at work reflect and embrace the Frank McKinney & Company Way and system?" I wanted my team to ask about every initiative, every decision, and every action, "Does this reflect the Way?" The Frank McKinney Way is a useful shorthand that keeps us focused on quality, standards, accomplishments, and striving to be better. This focus is also reflected in objective number three: "860/4555 to reflect the FM&C Way post-completion—every day, every showing, until sold." I believe we set ourselves apart by setting higher standards than anyone else in our field. Because we pay such attention to detail for

FRANK McKINNEY & COMPANY, INC.	
2004: A Year Where Applying the Very Essence of the FM&C Way Results in Sales & Systems	
Annual Objective Plan—Year-End Review	
OBJECTIVE	COMPLETION DATE
(1) Do your initiatives, decisions and actions at work reflect & embrace the FM&C Way & system?	2004—Very Good to Excellent in 2004
(2) 860/4555—Construction 99.9% complete and reflecting the FM&C Way *(100% when sold).*	By 4/9/04— Done Q2 (by 6/30)
(3) 860/4555 to reflect the FM&C Way post-completion—*every day, every showing, until sold.*	When Sold— Done Q3 (8/4, 8/18 & 9/13)
(4) Sell and close 860 *and* 4555 & celebrate when each one of our properties sells!	By 12/31/04— Done Q3 (8/4, 8/18, 9/13)
(5) Complete renovations related to Operation As-Is Sale at 701.	4/16/04— Done Q2
(6) Implement new integrated accounting, budgeting, bidding, & scheduling program.	12/31/04 w/ quarterly progress— Not done in 2004
(7) Secure, build out, and move into permanent office space.	12/31/04— Not done in 2004
(8) Negotiate w/suppliers & subs with the confidence of the FM&C name.	2004— Very Good in 2004
(9) Perform quarterly Objective Plan, marketing plans, & employee performance reviews.	3/31, 6/30, 9/30 & 12/31— Done in 2004
(10) I ask that we share our blessings with one worthy cause (employee driven choice).	12/31/04— Done in 2004
Note: The best year in the company's 19-year history!	

the entire time our estates are on the market, our houses look better a month, six months, even a year after completion. (You'll learn more about marketing maintenance in Chapter 9.)

You'll also notice that not all our objectives were fulfilled in 2004. That's going to happen, and when it does, you can reset the objective or roll it over to the next time period—in this case, the following year. In 2005 we made great progress on all of the objectives we failed to complete in 2004. We moved into our new offices in March 2005, and we implemented the final stage of our new accounting, budgeting, bidding, and scheduling systems. Notice also that celebrating the sales of our properties and sharing our blessings with others are both on our objective plan. That helps connect our objectives with our passion and vision. Your objectives need to lead you and your associates to experience the emotions and excitement of your vision and passion statement.

There are three requirements for objectives.

1. They must be *tangible*. Objectives are ways of bringing into existence the goals and emotions of your vision and passion statement. Therefore, they must be concrete, clear, and understandable by you and your associates.

2. They must be *quantifiable* or *measurable*. If you can't measure your progress toward an objective, how will you know when you've achieved it? Measuring is the only way you can determine how close you are and how far you must go to achieve your result.

3. Your objectives must be *manageable*. There always will be some things that are in your control and others that are not. Your objectives need to be within your control so you can monitor and manage them. For example, you can't set an objective to have the perfect buyer walk in the door the day you complete your construction. You don't control when your perfect buyer will show up, unless you already have someone in mind and plan to invite him/her for that specific day.

Setting manageable objectives for your career, the year, or individual properties will give you targets to shoot for when you start each day. By measuring your progress against them, you'll know when to reward yourself and when to increase your efforts. It's in the journey toward your objectives that you'll master the lessons of the Maverick approach.

BUILD THE SYSTEMS THAT WILL HELP YOU SUCCEED TIME AND TIME AGAIN

Just like many other things in life, real estate investing is about doing something well again and again. But to do so, you need to build systems. Think about an assembly line: Every person knows exactly what to do to build his or her part of the product. You should bring that same systematic approach to real estate investing. That means developing systems for planning, accounting, scheduling, research, constructing, and so on. Most people's system is to get out of bed, pull on their clothes, and take the day as it comes. They react to what happens instead of focusing on what they really need to accomplish. When you create, implement, and follow systems, you can handle the curves life throws you while still keeping your eye on the ball of the property, closing, completion date, showing, or sale.

This is a lesson that took me a while to learn, as I'm a "shoot from the hip" kind of guy myself. I'm always in the field, and I enjoy making moment-to-moment decisions about the creative aspects of my projects. But I have learned from hard experience that systems ensure your success in the long run. When we first began creating oceanfront estates, we didn't have nearly enough systems in place, and it made the process of construction and showing truly difficult. I felt like the stage manager for a play that's getting ready to open on Broadway. Two hours before curtain there would be chaos. People would be running around, set pieces would be dragged from one side of the stage to the other; there'd be lots of panicked voices and flaring tempers. Everyone would be moving a million miles an hour in ten different directions, banging into each other. Now, when the curtain went up, all you, the customer, would experience is a smooth performance. You wouldn't see the poor stage manager and the crew collapsed from exhaustion backstage. When we were first building our oceanfront estates, I was that unorganized, poorly systemized stage manager. When the curtain came up, customers still got a Frank McKinney product, but getting there was very painful.

My brother, Bob McKinney, is very good at systems, and he's been an invaluable addition to my team. He and I work on projects in Florida and Indiana (our home state), and he also is very successful investing and brokering real estate on his own. With Bob's help, we've created systems that allow us to know with certainty that the accounting is handled efficiently, bills are paid on time, materials are ordered and tracked, subcontractors are managed, the schedule for construction and selling is followed, and so on.

Our systems include spreadsheets that list objectives, the completion date for each as specified in the contract, and who holds responsibility for the objective. On the next page is an example of a milestones spreadsheet that covers a particular estate from contract to closing. (In the full version, we color-code each objective so we know whether it's pending, in process, or completed.)

Developing systems right at the beginning allows you to focus on what's really important instead of getting bogged down in endless details. If your brain is like a 10-piece pie, you have to devote only two pieces to making sure the systems are working (once you've set them up), leaving the other 8 pieces for creativity, researching new opportunities, and marketing—all the aspects of the business that benefit the most from your attention. This book is a result of my taking what used to be an off-the-cuff, creative approach to buying and selling real estate and systematizing what I have done for the past 20 years. If you take advantage of the work I've already put in, you can use my systems to increase your results and your peace of mind.

A system takes elements that repeat themselves over time and makes their accomplishment automatic. Accounting is a system because you know you have to make payments, keep track of expenses, and so on. Certain aspects of renovating can be systematized: You know you will have to get inspections, make repairs or build additions, landscape the grounds, and so on. For example, you can't hang drywall until plumbing and electric have been laid in, and the painters can't paint until the drywall is hung. If you create a flow chart showing what has to be done in what sequence, that's a system.

Operation: Close 1370 (Contract Fully Executed 7/25)		
MILESTONE (CONTRACT LINE #)	CONTRACT COMPLETION DATE	RESPONSIBILITY
Buyer's Attorney Contract Review (103) (E+2)	5:00 PM Tues. July 27	Scott
Deposit $ to Buyer's Escrow* (19 & 20) (E+3)	5:00 PM Wed. July 28	Buyer, Scott, Bob
Inspections via Greg Manning Company	9:00 AM Thurs. July 29	Bob, John, Ray, Manning
Proof of Financing Application (43) (E+5)	5:00 PM Fri. July 30	Buyer, Bob, Scott
Inspections to Have Occurred (Addendum 2.(a)) (E+8)	5:00 PM Mon. Aug. 2	Buyer, FMC, Bob
Inspection Expires (Addendum 2.(a), (b)) (E+10)	5:00 PM Wed. Aug. 4	Buyer, FMC , Bob
CCCL Contingency Expires** (1st Addendum to contract)	5:00 PM Tues. Aug. 10	Buyer, Bob, Scott
Seller's Desired Closing Date	Fri. Aug. 27 (post Maverick Premiere)	Buyer, Bob, Scott
Financing Approval Contingency*** (39, 40, 41) (E+30)	Tues. Aug. 24	Buyer, FMC, Bob
Close Sale (55) (E+45)	Wed. Sept. 8	Scott, Bob, Frank, Buyer

*Upon confirmation of receipt of full deposit, Bob will send 1st e-mail to Buyer.
**Bob to send 2nd e-mail to Buyer.
***Bob to send 3rd e-mail to Buyer.

There are many programs such as BuildSoft® that provide the necessary software to create such systems. As you develop your real estate investing plan, look for anything and everything that can be put into a system, from researching properties to obtaining financing to closing to renovations to marketing to making the sale. Whatever doesn't require your artistic input should be systematized as much as possible.

CHOOSE TO ADOPT THE MAVERICK WAY OF LIFE

Being a Maverick isn't something you wake up one morning and decide, "Okay, I'm a Maverick." The only way you know you're a Maverick is if you go out and take the actions a Maverick would take. It requires discipline, time, and commitment across the board. You can't expect to create and implement the Maverick approach in your business from eight to five and then turn it off when you go home. You have to be willing to make this a way of life. Of course, you don't have to be as rigorous at home; when I leave work I still might put on my SpongeBob SquarePants pajamas and watch *Sports Center* with my daughter. But if you adopt the disciplines of the Maverick approach, it's not just your real estate life that's going to change. You'll find yourself stretching and growing across the board.

I believe there are six key qualities every Maverick must share:

1. *You must hold yourself to high standards even when others don't or won't.* Remember, as a real estate entrepreneur/investor/opportunist/artist (whatever you choose to call yourself) most of the pressure to succeed must come from within. And this internal pressure is good. I hope as you're reading this book you feel the pressure building inside you, because if not, you probably won't succeed with this approach. Only you can hold yourself to the standards required for a true Maverick. With each project and each calendar year you must feel a drive not only to sustain your success but to outdo it, better it, stretch beyond last year's efforts to create something greater within yourself and your career. It's not easy to continually put in the work needed to exceed your results time after time. But it is

extremely rewarding, and it will lead you, over time, from $50,000 fixer-uppers to $100-million-plus mansions.

2. *You must ignore many outside influences and create your own reality.* If you spend too much time focusing outward on extraneous information and the day-to-day distraction of news, rumor, gossip, or punditry, then public opinion or general perception can sway you. And as a Maverick, you usually want to go dead against that. You succeed as a Maverick not just because you go your own way but because you know your market, you know people, and you know what's really true despite what the experts are telling you. Your greatest opportunities will come from going against conventional wisdom, against the crowd, and looking for the exceptions rather than the rules. This is not a path for those who want to follow the herd; it's also not a path for those who want to go against the herd just to be rebels. Certainly, be aware of what the experts are saying about the real estate market in your area or the economy in general, and of course pay careful attention to any information about specific properties you may wish to acquire. But listen to everything with, not a grain, but a huge boulder of salt. Always look for the ways that, by going against the common wisdom, you can make a new market.

3. *You must focus completely on your goal and not let others distract you.* When you're just starting out, well-intended friends and colleagues may tell you that what you're attempting to do is crazy, or won't work. Or they may say, "If you follow this other system, or get into this investment instead, you'll make a lot more money!" They may or may not be right, but the *only* way you'll succeed with the Maverick approach is if you commit to it and follow its precepts. This is not a dabbler's path, and it rewards those who follow it with great success. Tell your friends, "No, thanks," give the Maverick approach your full focus, and then enjoy the results.

4. *You must be massively disciplined, financially and otherwise.* To start your career as a Maverick, you must develop discipline. One of the key ways this shows up is in your creditworthiness.

When you are starting in real estate, you not only have to save for the down payments on your properties, you also must keep your credit report clean so banks will lend you money. You have to pay your bills on time, keep your credit cards under control, and be conscious of what you spend and where. But being creditworthy is just one example of the discipline you will need as a Maverick. You also need to get up early day after day and drive to see maybe hundreds of properties before you find the one that will fit your requirements, put in dozens of bids that aren't accepted, and negotiate time and time again with bankers, brokers, owners, and buyers. Discipline is an essential trait of a Maverick.

5. *You must adapt to changing circumstances.* The Maverick approach is all about change. Yes, its basic precepts will work for properties at every price point from $50,000 to $100 million and over, but one of its precepts is also to keep growing and evolving. Every deal will present you with slightly different circumstances; that's what makes it interesting to go to work every day. But you must be willing to adapt and learn from the changes you will need to make. Only by adapting can you continue to grow and learn.

6. *You must stretch the boundaries.* There are areas where even a Maverick has to play by the rules—inspections, taxes, laws, and contracts are a few that come to mind. But even when you have to play by the rules, you can still stretch the boundaries and look for how to shape the deal to fit your vision. This can apply to the terms of the sale, or your financing with the bank, or anything else. Once you decide, "This is the way the deal needs to be for me to reach my goal," then you work on stretching the boundaries to make the deal work. And if you can't make it work, then you walk away. Remember, a boundary is like a piece of old elastic. Once it's stretched, it will never come back to its old perimeter again. When you stretch your personal boundaries or the boundaries of a deal, you have expanded what's possible from that point on. Keep expanding and you'll be creating that $100 million house faster than you think.

Finally, as I said earlier, the Maverick approach requires that you put time into making it work. There is no substitute for time. You can shorten the amount needed to do a deal or to learn a strategy, but to create anything requires an investment of our most important commodity—the minutes we have here on earth. The Maverick approach is a long-term one. It isn't like day trading stocks, so if you need the rush of immediate gratification from seeing your brokerage account grow every day, this is not the path for you. With the Maverick approach you will be creating enormous value over time, building your net worth from year to year until you're ready to do something else or retire and do nothing. Remember, it took me 20 years to get to the point of building $100 million houses. It also took me that long to codify the Maverick approach so you can benefit from my journey. But you, too, will have to walk the path from point A to point B, to put in the time to create the vision and passion statement, to devise the objective plans, to build the systems, and to implement the Maverick approach precepts in your life as well as your business.

The Maverick approach is all about adding value. Everything is designed to take something that is undervalued, improve or add value to it, and then sell it at a price that represents new heights for the marketplace. But in order for this approach to work in the outside world, you must apply its value-added philosophy inside yourself as well. By committing to its precepts of high standards, stretching boundaries, having a vision and passion, and building plans and systems for attaining clear objectives, how much more value will your life have? How much happier will you be? How much more can you do for your family, your community, your world? What kind of a legacy can you leave when you live by the Maverick approach of always adding value? And how much of an investment of your time, energy, and passion would that kind of life be worth?

To be a true Maverick requires dedication, street smarts, and courage. But if you choose to follow the Maverick approach, if you apply its precepts in your business as well as your life, if you commit to taking the time to achieve your goals, then the rewards—of financial success as well as personal satisfaction—can be enormous.

Our magnificent two-acre Gulf Stream oceanfront estate.

3

Think People First, and Profit Will Follow

The ultimate key to the Maverick approach is simple: *Real estate is about people, not property.* Unlike stocks, which you can buy and sell using a computer without ever seeing another human being or knowing anything about the company, to do well in real estate you must understand people's needs and desires. How many of us go into a transaction focusing on what we want from the deal? That's human nature—and it's important. Unless you have a clear idea of how you want the deal to work out, or the outcome your interaction with this individual will provide, then you're unlikely to get the results you desire. But the other part of the process, and the part that ensures you will get what you want, is to *find out what the other person wants from the relationship and give it to them.*

"Wait a minute!" you're probably saying. "If I give the owner what he or she wants for the house, I won't make my required profit numbers. If I give the seller the discount he or she wants, then I'm going to lose my shirt. If I give the banker/broker/contractor/mortgage agency what they want, the deal just won't work. How can I give the other person what they want and still get what I need from the deal?" Questions like those indicate that you're still in the "profit only" mindset. For you to earn recurring profits, you need to discover what people need, which often has little to do with a specific number, dollar figure, interest rate, or set of terms. You need to walk a while in the other person's shoes so you can learn what will give them the satisfaction they will need to close the deal.

WHAT PEOPLE REALLY WANT

Residential real estate is a "high touch" business. Most people are purchasing or selling a part of their lives—the house where they've lived, raised children or been raised themselves, or the ideal spot where they can do those things for the next several years. When you invest in property, you're dealing with a human being's fundamental emotions.

Any discussion of what people really want must start by differentiating between *needs* and *desires*. Everyone needs a place to live, a shelter from the elements. But then you move into what I call secondary needs: (1) the need for *security*—having a shelter you can pay for, and, if you own it, one that provides you with financial security as well, and (2) the need for *comfort*—having enough room and/or amenities to make your life and your family's lives comfortable. I believe that those two needs—comfort and security—must be addressed when it comes to first-time buyers.

First-time buyers are usually renters or those leaving the comfort of their parents' homes. Renters have satisfied the need for a roof over their heads, which provides them with security, but they're not building any equity that could contribute to their long-term financial future. They also may or may not have satisfied their need, or their family's need, for comfort. Their apartment or rental house may not be big enough, or in the wrong neighborhood, or perhaps it doesn't have a back yard or garage or other amenity that would make the family's lives better. If you are looking to sell to a first-time buyer, you need to keep their needs for security and comfort in the forefront of your mind. When a first-time buyer sees how your property can fulfill these two needs, you are more than halfway to making the sale.

In 1986, before I ever bought my first fixer-upper properties, I got to know the neighborhoods and the people who lived in them. In those years, mortgage rates were more than 10 percent, and moving from renter to buyer could seem impossible for these people (unlike today, where there are many creative mortgage products, lots of ways to qualify, and dozens of TV commercials and e-mail solicitations telling people how easy it is to get a loan). Renters were going to be the market for my properties, so I asked myself, "What would I need to know to be interested in buying my house?" I'd need to see how I could afford to buy a house for about the same money I'm spending on rent. I'd also need to know how to get a mortgage when I'd never done it before, and that my down payment could be less than the first, last, and security deposit required to move into an apartment. To answer these questions, I started giving free seminars I called Mortgage Qualifier Programs.

Would I do the same thing today? You bet. Even now, with easy financing available, people are still renting instead of buying. This can be due to a number of factors: They have bad credit, they don't have steady employment, they want to live in a particular area but can't afford to buy there, they're in the area temporarily, they have other financial priorities such as higher education or supporting family members financially, and so on. Certainly there can be valid reasons to rent; however, if fear or a lack of good information about home ownership is the reason someone is still renting, as a potential seller you can help potential buyers get past the fear with a little education and encouragement.

What do most first-time home buyers need as far as comfort is concerned? Typically they're looking for the best house they can afford, with at least three bedrooms and two baths, a kitchen, a living/family area, a garage, and some kind of yard. The house also should be in good enough shape that the buyer can move in with very little work. The other way you can provide comfort to a buyer is to make the process of buying your house as easy as possible. Remember, purchasing a home for the first time is the biggest investment most people have made to that point. Not only is a lot of money on the line, but the process itself also can be extremely intimidating. Anything you can do to make it easier will help fulfill the buyer's need for comfort. When showing the house, make sure you point out all the features that will make their family happy. Have a contract completely filled out and ready to sign, except for price and closing date. Walk the buyer through the contract yourself and explain it in English. Provide manuals for all appliances and instructions for everything in the house, ready for them at closing. The easier you make the buying experience, the more certain your houses will be to sell quickly at the prices you desire.

THE DIFFERENCE BETWEEN NEED AND DESIRE

Imagine you're walking through the supermarket to buy some cereal. You look at all the choices on the shelves—everything from sugary flakes to granola, in generics and name brands. Need says, "Buy the store version of All-Bran—it's healthy and inexpensive." But somehow you gravitate toward the Fruity Pebbles. You read the box and see it has vitamins and minerals and grains (along with a ton of sugar). "Little Johnny will like this more than All-Bran," you think. Funny thing is, when you get home you sit down and have a big bowl of Fruity Pebbles yourself.

All buying begins with need but is driven by *desire*. It's pretty clear immediately whether your property will meet a buyer's needs: If your house is the right size, offered at the right price, on the market at the right time, and you make the buying process easy, then the buyer is guaranteed to make the deal, right? Of course not. Desire is what causes one family to purchase a minivan while another chooses a convertible. Desire drives most home-buying purchases, too—people want to live in a bigger or smaller house, or a different neighborhood, or better schools, and so on. Desire causes one buyer to salivate over your property while another overlooks it entirely.

Once you get past the needs for price, security, and comfort, every factor in the buying decision is driven by desire. Most people want to love where they live. Is the kitchen big enough? Does it have the right amenities? Is there a great back yard? Is there a fireplace, or a screened-in porch? Are the colors right? Are the appliances new?

Are the master bedroom and bathroom large enough? Is the landscaping inviting? All of these are desires rather than needs. The emotional return people get from their homes is more important than any financial return from appreciating property values or tax advantages of home ownership. You as the seller need to understand the fundamental desires of your buyers so you can provide them with the ultimate experience in their price range. For example, first-time home buyers may not care about granite countertops or a Sub-Zero refrigerator, but they may absolutely love the white picket fence you put up around the property. No sense in spending your renovation dollars on improvements that are (1) not what the buyer wants, or (2) more than the buyer needs.

To understand your potential buyer, you must do research. Start by going to the areas in which you are looking to buy. (We talk about choosing your neighborhoods in Chapter 6.) Look at the prevailing style of the houses in the neighborhood—sometimes you can vary the style a little, but the people who live there (who are your target buyers) already have set the overall look. I like to get to know the neighbors on the street, and if possible find out what they think about the community. I also suggest you go to as many open houses as you can. Whether you're interested in the house or it's way out of your price range, if it's in the neighborhood, get yourself in the door. See what amenities and features people comment on when they walk through. What gets them excited? What don't they like? What do realtors point out to their clients? Don't just look at the house yourself but listen to the potential buyers. Getting to know the desires of your marketplace is some of the most important research you can do.

You also can enlist real estate professionals to help you. Talk to realtors in the area. Find out which houses are selling and which are just sitting on the market, and why. Tell the realtors, "I'm renovating a house in the area and I'm on a budget, but I want to do the right thing. What do people like to see?" Talk to more than one realtor and listen for recurring themes; that way you know there's some validity to their opinions. Have a broker provide you with descriptions from the Multiple Listing Service (MLS) of comparable properties for sale in your target neighborhood. I also suggest you talk to professional appraisers and ask them the common features and amenities they see in houses in the area. Finally, because you will be looking to create properties that stand out from the norm, ask the appraisers and realtors what *un*common amenities add to the value of certain homes. In most neighborhoods there are a few houses that realtors and buyers love. You'll hear, "Wow, that house is beautiful. Have you seen it?" Learn what appeals to buyers in the area, and why.

There are a few things you can do to help your property meet the conscious and unconscious desires of every buyer. First, the house must look and smell absolutely clean. Nothing makes a buyer happier than the idea of being able to move into a clean house, and nothing turns them off faster than dirt or a less-than-clean smell. Second, people like new things. A house is a huge purchase, and even if it's a renovated property, as most of yours will be, anything that says NEW will help you make the sale. When I put new appliances into the kitchens of my fixer-uppers, I would leave all the tags and the efficiency guides in place so people would see that the refrigerator, stove, or microwave was brand new. Something else that says NEW is that new carpet smell. Unless you have hardwood floors throughout your property, see if you can put new carpet in a few rooms. Remember, anyone can satisfy a buyer's needs. How you fulfill and even exceed the buyers' needs *and* desires will determine whether they will spend $10,000 more for your house rather than settling for the cheaper house down the street.

MEETING THEIR ASPIRATIONS

Say you're ready to move out of the first-time home buyer market and into higher-end properties. These houses are usually "move-up" homes, bought by people who already own a home but wish to move into something better, larger, or in a different neighborhood. Desires play a very important role in a move-up home—people will have definite ideas of how many rooms they want, the amenities, size of the yard, the neighborhood, and so on. The purchase of a move-up home is driven by the buyer's *aspirations*. They're looking for a home that will make them feel like they have become the people they aspire to be. Their home is a statement of who they are and what they have achieved.

What are the things that mid-level buyers love? Great kitchens, master suites with beautiful bathrooms, four bedrooms or more, three-car garages, and more square footage (a significant factor to many mid-level buyers) are some of the fundamentals. If your house doesn't have the right configuration, you're going to need to compensate in some way—either in price or by providing other amenities. For example, you can make up for the fact that the kitchen isn't huge by creating a pass-through into the dining room, or putting in a Sub-Zero refrigerator or Viking range. If there's not enough room for a pool, perhaps you can fit in a deck with a Jacuzzi. Again, open houses, neighborhood drive-throughs, and talking to realtors and appraisers will bring you the information you need to determine what features and amenities will meet your buyers' aspirations.

With the move-up house, the buyer's experience is absolutely key. We talk about creating this experience in Chapter 9, but your goal must be to touch the buyer's five senses every time they enter your property. They must feel that your house is the embodiment of their dreams come true. They should see themselves coming home every night and being proud of what they've accomplished. They should feel this is where they want their kids to grow up, or bring their friends for social events. In a very fundamental way, the buyer for the mid-level house becomes completely identified with it; the house is how the buyer sees him/herself at his/her best.

Any mid-level home purchase will be discretionary. The proportion of need to desire is lopsided—less need and a lot of desire. If you look at your property as something that doesn't just satisfy needs and desires but also provides an exceptional experience when people come home every night, then you'll have buyers lining up for your houses and paying the top dollar you want.

CREATING THE ULTIMATE EXPERIENCE
FOR THE ULTRA-WEALTHY

Ultra-wealthy buyers rarely have needs that they haven't taken care of long ago, and they're used to satisfying any desire as soon as it arises. Most buyers at this level already have one or more homes and more than enough money to buy whatever they want whenever they want it. Unlike the mid-level buyer, the homes of the ultra-wealthy do not represent their aspirations, because the ultra-wealthy have already arrived and they are well aware of this fact. With the 50,000 or so people in the world who can afford properties of $10 million or more, you must create not just desire but *subliminal euphoria*. Your property must provide an experience that they didn't consciously know they wanted, but once they have it they won't be willing to settle for anything less.

I have become something of an expert in the psychology of ultra-wealthy buyers. For the past 15 years I have studied their desires, their requirements, and what makes them decide to buy. I have taken potential clients through thousands of showings. Early on sometimes I pretended to be the contractor or the pool guy, or even hid in the closet or under the bed, just so I could hear the unedited comments of prospective buyers. I learned what impressed them and what turned them off, their subliminal preferences, and the nuances that created the most impact. I spoke with realtors and buyers, getting feedback after showings and even after sales, asking why a sale did or didn't go through. The primary thing I learned was this: *When you deal with the ultra-wealthy, you are no longer building homes; you are creating works of art.* The entire property must make buyers feel that it was created just for them. You no longer are meeting needs and desires, you are *creating* them. Like great art, your property must expand the buyers' vision to encompass a new level of luxury and beauty.

The list of amenities required by the ultra-wealthy buyer is long and detailed, and anything that doesn't satisfy their requirements must be changed before the sale occurs. (I had one woman who refused to walk further than the front door of one of my estates because she didn't like the covers on the air conditioning vents.) But

I've found that all of the many requirements, desires, and wishes of the ultra-wealthy can be put into four categories:

1. *The ultra-wealthy want security.* They must feel the property is completely protected from unwelcome visitors, pressures of the outside world, and any hazard to themselves and their families.

2. *The ultra-wealthy want convenience.* They want their homes easy to manage and automated: LCD TV screens that appear at the touch of a button, kitchens set up for catering as well as home use, space for assistants, servants, and other people who make their lives easier, and so on. The ultra-wealthy are often extremely busy, and they don't want to deal with problems with their homes. Therefore, everything must work flawlessly from the moment they walk through the door, often with just the touch of a button.

3. *The ultra-wealthy want the best.* Every aspect of the property and the house must be composed of the finest materials, put together with taste and style in a manner that exceeds what they have come to expect.

4. *The ultra-wealthy want to be unique.* They love one-of-a-kind pieces, original artwork, new items that no one has ever seen or used in that particular way before. Their experience must not have been duplicated by anyone anywhere else.

In selling to the ultra-wealthy, it's all about creating the experience of owning one of the most magnificent mansions in the world—a work of art. Every showing must immerse their five senses while fulfilling at the highest possible level the four categories just listed. With ultra-wealthy buyers, you are constantly pushing the envelope. They've seen the best already—in their friends' homes and quite possibly in their own home or yacht, or in the five-star hotels they visit around the world. But your estate must represent a step beyond anything they imagined. You must give them the experience of subliminal euphoria every time they are exposed to your property, from brochure to web site to the front gate to every square inch of the land, house, guest house, beach, pool, or dock.

There are fewer than 50,000 people in the world who can afford a multimillion-dollar estate, so it's absolutely essential to learn as much as possible about the individuals who are interested in your properties. Today, of course, you can obtain a great deal of information about individual buyers. This is especially important as (1) deals on multimillion-dollar estates tend to be quite intricate, (2) most of the ultra-wealthy buyers are used to complex negotiations, and (3) they're used to coming out on the best side of the deal. So you need to know when to play hardball, when to accommodate requests, when to offer other terms, and so on. To do so you must know as much about your buyer as you can.

For instance, in 2004 I was selling a $7 million direct oceanfront estate in Ocean Ridge, Florida. (This property is in one of the few undeveloped communities in Palm Beach County, and one of the lowest-priced estates I had sold in a while.) A gentleman had come to look at the property and really loved it. He had made me an offer of $6.5 million, and I had countered with $6.7 million, which he said was too high. I had done quite a bit of research, and I knew he had just sold his company and was in the position to make a cash purchase. I also knew he made decisions quickly. So I had e-mailed him an offer to split the difference and settle on $6.6 million, and I laid out the final terms I would accept for the sale. I also told him I was continuing to show the house and believed it would not be available for much longer. (This was only two months after the house had gone on the market.)

Then I used a little truthful psychology: I called this man in the middle of touring the property with another couple who was on the verge of making an offer. "I just wanted to let you know that the people I told you were coming back are walking through the house now," I said. "Have you thought about my last offer? Because I can call off the showing right now if you say the word."

I could feel the tension on the phone. He said, "I offered you $6.5."

"That's right," I replied, "and I told you that I felt $6.7 was reflective of the value of the estate."

"Okay, okay! $6.7!" he answered quickly.

I said, "No, in my last e-mail I said I'd split the difference with you. I will take $6.6 million, with the terms I described."

"Fine, do it. Just get those people out of my house," he answered.

Had I not known this man's circumstances and psychology, I might have continued the offer/counteroffer dance until we came to a number agreeable to us both, or I might have lost the deal altogether and sold to the other couple. But because I knew how much the subliminal euphoria was driving his desire for the property, I held fast. The result? I got the deal I asked for—in fact, he wanted it so much he would have paid $100,000 more.

Nowadays you can check public records on someone's company, job, career, promotions, marital status, impending lawsuits or judgments, family events, and so on. The more information you have, the easier it will be to create a deal to satisfy the wants, needs, and desires of your buyers while providing you with the best results possible. We talk more about creating subliminal euphoria in Chapter 9.

WHEN YOU'RE THE BUYER AND
SOMEONE IS SELLING TO YOU

It's just as important to put people first when it comes to buying properties that you will eventually resell. Remember the most important rule of real estate: You make your money the day you buy, *not* the day you sell. Sellers have the same kinds of needs, desires, and aspirations as buyers. You have to know what's most important to the seller so you can structure your deal based on that knowledge. If you find out what the seller truly needs and do what you can to provide it, the relationship you create may help you acquire the property on favorable terms. Why does this person need to sell? Are they moving up or downsizing? Has their life situation changed? Has their company transferred them and they need to sell quickly? Have they inherited a house and want a no-hassle closing? Have they recently retired and no longer want to pay property tax on a house that's too big for them? Do they have mounting medical bills and need a specific amount from the property sale? If you can discover someone's real needs and desires, you will go much further toward understanding the terms that will make or break the deal. Do your research. Talk with the broker, the neighbors, and the seller if possible. You must get inside the head of the seller to figure out what's *really* important, and then to use that information to make the best deal possible.

In 2000 I created and sold a beautiful mansion in Manalapan for $29 million. It is probably the nicest house I've ever seen on the ocean—three acres of land, 30,000-square-foot house, 11 bedrooms, 16 bathrooms, a 12-car garage, tennis court, guest house, and a motorized walkway to the beach. When I sell a property I assume I'll never deal with it again, but in 2002 I noticed a FOR SALE sign on the wall of the estate. The man I had sold it to had it on the market for $40 million. I thought, "This guy's going to flip it and make $10 million without any effort. Guess I should've asked for more when I sold it!" But after two years the mansion was still on the market. Even though I had two major projects and a smaller deal in Indiana in the works, I thought, "Wouldn't it be great to own that house again? There were a lot of things I'd do differently if I had the chance—better materials, even better design, and so on."

The asking price on the property had dropped from $40 million to $27 million. Since I had sold the house to the owner for $29 million, I knew this gentleman wanted to move on and was willing to take a loss on the property. I also remembered the first deal had been extremely fast, closing in just about a week, and the owner was a quick decision maker. (This is a key lesson in buyer's and seller's psychology: Anybody who's quick on the way in also will be quick on the way out.) I had maintained a relationship with the owner of the property, so I asked him to give me a call, which he did. Turned out he had already bought and moved into another house in Florida, and he hadn't lived in the property for a year and a half. He and his wife had adopted two children and they wanted more of a neighborhood "feel" for their family. "I love the house, Frank, but I'm ready to sell it and move on," he told me.

I inspected the property (which was in beautiful condition—I wasn't going to have to do a lot of deferred maintenance) and ran my numbers. I had to plan how much I would put into renovations, carrying costs, and all the standard factors we discuss further in Chapter 7. I also took into account the properties I was already building. (Remember, I build these houses on spec, using all my own money, and I don't get paid until the properties sell, so a lot of my capital was already tied up.) Then I reluctantly sent the owner an offer of $19 million. "I know this is lower than you want, and if you wait you'll certainly get more, so don't take this if you can wait," I added.

Within a day or two he sent a counteroffer of $21 million. "That's as much of a loss as my wife and I want to take," he wrote. But I knew three things about this seller: (1) He made decisions quickly; (2) he had moved out of the house already, and (3) he was willing to take a loss of $8 million on a property whose value had skyrocketed since he had purchased it four years earlier. Based on that, I felt I could stand pat with my $19 million offer. (Actually, that was all I could afford to pay with the inventory we had at the time. I reminded myself, "Those are leaves growing on the trees, not money," and there was a limit.) I told him I would pay $21 million when one of my other properties sold, or $19 million right now. I also offered him convenience. The owner had had several other deals on the table during the tenure of the listing, but they had fallen apart due to contingencies, financing, inspections, and so on. The deal I offered came with no strings attached and a quick closing. Because I knew the house and had seen its current conditions, I didn't ask for any inspections, only a survey. Within days he took my offer of $19 million and included some of the furnishings as well. I was able to make the deal because I knew what was most important to the seller and offered him not just money but the convenience and terms that suited his other needs. If you get to know the people who are selling the properties you want to acquire, often you can satisfy their needs with something other than cash—time, terms, ease of sale, and so on. When you find out the seller's needs and seek to fulfill them, you will make better deals for you both.

SATISFY THEIR EMOTIONS AND YOU WILL HAVE A DEAL

Residential real estate is an experience rather than a commodity. Every house represents a place to raise a family; an investment for old age or financial security; a sign of success; proof of their taste; a symbol of worth. There's a reason owning a home is called "owning a piece of the American dream." Your buyers and sellers have their own versions of what that dream is. Your job as a Maverick is to discover that person's dream and see if your deal or property will fit it.

A book called *The Experience Economy* describes how companies like Disney and the Ritz-Carlton succeed by creating unforgettable experiences that generate powerful emotions for their customers. People will pay a lot for experiences. When you go to Disney World, what do you get for your park entrance fee? The feelings you and your family experience while you're visiting Cinderella's Castle or the Pirates of the Caribbean ride or Epcot. At the Ritz-Carlton, you pay a very small amount for the hotel room and a lot more for the luxuries that make staying at the Ritz different from the Econo-Lodge. People also buy products that give them emotions. With the OnStar service available on many new cars, you get a year's membership free, but after that you pay $17 a month. People occasionally use OnStar for directions or phone calls, but what is the primary reason you pay for the service? If you ever have an accident, OnStar will contact the police or ambulance or your family. The $17 pays for peace of mind—an emotion.

You, too, are in the business of discovering and satisfying the emotional needs of sellers and buyers. People may tell you what they want is tied to a particular dollar figure or deal structure or profit potential or interest rate. Don't believe it. Dollars are always important, as is profit, but every deal will have a strong emotional component. And discovering someone's emotional needs in a given situation and then seeing how you can fulfill them will go a long way toward getting you the deal you want.

If you get to know people—what they want and don't want, what they fear, what they desire—your chances of success will go up exponentially. Never say, "It's just business"; that will kill your deals faster than anything else. While it may be business, it involves emotions and experiences, not just a certain amount of money in the bank. Think of the emotional needs of buyers and sellers as yet another deal point that must be satisfied in order for the deal to go through. I guarantee that if you meet someone's emotional needs first, you will find that the financial side of the deal will swing your way far more often.

Two-story oceanfront master suite in Manalapan.

Photo credit Corey Weiner/Red Square Photography

4

Create Vital
Relationships Up Front

I'm a strong believer in the power of relationships in real estate. Even Donald Trump, who is a very tough negotiator, has extremely strong relationships with almost all of the people he works with. These relationships aren't just based upon mutual gain, but upon shared experiences and a lot of respect on both sides. Good relationships are better than money in the bank because they will earn you *more* money, along with greater success. When you put in the time and effort to develop vital relationships up front, people and institutions are more likely to let you take greater risks, give you better terms, tell you about great deals, and so on.

Strong relationships will give you the freedom to build your real estate career the way you want, rather than the way everyone else does. I've been able to go from $50,000 projects to $100 million mansions without much overhead or going public, and with a relatively small team of people at my company, because I have built strong relationships in the community. Developing vital relationships must precede your first investment and follow every sale. I've been with the same bank, Bank of America, for 24 years. I deal with the same realty firms consistently. I use many of the same appraisers, contractors, and subcontractors. I've also developed strong relationships with local governments, Chambers of Commerce, and zoning boards. I contribute to my church, the local schools, and many charitable organizations in town. All of these vital relationships don't necessarily pay off monetarily, but I reap boundless personal and professional rewards from them nonetheless. In the same way a house needs to have strong foundations, your real estate investing career needs strong relationships to support its growth.

TURNING THE "BIG, BAD BANK" INTO YOUR PARTNER

As a real estate investor you must have access to capital, and a bank is actually one of your best sources for lower-cost money. Before you go to friends, family, or hard-money lenders, or max out your credit cards to fund your deals, you should approach traditional lending institutions first. That's right, go to those who make their living lending YOU money! Now, very few of us feel empowered when we go to get a loan. It's easy to see the bank as an obstacle rather than an ally. Of course, with the wide variety of mortgages available today, it's somewhat easier to obtain financing than it used to be. But to get the best terms and be able to step outside the norm with your Maverick deals, you must build relationships with a bank or mortgage company.

In 1982 I took out a personal loan from Bank of America for $2,500, the smallest secured loan they would allow me to take (and the largest loan I could qualify for at the time). I didn't need the money—I simply wanted to create a positive credit history. I paid off that loan not a day early or late, and regarded the interest as an investment in the relationship. After using my own savings and some investor money as down payments, I went back to that bank to borrow $100,000 for my first real estate properties. Through the years I continued to borrow and repay, increasing the size of the mortgages while repaying the loans early or on time. While I am always pushing the envelope when it comes to my next deal and still have to educate my bankers almost every time I propose a project, because of our long-term relationship they're more likely to give me the terms I need.

Whether you work with a mortgage company or a national bank, you must always build a strong relationship with your local bank branch. Why? First, business professionals in a community talk to each other. If you become a great customer at your local branch, you're starting to build a good reputation as a legitimate businessperson. Second, every lending institution will look at your credit history and banking relationships when evaluating your worthiness for a loan. Having your local lending officer as a reference will help you with whatever bank you choose as your funding source. Third, if your bank is a branch of a larger financial institution, the local recommendation may give you access to greater capital. When I sought my first multimillion-dollar loan from my bank's national headquarters in North Carolina, the referral came from the branch here in Palm Beach County.

Your first step is to research the banks in your area. If you're interested in doing a lot of real estate deals I would advocate going with a bigger bank, because it will have higher lending limits. On the other hand, if you're just starting out, you may want to go with a community bank. A community bank is a small, local bank, usually with one or two branches, that often is owned by a family or group of investors. I love community banks—I used one when I was first getting started. In those days the CEO himself would come to my properties and see what I was doing. Eventually, however, I outgrew the bank's loan limit. (The amount a bank can lend will be based upon the assets they have. The loan limit for an individual investor might be a couple of million dollars.) So if you choose to go with a community bank, ask them up front, "What's your loan limit?" That way you'll know whether their loans will suit your planned levels of investment.

The best of all worlds is to create the feeling of a community bank inside a big bank, which is what I've developed with Bank of America. You develop this kind of relationship by opening a checking account, a savings account, a business account, and then get some kind of loan—a car loan, a first or second mortgage on your own residence, or a home equity line of credit. At the least, take out a small personal loan and pay it back religiously. Start building your creditworthiness right now, so that you will have proven your ability to take care of the bank's money later.

BUILDING RELATIONSHIPS WITH BANKERS

Banks and mortgage companies are composed of people, so get to know the people in your branch, particularly the loan officer. Introduce yourself as soon as you open an account. Make a point of saying hello when you make a deposit or cash a check. (I know you can do those things by ATM and electronic banking, but when you're building the relationship you may want to create reasons to go into the bank.) Once you've gotten to know the loan officer, spend some time discussing potential loans. Let the bank officers know that you're interested in real estate, so they can tell you about loans that might fit the bill.

In every loan officer there is a number cruncher who thinks inside the box, and a human being who considers venturing outside it. When it comes to evaluating your loan application, the number cruncher has to believe that your loan proposal makes sense for the bank. But if you've developed a relationship with the loan officer, the human being can weigh in on the loan decision also. The human being may help you get better terms, process the loan application a little faster, or recommend you more forcefully to the loan committee at your branch or the bank's national headquarters.

Another key person with whom you should develop a relationship is the real estate owned (REO) officer, who is in charge of property on which the bank has loans that are going into foreclosure or are in foreclosure already. The REO officer takes calls from people who are interested in acquiring these properties at a discount. (This is known as short selling.) Banks have no interest in actually *owning* the properties upon which they hold mortgages. The more foreclosed property a bank has on its books, the worse the REO officer (and the bank) looks. Therefore, it's possible to make some very good deals by negotiating repayment of the outstanding mortgage debt for less than the amount currently owed. I myself did a few of these deals when I was first starting out; many real estate experts make a career of short selling. If you're interested in short sales, do your research on how many properties the bank has in foreclosure, the discount rates on the loans, and the offers the bank has accepted in the past. With that information, make your offer to the REO officer. Be persistent but kind. Don't assume you can offer the bank bottom dollar because they're desperate. To build strong relationships with the REO officer—and with anyone—you have to go back to what I said in Chapter 3 about putting yourself in the other person's shoes. REO officers will have to justify to the bank any offer that's below the outstanding mortgage debt. You need to help them by being clear about the reasons behind your offer, for example: "I went by this property and the house has fire damage, the roof's half gone, and there are vagrants living in the building. It's going to take me $50,000 to make the house habitable. Here are the estimates from local contractors. That's why I'm offering you only $50,000 on a $100,000 mortgage." Doing your research, being up front with the REO officer about your offer and the reasons behind it, and above all, developing a relationship that extends beyond just the current deal will serve you well.

Once you meet and get to know the REO officer and other loan officers at your bank, you must work at building the relationship. Invite the bank officers to lunch. Take them to see your completed property. When you hold your open houses, have a special showing for them and/or ask them to come by. If you get to the point where you have grand openings or events or you hold seminars (like the Mortgage Qualifier Programs I taught early in my career), make sure to thank your bankers and lawyers and anyone else involved in the project. This commercial costs you nothing, but it's a huge acknowledgment for people who rarely get recognized. Your efforts to build a relationship with bankers will make the difference between being seen as "another real estate investor" and "the one who brings us great deals, even if they look a little outrageous at the start." Because today I require such large loans, with every deal I have to re-educate the people from the bank's headquarters. My local bankers know what I have to propose is probably going to work, but the local bank has only so much they can authorize. So I tell my local banker, "Joe, get the suits down here and let me do my thing," because I know I can sell them on the deal.

I look at any lender as being like a fairly large person—maybe a 250-pound linebacker or a Goliath—who holds the key to the vault.

He loves to make you jump through hoops, but to stay in business he has to open the vault and lend people money. The bank has the power of money, but they need to loan it to customers who will return it to the bank with interest. Never underestimate your power as a good customer; it will help you create an equal relationship with your financial institution.

GETTING OUT OF THE BANKER'S "BOX"

Like all other big organizations, banks will do their best to put you into a box, so they won't have to think when it comes to accepting or rejecting your loan application. You sometimes can use this tendency as an advantage in making your loan deals. For instance, there are different guidelines for someone buying an investment property rather than a primary residence. If you're purchasing a duplex and planning to rent one-half while living in the other, your loan could be considered a mortgage on a primary residence. In some circumstances you get better rates if your investment property can be considered a second home. If you declare yourself a real estate investor, there will be different lending departments, requirements, approval process, terms and rates for residential, commercial, single-family homes, or apartment buildings. Private client status, where you have significant assets on deposit and/or a significant loan portfolio and track record with the bank, can give you the flexible access to capital required when you are making multimillion-dollar deals.

To get yourself out of the bank's "boxes," it's often useful to get your banker out of his/her box—the bank. Most financial decision makers never leave their offices, but since a Maverick's deals almost always fall outside the norm, you need to convince the bankers to buy into your vision. Ask them to come and visit the property you wish to acquire. Paint a clear picture of what you're proposing and why the loan you're requesting is justified. Once they make the loan, invite them to see the work in progress. When I was working on one of our $20 million houses, I called my banker and said, "Joe, I just had the aquarium bar put in; you've got to come by and see it!" He came by the property and we had lunch, and then I showed him the aquarium bar, the $250-per-square-yard carpet, and the waterfall that poured into the swimming pool. Getting your banker out from behind the desk to see your completed projects is absolutely essential in creating a positive reputation with the bank.

Bankers must have boxes; that's their nature. But a Maverick's entire focus is either to break out of the box or at least to push out the sides gradually with successful deals. Your ultimate goal is for your bankers to believe in what you can accomplish. As a result of my long relationship with Bank of America, we've learned together how to throw away the box because I've insisted they visit my properties, see what I envision, and understand why my proposals actually offer lower risk than their models indicate. Then I've justified their confidence by producing profitable results time after time.

WHEN RELATIONSHIPS EVOLVE

One of the hardest things about working with an institution like a bank is that, while the institution remains, the people within it may leave or get promoted or transfer to other positions in other branches, and you have to build a relationship with a new loan officer or private banker. In these cases, the other relationships you've already developed will benefit you while you rebuild a personal connection with the new officer. However, even if the people in the bank stay the same, the relationship with the bank will keep changing with every deal you make. Successful projects will make it easier for you to borrow the next time. Your good payment record will make you a valuable customer. Eventually you may get to the place where you can hold out for better terms, lower interest rates, and so on.

The terms you get from the bank also are a moving target, affected by your past history and your current status (your level of liquidity, value of current holdings, and so on). For each new loan you should ask that your interest rate be less than the previous deal by perhaps an eighth or a quarter point, with a little bit longer term and higher loan-to-value ratio. Whenever a bank says, "Your last loan was a very good offer," I'll usually respond, "That was then, this is now." By using every loan as a new step in the evolving relationship with my bank, I have been able to get some of my loans for my big projects for around two percent interest. (Donald Trump may pay 1 percent, but he gives his lenders an equity stake. I'm happy to pay 2 to 5 percent in exchange for 100 percent of the profits.)

A word of caution, however: When your deals close and you get your payday from a project, make sure to *pay off your loan first*. It may be tempting to put all the money into a new deal and let your line of credit ride, and you can certainly invest some of the proceeds of a sale in another deal, but that should be your last resort when seeking money to invest. If you've been a great customer and paid off your loan, and you're sitting there debt-free while you look for another project, the bank is usually going to come after *you*. They're going to want the profit potential you represent, and they're far more likely to agree to the terms you request. Recently, when I was setting up a $100 million deal, I made just one phone call to my bank to say, "I want an aggressive loan with these terms and this particular loan-to-value. I've already started negotiations and I assume you'll be on board." They called me to hammer out the details, but I got the loan with little argument. Now, I don't ask for absurd terms; I know I've got to put money into the deal myself, and I have to pay interest and perhaps some kind of small financing fee. But my relationship with this bank has evolved from that first $2,500 loan to where the bank values my business to the tune of a $100 million commitment.

While you value your bank, you've also got to be willing to take your business elsewhere. You may outgrow their ability to cover the size of the loan you want, and you may need to look for a new bank that can accommodate your needs. Or the relationship just may not be working anymore. Banks and many other businesses are service providers; the way they stay in business is by serving their customers. But sometimes they forget that fact. Even with my bank, there have been times when they've tried to put me into a box that was wrong or too small, and they weren't willing to change. So I told them, "The status and brand I've developed need to be taken into account. If not, I'm going somewhere else that will give me better terms." And I've gotten the loan from another bank. This willingness to go elsewhere has helped keep my main bank honest. They saw what they lost when I left, and they were more willing to negotiate with me on the deals I wanted to put together. (On the other hand, you and your bank shouldn't part company over an eighth of a point on a loan. We talk about negotiation skills in Chapter 7.)

For my entire career I have brought one fundamental attitude to any relationship: I believe that Frank McKinney & Company is a privilege to do business with. I'm not talking about the kind of privilege that says, "Bow down to me." It's just that we are committed to being the best at what we do. When we walk into a bank, we have a belief in the way we approach our business that makes it much easier to deal equally with the suits who control the money. As a Maverick you can adopt the same attitude. If you're a good candidate with a good track record and good credit history, then it's the bank's privilege to loan money to you.

In the same way, when a client comes to view one of my estates, if he or she decides not to buy, that's their choice, but I know that nothing else on the market will stack up to this beautiful property. Part of being a Maverick is recognizing the value of what you have to offer and educating others to appreciate that value as well. Your job throughout your investing career will be to continually raise the bar for yourself and your properties, and each time you do, you will be educating the people and institutions you deal with and bringing them up to the new level of achievement. It makes for exciting times as you move upward with the Maverick approach!

CREATING A TEAM WITH REALTORS

Realtors will inevitably be a part of your team when you invest in real estate, so get them on your side early. Having a good relationship with realtors can benefit you in two ways: Realtors can bring you properties at every price point. Realtors also provide you with access to powerful tools for selling your property, including the Multiple Listing Service (MLS), out-of-town buyers, perhaps a web site to list and show your property. When I was starting in low-end properties, I sold them without a realtor. The law in Florida says you can sell your own property without a real estate license, as a FOR SALE BY OWNER (FSBO). At that point my deals were small and every cent of profit was important to me, so I didn't see why I should pay commission on something I could do very well myself. But I lost out on a lot of other benefits by selling my own properties. Many people never saw my houses unless they checked the newspaper for open houses on the weekends. When I increased the number of properties I was showing (at one point I was renovating and selling upwards of 20 properties at once), I couldn't be at all those open houses at the same time. At that point I decided it was better to find a realtor I could trust and negotiate a decent commission than to keep stretching myself so thin.

Even if you choose to sell your own properties (either as a FSBO or by becoming a realtor yourself), I still advocate developing relationships with the realtors in your area. The industry is set up for people to buy and sell through realtors, so to gain access to those people and properties, local realtors are your entry. Even today, when I'm selling only one or two properties at a time and have enough name recognition that I could probably sell them without a broker, I feel it's better to list than not list. In my case we're talking about millions of dollars of profit and hundreds of thousands in commissions, but if the realtors can find the right clients so I can sell my properties quicker and at full price, the savings on the monthly carrying costs helps to offset any broker fees.

That's not to say you can just turn your property over to someone and expect them to do all the work. There are A+ realtors, who work hard and do a great job marketing and selling your properties; B realtors, who do an okay job; and also many C− realtors, who do little more than list your house and do minimal marketing. You can't just turn your property over to a realtor expecting them to do a great job. You must choose your realtors wisely, develop strong relationships with them, and then monitor their efforts on your behalf.

Some people who embark on an investing career choose to get their real estate license first and perhaps join a brokerage firm for a few years. That way they can broker their own properties and save on commissions. They also learn about contracts, deals, and the legalities of buying and selling properties. You may want to get your license, too. But regardless, you need to take great care whenever you choose a realtor or realtors to represent your properties.

It's better to start looking for your realtor before you purchase your first property, instead of waiting until your property is ready to show. When you do your market research to decide the neighborhoods in which you want to buy, you can research real estate brokers at the same time. Some brokers are willing to help you with market research, comparative analysis, and value assessment. (That shows a dedication to relationship-based business.) Realtors also can be a resource for value verification when you find a property to consider for purchase. You must be sensitive to abusing the time of a realtor. After all, they're in business to make money, and their time isn't free, but you can start investigating which realtors will make a good match for you and your business.

When it's time to select your realtor, you should interview two to three candidates to determine your final choice. Here are six things you should look for.

1. Find realtors who specialize in the area, or in the specific kind of property you want to buy and sell. You can find these people by driving around and looking at FOR SALE signs, or by checking real estate brokerage web sites to see which realtors are representing properties at similar price points in the same area.

2. When you've got a list of prospective realtors, look at their marketing materials. Pick up the local realty magazines. Look at the ads in the daily and Sunday papers. Check realtors' web sites to see if you like the ways they market their properties.

3. Choose the realtors you feel are doing the best job and set up interviews with them. Ask how many buyers they bring to the properties, and what percentage of their in-house listings they actually sell. Some realty companies just put houses in the MLS and wait for other realtors to call them with buyers. You want a firm that actively sells the properties they represent.

4. Ask about sales avenues and success rates. Where do they advertise? Do they use newspapers, magazines, web sites, commercials, and targeted direct mail? What kinds of lists do they mail to? What's the average time houses in your price range are on the market? How many showings do they hold per month? What's the in-house conversion rate—the percentage of listed properties that they actually sell? A good realtor should have these answers on the tip of the tongue. If not, find another agent to consider.

5. Check references and referrals. If you can, find out the average percentage of in-house selling for realty offices in your area.

Get the statistics on the sales of this particular broker. What's their closing ratio? How long have they been in the business? How many properties are they representing at the same time?

6. Finally, you must believe this broker can do the job. Do they have the right personality for sales? (I've actually hired two people who were originally marketing directors. They got real estate licenses so they could represent my properties.) Are they professional and educated? Do they know the facts about their properties, and are they willing to put in the time to learn the facts about yours? Do they refuse to stretch the truth in order to make a sale? If you can't be there for a showing or a closing, are you confident that they can handle it on their own? Are they open to partnering with you in selling your property, taking your advice and direction without getting upset? Your confidence in their ability, honesty, passion, professionalism, and willingness to work with you should be factors in your choice.

When you select your broker, you will sign a listing agreement for a certain period of time. You can negotiate the amount of time the listing agreement will cover, and you *must* negotiate and put in writing the specific avenues—newspaper, magazines, web, MLS—through which the realty company will market your property or properties. (You will be doing your own marketing in addition to anything the realtor does; we talk about that in Chapter 9.)

In the same way that educating your bank is your responsibility as a Maverick investor, a large part of your relationship with realtors is education and direction. My current brokers, Premier Estate Properties, are affiliated with Christie's auction house. They're reputable, they don't take listings under $1 million, their client base is composed of my target buyers, and they pay particular attention to high-end spec builders like myself. I've been with them for many years, and I use them for very specific tasks, which I add to the listing agreement. The addenda to our listing agreements are longer than the standard listing form. They mandate the frequency with which advertising takes place, the specific periodicals and magazines where ads for my estates will appear, the placement of ads (right or left side of the page), full-page versus half-page, how many times we're featured on the cover of their magazines, how many times the search engine that drives customers to my web site is updated on their web site, and so on. And this is simply to drive prospective buyers to me, as I myself do the actual selling of my properties. You can put into your listing contract any specific efforts you want your realtor to make. If the realty company takes out glossy ads in magazines, places newspaper ads, creates color brochures, does virtual or video tours of properties on their web site, you can write into the contract that your property or properties will be included every single time in all those marketing avenues. Because you will be an active participant in selling your property, put in writing that you will be notified prior to every showing of your house. Remember, you may only be one customer to the realty company, but you're your *only* customer. You need to make sure your realtor knows that you're not just a home owner looking to sell one house and then move; you represent a lot more business and more commissions to them in the short- and long-term. (You will probably have to remind your realtors of this fact again and again.)

Once you sign with a realty company, you must continually monitor the efforts made on your behalf. They should give you a report of every showing of your property. And you must be willing to pull a listing from a realty company if they're not bringing potential buyers to your door. However, you do need to give them enough time to prove themselves; it's going to take a while for the brokers to get used to you and your unusual requirements for marketing. The minimum commitment I would suggest for your initial listing with a brokerage is six months; with higher-priced property, you should stay with them for a year. And while you should maintain control of the sale of your property, make sure you let your brokers do their job. You set up the plan, put your criteria in place, and then let them run with it. Don't bug your broker to death, asking every hour whether they've found you a buyer or set up a showing, because then your broker may fire *you*.

If you're just getting started, listing with a realtor is often the best choice because of the resources and, more important, the education you will receive about your marketplace, as well as selling, showing, and so on. Once you've gotten your education, you may be able to strike out on your own. I find a hybrid works best, where I list to gain access to the resources of a brokerage while taking charge of the marketing side myself. Regardless, as a Maverick investor, you must be actively involved in selling your property. Don't leave it for the brokers to sell without monitoring their progress.

By the way, you also should build relationships with brokers who bring buyers to see your properties. As I said earlier, upward of 75 percent of properties are sold by agents other than the listing broker. Every showing is an opportunity for you to build relationships and learn more about your market. I ask brokers for feedback. What did they like about the house? What did their clients like? Was there anything they'd like to see changed? You never know when an idea will help you earn more money on your next property, or whether the next broker who shows your house will be a broker you will list with in the future.

A broker's primary responsibility is to bring you buyers and to support the market you're creating. Your broker needs to feel the same passion as you do about your property and walk in step with your marketing and selling efforts. They also must be willing to constantly raise their standards and keep pace with you as you move ahead in your Maverick real estate investing career.

RELATIONSHIPS WITH YOUR SUPPORTING CAST

Your success in real estate will be determined by your success assembling a team of people to support your efforts. In addition to a banker and a broker, you'll probably need a bookkeeper and/or an accountant, and, unless you do renovations yourself, you'll need plumbers, electricians, contractors, laborers, painters, and/or landscape gardeners. You also might need help with marketing, and that may involve graphic designers, and perhaps media consultants. At the level of multimillion-dollar properties, I need a small army of laborers, artisans, an interior designer (my wife, Nilsa), home automation contractors, and so on. Most of my projects will soon be built by independent contractors hired for one project at a time, thereby reducing my liability as an employer. However, that doesn't mean I won't use the same people repeatedly. I have a great team of contractors and tradespeople, some of whom I've kept busy for years. But in late 2004/early 2005, when I sold my entire inventory, I had to let go several laborers and contractors and a couple of office staff. It wasn't easy, and I did my best to provide for them. I offered to send one construction worker to school to get computer and spreadsheet skills, which he needs to better himself. "If you do that, I'll pay for it," I said. "And if you don't, I'll give you plenty of temporary layoff assistance." (I don't use the word "severance" because it's not permanent.)

Some investors try to build relationships (and get better rates) by promising their contractors future work, but most of the time this ends up being smoke and mirrors. If you want to establish a long-term relationship with a contractor, be honest. Try saying, "I know you've heard this before, but I have a business plan that shows me doing five renovated houses this year. Somebody's going to be doing the work. It's either you or somebody else. Let's make it work out so that it can be you."

Of utmost importance in any professional relationship is to pay people as agreed and on time. I also like to throw in little bonuses here and there. However, I firmly believe that you should never put the promise of a bonus in writing. Bonus amounts, and even whether you offer a bonus, depend on how much money you made on a deal, how fast the property sold, and a dozen other factors. I also suggest that you are generous, based on your level of deals and the number of people you have working for you on a project, and the hourly wages you pay them.

Creating relationships within your team doesn't mean letting them be mediocre. You have to hold people to account and push them to do their best. My job is to create, use my vision, plan logistics, to budget, schedule, push, drive, and otherwise encourage the people who work on my projects to deliver the highest possible quality on time and on budget. Ultimately, my most important job is to bring the whole team on board with the Maverick approach, which is striving for the best, pushing the envelope, being assured but not arrogant, and never being satisfied with the status quo. When your team is enrolled in the Maverick approach, your results will reflect the quality of their work.

RELATIONSHIPS WITH THE PUBLIC

In 2004 four hurricanes hit Florida, two of them coming straight through Palm Beach County. At the time the third hurricane was heading our way, I had a sale pending on a $50 million property, with closing scheduled for the next week. I stayed at the property to make sure the house was protected from major damage. When the "all clear" was sounded, there was a lot of cleaning up to do, and power was off throughout the area. As you can imagine, I wasn't the only one who needed help, but because I have such strong relationships in my community, I was able to call in a lot of favors. I talked to the municipality to get the electricity restored; I called contractors and laborers and worked with them to clean up the fallen trees and foliage. When the client who was buying the house called me, worried about the deal, I said, "Come out and inspect all 30,000 square feet of this property. You'll see there are no leaks and no damage, and everything is back in shape." Within 24 hours of the electricity being restored, I handed the keys over to the new owner. But I never would have been able to get the house ready in time without the strong relationships I had built through the years.

Building relationships with people in your area will pay you back a hundredfold. Every person you meet may one day be a potential buyer and seller, someone that helps you get zoning cleared or leads you to a great subcontractor or other resource. You can build these relationships in the grocery store or the dry cleaner, with the people at your church, on the Chamber of Commerce and local government boards. There are six keys to building great relationships.

1. Relationships need to be genuine. People will know whether you're interested in them for themselves or merely in what they can do for you. Develop a genuine interest in people and you'll find they will return the same—along with helping you out when needed.

2. Relationships need to provide value for both people. Make sure you are looking for ways to help others. If the plumber comes to your property on Saturday because some child put a toy down the toilet during an open house, pay him extra or send a recommendation letter or a thank-you gift. Favors are part of building business relationships.

3. Be honest. Don't say you can do something if you can't, and don't promise future benefits to get help now: "If you give me

a great rate, we'll be doing a lot more business together." Never promise anything you can't deliver.

4. Courtesy and gratitude are some of the most valuable currency in any relationship. Make an effort to thank people, especially when they provide a service. After my showings, I'll write thank-you notes to all the brokers who brought clients to see my estates. Part of doing business is the follow-up, which should almost always include a personal handwritten thank-you.

5. Pay attention to the little things. Return phone calls in a timely manner, even if you have a personal assistant or secretary. It will keep you grounded while maintaining vital relationships.

6. Do what it takes to maintain relationships over the long term. For example, at one of my oceanfront estates we made a mistake in using regular high-grade finish on some outside cabinetry. (Usually we use marine-grade finish so the wood withstands salt and ocean air.) After a couple of years the cabinets were starting to warp, and the owner called me to complain. Like most other builders, I offer only a year warranty on properties, but we replaced the cabinets, anyway. We did what was needed to maintain the relationship.

In the same way you begin your real estate career by accumulating capital to invest in your first property, you must accumulate human capital by continually investing in your relationships with your community. Just as your money grows with each property, with proper nurturing and attention your relationship capital will grow, too, increasing your net worth and the quality of your life as well.

Our first $10-million-plus estate.

Chateau D'Amoureux, Delray Beach, Florida

SOTHEBY'S
INTERNATIONAL REALTY

Source: www.frank-mckinney.com

5

Don't Just Learn
Your Market—Create It

I was never the best student in school; formal education through classroom learning was not something at which I excelled. But I have always worked hard to learn whatever I needed, starting from the ground up. My most important education by far has been learning about the market for the different real estate projects I have undertaken throughout the years. You need to learn as much as you can about your market before you can shape it and ultimately create something entirely new, which is the true goal of a Maverick.

There are four aspects of learning your market.

1. Choose the investment category (renovation, new construction, short sales, foreclosures, tax sales, buying to rent, etc.), the kind of property (single-family, duplex, condos, townhouses, pre-construction, etc.), and price point (entry-level starter, mid-price move-up, high-end, etc.) you will focus on.

2. Choose the community and neighborhood in which you want to invest.

3. Know the general market trends that will help you "ride the tide" of economic ups and downs.

4. Know what's most important to your buyers at their particular price point.

Once you know your market, you can move to the step that sets a Maverick apart: envisioning and creating a market that breaks new ground for the area and the buyer. A Maverick's market is built not only upon people's varying definitions of the American dream, but also upon their sense of who they want to become while they pursue it. Whether for oceanfront estates or entry-level fixer-uppers, the market you create is never based on how much things cost. Instead, it is determined by how much people are willing to pay when your property fulfills their dreams.

CHOOSE YOUR INVESTMENT CATEGORY, TYPE OF PROPERTY, AND PRICE POINT

At the age of 21, when I first considered property investing as a business, I had very little cash, so I decided the quickest way for me to accumulate capital was to buy and sell distressed properties. I called this my "cash accumulation" stage. I thought once I had built up enough capital, then I could decide which direction to take my real estate career. However, I liked the cash accumulation stage so much that I never left it. I simply continued to buy, build, improve, and sell properties in increasing numbers and at higher price points. Today, while I consider myself a real estate artist, I'm still an entrepreneur and a real estate opportunist who buys undervalued real estate opportunities, creates value where there was none (or enhances where there was little before), and resells to those who recognize the property's new worth.

If you're just starting your real estate career, I suggest that you enter a cash accumulation stage first. Cash accumulation can occur in two different ways. First, you need to save as much of your own money as you can. This is not fun or sexy, but it is essential. Drop the "latte a day" habit. Avoid the instant gratification of malls and

Internet shopping. Bring your own lunch to work. Get a second job if necessary, and put aside every dollar you can. Make sacrifices today for a better tomorrow. Second, talk with your friends, business associates, and family to see if they would be open to investing small amounts in your real estate ventures. Initially, private family type money can have far fewer restrictions than bank money. It also can give you a cushion should your first few deals take more time and capital than you estimate. On the downside, money borrowed from friends and family can carry strings and emotional baggage that bank money never will. But it's still important to develop access to investor money early in your career. Then you can start with small, low price point properties found through foreclosures, tax sales, sheriff's sales, and so on. If you find undervalued properties, improve them quickly, and then sell them at an adequate profit, within a few years you can accumulate enough capital to move into bigger deals with more potential.

Your first decision is to select the kind of real estate investing that's best suited to your personality and goals. You may hate renovation and building and love landlording, or vice versa. You could be a great salesperson and lousy at the details. You may relate well to first-time buyers and be intimidated by the super-wealthy. To choose your strategy, start by asking what's most important to you when it comes to investing. What do you want, and what do you enjoy? A big net worth (who doesn't)? Quick and frequent rewards? A nest egg for retirement? The excitement of doing deals? The security of monthly income? Identifying what's most important will help you choose a strategy that will satisfy your emotional as well as financial needs.

You also need to know up front what the approximate costs in time and money will be for the particular strategy you choose. For this reason some people who are just starting out prefer flipping (buying and selling without improving), as this strategy can produce a quick payday. They're willing to take less than they could make if they increased the value in the property, in exchange for getting their money much faster. However, you don't want to be forced into flipping just because you didn't plan for the resources required to improve the property. You must take into account the cost of time and money you'll need for your chosen strategy.

Here's a scaled down list of possible real estate strategies.

- Buying bank foreclosures, tax sale properties, and so on.
- Buying distressed properties directly from homeowners—WE BUY HOUSES FOR CASH.
- Short sales—buying properties or mortgages for less than face value through a lending institution.
- Buying to rent (being a landlord).
- Lease-option—buying or selling the option on a piece of property with the goal of selling the property at the end of a certain period of time.
- Quick turnaround deals—flipping, wholesaling, and so on.
- Building new houses or commercial buildings from scratch.
- Commercial property—office space, warehouses, and so on.
- Creating value—buying undervalued properties, improving them, and then selling to buyers who appreciate your product.

I've used most of these investment strategies at one time or another, depending on my situation and the current climate of the marketplace. I've owned commercial real estate. I've rented houses. I've flipped properties, including the $50 million estate I sold in 2004. I've used lease-option deals in a tough market when I wanted to make some cash quickly while locking in a sale. But whether I was buying and selling distressed property or building multimillion-dollar mansions from scratch, my primary objective always has been to buy undervalued properties, improve them, and sell the results at values that set new benchmarks for the market. As a real estate opportunist/entrepreneur, you must evaluate the market and decide which strategy is best for you. However, I recommend focusing on one strategy at a time. You'll be better off choosing one type of investing and getting really good at it before you try another.

Once you've chosen a strategy, you must select the category of real estate you'll focus on. Most of my properties have been single-family detached homes simply because that's where supply and demand are greatest. However, the Maverick approach can be used on almost any kind of property—condominiums, townhouses, duplexes, apartment buildings, and commercial buildings. Indeed, if your financial resources are limited, or the prices of single-family detached houses in your area are high, townhouses and condominiums may provide a great entry into the investing market. (Not long ago my sister bought and sold a townhouse in San Diego—one of the nation's most expensive housing markets—using the Maverick approach.) Duplexes are another great choice, because you can live in one side for free and rent or sell the other side. You also need to determine the price point at which you can invest. If you're just starting out, you probably won't go straight into million-dollar-and-up homes, but that still could be your eventual goal. If so, find out how much capital you will need and start researching the psychology of your target buyer. Of course, as you increase your capital by accumulating profits from successful deals, you'll be able to look at more expensive properties. But make your learning mistakes on the fixer-uppers! Plan to start your investing career with properties at the lower end of your price range, no matter what your desired ending point may be.

The strategy outlined in this book is adding real value to a piece of property through improving it or building a new house. I am an advocate of this approach because it's proven to produce the best returns consistently, and it works at every price point, with many different kinds of property, and in every market. This strategy is the first-class stamp that you can use to build your real estate empire. With buy-and-hold strategies, where you buy property and rent it out, investors can occasionally find themselves real estate rich and cash poor. You can avoid this with the Maverick/value-add approach, as your goal is always to buy at the right price, improve in a reasonable amount of time, and then sell quickly at a price that represents the additional value you have created.

One final point: A I mentioned in Chapter 4, to really learn the business, you might want to get your real estate license. You'll learn about real estate law, listing and escrow agreements, contracts, and so on. You also can affiliate yourself with a national real estate firm like Coldwell Banker, Re/Max, Prudential, or Century 21. The local offices of these firms will give you insights into your area that are almost impossible to get otherwise, and certainly would take you far longer to acquire on your own. You'll learn about the brokerage side of the business (which will help when you negotiate commissions), master the MLS, see how brokers market their properties (and how you might do it differently), and get hands-on experience working with contracts and the legal side of real estate. Being a broker for a few years also can provide income while you're investing; you can get paid a commission for learning the business on someone else's time! Having your license will give you more freedom because (1) you can be your own broker if needed, and more important, (2) you can deal with other brokers from an insider's perspective.

CHOOSE YOUR AREA

To date, all of my real estate dealings have been in South Florida, and concentrating my focus there has paid off handsomely. I went from single-family homes to entire neighborhoods to ultra-high-end real estate, all within about 75 square miles. Other real estate gurus may advocate looking for specific kinds of property (foreclosures, tax sales, fixer-uppers) in a wide geographic area, going for the deal rather than the location. But if you want to really learn your market, it's better to concentrate your focus. Think how well you already know your hometown. You know the good and bad neighborhoods and the local amenities—shopping, transportation, entertainment, and so on. If you've renovated your own home, you also may know about zoning or local government or the permitting/inspection process. The knowledge you already have will help you enormously in your investment purchases and sales.

Eventually you may need to expand your geographic focus to include more neighborhoods and properties at different price points. I would suggest expanding it gradually and continuing to do thorough research. Remember, you're not just exploring an area, you're learning to apply the same tools to any location. It's this first-class stamp mentality that sets the Maverick apart. While you can apply the Maverick approach no matter where you are, where you want to invest, and at whatever price point, focusing your efforts in one particular area will give you greater ability to shape your local market.

BECOME AWARE OF GENERAL MARKET TRENDS

With the stock market crash of 2000–2001, more people saw real estate as a less risky investment alternative for their long-term financial goals. But just like the stock market, real estate is subject to the general economic climate, local and national news, rising and falling popularity of certain geographical locations, and so on. As a Maverick investor, you must be aware of general market trends so you can (1) protect yourself from negative consequences and (2) take advantage of trends by either going against them or staying in front of the overall tide.

Start by keeping tabs on market cycles and economic data. The coming retirement of the baby boomers, as well as the move of echo boomers from starter homes into larger properties, will have an impact on real estate growth in Florida, the Southwest, and rural areas throughout the country. In addition, the availability of a wider range of mortgages and low interest rates is allowing more people than ever before to purchase their first homes. This adds up to a rosy picture for real estate in general. That's the plus side. On the minus side there is general unease about consumer debt, higher-risk mortgages, and rising interest rates. Even ultra-wealthy buyers can be affected by overall economic and social conditions. Not because their level of wealth will materially decrease—it won't—but when there is a lack of clarity in the current economic climate, the ultra-wealthy are less likely to buy. Remember, for the ultra-wealthy any home purchase is discretionary and strictly based on desires and wants. If the overall economic or social situation is unclear, the ultra-wealthy will stay put.

As a Maverick, you need to make a point of gathering good information on real estate and the general economy. Some potential sources include the National Association of Realtors® (NAR) web site, your local newspaper, a national newspaper like the *Wall Street Journal*, local real estate investment clubs, and selected financial magazines. Look for statistics such as (1) average and median price for homes in your area; (2) general trends in mortgage rates; (3) percentage of homes on the market; and (4) length of time it takes them to sell. You are looking for information, not interpretation. Don't let any sensationalism or doom and gloom get to you, and take any information you read with a grain of salt.

I subscribe to the newsletters of several real estate professionals who specialize in different investing strategies. I also love reading the newsletters of real estate investment clubs because I can catch up on trends, see what people are investing in successfully, hear stories of strategies and mistakes, and so on. You don't have to be a member of most real estate investment clubs to receive their newsletters. I suggest doing an Internet search for clubs in your area, and then asking to be put on their mailing lists. Investment clubs are often great places to network and become active in your local market even if you're still saving for a down payment or searching for your next property.

You also should keep up on different lending options. Nowadays the 30-year fixed rate mortgage is only one of a host of loans that can be used on primary residence mortgages. Some of these new loans (which include 15-year fixed rate, adjustable rate, interest-only, minimum payment, piggyback loans, etc.) you can use to finance your own deals, while others can be used by the people who buy your properties. Especially if you are going to invest in starter homes, it's important to know the available mortgage options so you can point buyers in the right direction.

Remember, general market trends will have an overall impact on the real estate market but a minimal impact on individual buyers. When someone needs a house, they need a house. General economic data, interest rates, or sky-high home prices won't stop them from purchasing if they need the space or have to move for other reasons. However, your knowledge of these things will help you more accurately assess the potential returns on the properties you purchase and look to resell.

The U.S. Commerce Department and the National Association of Realtors® (NAR) keep track of sales figures for single-family homes (both new and previously owned) both nationally and for 66 different communities across the United States. Here are a few things you can learn from the NAR web site, www.realtor.org.

- Average holding time for houses valued from $100,000 to $5 million.

- Median and average prices for homes sold in your particular area. (Median price means half of the homes sold in the area were priced below this figure, and half were priced above. Average price adds together the prices of all the houses sold in a particular year or month and then divides by the number of houses sold.) You also can find out how much of a price increase or decrease there has been in the median and average prices over the past quarter, year, five years, and longer.

- Sales figures for the number of houses sold, by month and by year, tracked nationally and by community. The numbers include sales of single-family homes, condominiums, townhouses, and co-ops.

As a Maverick you should be aware of general market trends but not be boxed in by them. Yes, it's good to know how fast or slow home values in your area are rising; you need to know where the herd is going so you can break away from it. That's why a Maverick knows the local market, general market trends, and any economic data that can influence the marketability of the houses he or she wishes to sell.

CHOOSE YOUR BUYER

A part of learning your market is getting very specific about your buyers. If you're just starting, I strongly suggest you consider first-time buyers as your clients. Everyone needs a place to live, and that means there will always be first-time home buyers. This is the most recession-proof segment of the marketplace. Even in the late 1970s and early 1980s, when interest rates were 21 percent and the economy was a mess, people still bought their first homes. In the hottest real estate markets today, there are first-time home buyers stretching themselves thin to get into a house. This segment of the market is going to continue to survive regardless of conditions, so why not take advantage of it through applying the Maverick approach?

First-time home buyers in your particular area may have some demographic or psychographic traits that you should understand. Are there ethnic neighborhoods in the area where you wish to focus your efforts, and should you create marketing materials for them? Are there special amenities that will encourage more first-time buyers to consider your houses? What will set your property apart? A patio with a trellis to keep the sun off in hot climates? A mud room in northerly regions? For mid-level buyers, kitchen and bath amenities will help you sell your property for a higher price. Are all the bedrooms wired for cable and high-speed Internet? Are the kitchen countertops made of high-end material? Can you create a master suite with a spa-like bath? Knowing the buyers in your particular market will help you design, improve, and sell your properties at better price points more quickly. If you improve judiciously (as we discuss in Chapter 8), buyers will be eager to choose your properties and pay top dollar for them.

Ultra-wealthy buyers are looking for a "wow" factor. They expect the best, so your job is to surprise and delight them with new levels of what the best truly can be. This wow factor has to start at the property line, with the landscaping they see as they approach the gates. It includes the rarity as well as the beauty of the foliage, continues with the golf-course quality grass that lines the driveway, the coral caps on the property walls, the marble driveway, the lanterns (we used real gas jets in the lanterns on our last property), and so on. One of our recent estates included a dock for the owner's boat on the Intracoastal Waterway. The dock we built could accommodate a 126-foot yacht, and I installed 200 amps of power (the wattage available in the average American house) on the dock, so that someone could literally live on their boat.

Almost all potential buyers love our oceanfront estates. A few don't, and that's fine; I know that there will be buyers for my masterpieces. I understand the minds of the ultra-wealthy and I'm willing to push the envelope to provide their dreams of the perfect home that will represent everything they ever could be or become. You, too, need to understand the dreams of your clients and provide them with the best experience their wallets can buy.

CREATE A MARKET THAT BREAKS NEW GROUND

Creating a new market is where a Maverick excels. Creating a market isn't about providing what's already selling but about establishing a new definition of what's possible, based upon what people truly want. But you must overcome the fear associated with encroaching upon uncharted territory. Creating a market will make you more profit as long as it's done with intelligence. It requires both knowledge and vision: knowing what is already present in your targeted area and envisioning the next step. Sometimes this vision can transform an entire neighborhood while setting a new standard for the area.

Let me use an example of a street in Delray Beach that became known as Bankers Row. This block of tiny, old, wooden houses was in complete disrepair in the late 1980s and early 1990s. The best thing about these houses was their location, approximately one mile from the ocean and less two blocks from downtown Delray Beach. I ended up buying and improving five properties on that block. I moved into one of them; it was the house I got married in and later sold to finance my first oceanfront deal in 1991. I bought that house for $75,000, and after renovations sold it for $225,000. Most of the other houses on that block I bought for around $20,000 to $30,000 and sold for around $100,000 each after improvements. Today, 15 years later, the house I lived in sold for $1.7 million, and most of the other properties on that street are worth at least a million each! That increase in value is not just as a result of rising property values and the great improvements I put into those houses. It also has to do with creating a whole new market in that part of Delray Beach. As I was renovating those Bankers Row houses in 1990, we formed a home owners association and taxed ourselves to improve the street and put in new streetlights that made the neighborhood safer and provided an upscale ambience. We also got the zoning changed to allow for businesses on the street. I believed that the proximity of this particular street to downtown Delray might make it a great option for mixed-use expansion in years to come. The other neighbors and I were proactive in making Bankers Row more livable and driving up values in the process. Bankers Row is now part of the Old School Square Historic Arts District, and it's surrounded by cultural and civic projects that have developed since I renovated those houses.

When you're creating a market, you can't just focus on your property or house and make changes up to your property line and no farther. You have to look at the entire neighborhood as part of your marketplace. For example, if you're buying fixer-uppers in marginal neighborhoods and the house next door is a dump, offer to cut their grass and trim their trees. I've even painted the houses next to my property so the neighborhood looked more in line with the new level of value I wanted to establish.

You also should get involved in the community. Lobby the zoning boards and county commissions for improvements to roads, sewers, streetlights, zoning changes, and so on. Volunteer your time for committees, boards, commissions, and the local Chamber of Commerce; they will keep you informed about future improvements that may help you sell your houses at higher prices. When you can tell a buyer, "Within a year there will be new streetlights," or "There's a new grocery store going in a half-mile from here," or "Next year the county is going to open a new elementary school in this district, with brand-new beautiful facilities, and that's where your children will go to school," you're much closer to a potential sale.

Creating a market is not always comfortable. You're asking buyers, local officials, realtors, and appraisers to stretch their ideas of what's possible, and this doesn't come naturally for most humans. A large part of your job will be showing others the value you have created and why your higher price is justified. You may need to teach people about your particular property, pointing out the unique amenities you've added and how you've upgraded the entire house and yard to a level worth the extra 10 or 20 or 30 thousand dollars above the average house price in the neighborhood. (Of course, this improvement level needs to be appropriate to your buyer and add value while still maintaining your profit level; see Chapter 8.) You also may need to educate buyers about the area. We have sold ocean-front estates in the coastal towns of Delray Beach, Gulf Stream, Manalapan, Ocean Ridge, and Jupiter, and we have information on our web site about each community: when it was founded, who founded it, how many people live there, how many houses are on the ocean, and the town's amenities (such as a private fire department and police department, in the case of Manalapan). Ultra-wealthy clients aren't just buying wonderful estates, but they're also buying a lifestyle and a community, so we show them exactly what they will be getting. For instance, in Delray Beach we talk about land values (other than Palm Beach and Manalapan, Delray is the highest-priced land in Palm Beach County), the downtown area, and all the amenities offered by having its quaint yet upscale shops and restaurants within walking distance.

The Ocean Ridge house is a perfect example of creating a new market. A broker called me and said, "Frank, are you interested in a piece of property on the direct oceanfront in Ocean Ridge?" I thought I knew most of the direct oceanfront land in Palm Beach County, but I had never seen the portion of beach the broker was referring to because the entire community is east of A1A, the main ocean road. When I took the turnoff for the small Ocean Ridge community and found the property, it looked like a throwback to the houses I had bought in the 1980s—abandoned, windows broken, sitting on a 70-by-300-foot lot (a small lot for the properties I build now). It was behind a surf shop and a little sandwich shop, and the road leading to the house went right by the only oceanfront trailer park in the United States. There was one paved road in the community (the rest were gravel); the water pressure was awful because the pipes serving the community were probably 100 years old. The houses were tiny, dark, most of them owned by absentee landlords, and worth no more than $200,000 to $300,000 each. The beach was gorgeous, but it was called Dog Beach because it was the only one in the county that allowed dogs to run free, with very predictable problems with cleanliness.

The owner of the property was asking $1.1 million. I knew there were a lot of drawbacks to the area, but I also saw it as one of the last opportunities in Palm Beach County to build an entry-level, smaller estate that still would raise the bar in terms of square foot costs while transforming the community as a whole. I calculated that, with the lot size and the kind of house I wanted to build, I would be asking $7 million for the final product. But to set that kind of market level I not only had to create an amazing house and grounds, I also had to upgrade the community around it. I started by befriending the neighbors and, working with them, we got the county commission to open a beautiful dog park nearby and move the dogs off the beach. We also persuaded them to pave the roads and put in a new water main and sewer line.

However, I knew that selling a $7 million house in a community with such humble origins wasn't going to be easy. I told the people in my company, "Once someone comes through the gates to this property, they've got to feel like they've entered Shangri-La. We've got to find the tipping point that will make them focus on the beauty they are surrounded with and ignore any possible negatives that may exist." And we did. Every element of the house and grounds was designed to transport the owner to another world of luxury and style in a relatively compact space. For instance, instead of the four-to-eight-car garage we usually put in our houses, this project had a two-car garage with lifts, so the owner could keep five cars in a two-car-garage space. In the main building we built a bar with a suspended acrylic floor that had moving water underneath. On the floor beneath the water was a mosaic of a great white shark, its jaws wide open. It looked like you and/or your bartender were standing on water with a great white below you, ready to pounce. Combined with the exquisite finishes in the kitchen, a master bath better than anything I had ever built, exceptional landscaping, and many other beautiful touches, the entire property transported buyers into another world.

Over the two years this house took me to complete, I had a few doubts. That's something you must guard against when you are creating a market. There will be times when you'll doubt that there will be clients to appreciate and buy your properties. I had to keep repeating to myself, "There are no other houses on the ocean, of this size, at this price, with this level of luxury in Palm Beach County." That property sold in 84 days for nearly the full asking price, to a buyer that would have paid more if we hadn't already agreed to a deal. Today the owner is happily enjoying his beautiful home that is now worth more than $8 million, and we have created a new market in the community of Ocean Ridge. We have been a catalyst for change and have increased values that will benefit other homeowners.

As this book goes into print we are in the design and permitting stages of creating the first nine-figure spec home in the United Sates. That's right: a home with a value in excess of $125 million. We are again eager to apply everything you have just read to create yet another market and do so in true Maverick style. Please visit our web site, www.frank-mckinney.com, to see the progress on this magnificent work of art.

There will always be those who challenge your ability to create a new market, even if it's something as simple as asking 10 percent more for your property than anyone has ever paid in that neighborhood before. If you're in an area where the most any house has sold for is $300,000 and you ask $330,000, you'll need to be prepared to explain your reasons. Always remember three things. First, it's a lot easier to drop your price than raise it. If you find you're charging more than the market is willing to pay, and you've built in enough cushion to your profit equation (see Chapter 7), you can lower your price if absolutely necessary. However, the second thing to remember is that if you've improved based on your analysis of the buyer's wants and needs, and if you've provided more value for the dollar spent, you shouldn't have to worry about selling your house at the price you want. The buyers will be there if you are patient. Finally, creating a new market is never based on dollars and cents but upon the financial and emotional returns your house will provide. There will be buyers who can appreciate your work and will pay extra for the value they receive. A real estate Maverick should be willing to say, as I have upon occasion, "Look, Mr. or Ms. Client, if you think this property is overpriced, then go find a house that's as well built, well accessorized and furnished, with this kind of view and these amenities. However, there isn't one. If you want this piece of art, the asking price more than reflects the value you have experienced." You must have that level of confidence in yourself, in your knowledge of your buyer and your market, and in your ability to create new levels within your marketplace. This is the very essence of the Maverick approach.

PART TWO

THE FOUR STEPS TO MAVERICK REAL ESTATE SUCCESS

Have you ever watched a great tennis player in action? I was a tennis pro when I first came to Florida, and I still enjoy watching players like Serena Williams and Roger Federer. What they do on a tennis court is magic, but in essence they're doing exactly what my seven-year-old daughter will do when she starts competing—serve, volley, lob, smash, and hit forehand and backhand shots. But Federer and Williams have practiced so much that they developed the skills that brought them to the pinnacle of the tennis world. Inventory some of those who have influenced your life who seem to be at the top of their game and see how the repetitive, upward spiral of application has gotten them there.

The Maverick approach is a guide to becoming the equivalent of a world-class tennis pro in real estate. While the four steps of the Maverick approach may seem familiar, *how* you take those steps is different. Using this system you will learn to go against conventional wisdom and follow an unorthodox yet proven path to success. If you've read and adopted the ideas and principles outlined in Part 1, you're ready to learn the steps of the Maverick approach.

Before we begin, there are three key points.

1. *Start and stay small until you are ready to break out.* There's nothing wrong with focusing on just one deal and making a small profit. I made a grand total of $7,000 on my first house after four months' work (much of which I did myself), but that project taught me lessons I apply to this day. I also made some mistakes with that house, but instead of costing me hundreds of thousands of dollars (as they would today), those mistakes cost me a couple hundred dollars—a much cheaper way to learn! Even if you're an experienced real estate investor and follow the Maverick approach to the letter, there will be a learning curve, so start small and make your mistakes with less costly properties.

   I also suggest you choose a category of real estate that will produce a lot of buyers—starter properties for first-time buyers, for example. If you're a veteran real estate investor with more cash reserves, perhaps mid-level homes are an appropriate small starting point. The principle remains the same: Start small so you can invest big later, and regard your first property as an investment in learning.

2. *Pay hyper-attention to your first deal.* I hear the same thing over and over when people talk to me about real estate. "Yeah, I bought one property, renovated it, and it was a complete bust—I lost money," they say. "Now I'm thinking of getting into buying and selling lease-options (or short sales, or tax deeds, and so on). Do you know anything about that?" These people had a lot of enthusiasm but little skill, and they plunged headlong into their first deal without adequate preparation and suffered a significant loss as a result. Now they're looking for the next big thing that will make them a fortune overnight.

   Most people want to move on quickly from a perceived failure, even if the problem lies not with the system but with their application of it. Therefore, you need to work extra-hard to make sure your first deal is a success. Enthusiasm isn't enough; you must have both the skill and the willingness to follow a system that's been proven to work. You must pay attention to every detail, not be tempted to deviate from the system no matter how attractive the property, and check off every item along the way to ensure you're doing things right. Carpenters say, "Measure twice, cut once." A Latin proverb says, "A good beginning makes a good ending." Frank McKinney says, "Pay hyper-attention to your first deal and you'll be more likely to succeed on your second, third, and fourth."

3. *Base hits are better than home runs, so don't swing for the fences.* Batting average in baseball measures how often a player gets a hit when he comes to the plate. But there's also a statistic called slugging percentage, which measures how many bases a player covers for every time at bat. Slugging percentage assigns a greater value to bigger hits—triples are better than doubles, which are better than singles, home runs are the best, and walks don't count at all. In real estate, some people go for slugging percentage: They want to hit a home run every time, meaning they want to triple their money or more with every property. They see a property and think, "Wow, I could make a million bucks on this if I just buy it right and sell it next month." But because they're swinging for the fences, so to speak, they're also more likely to take bigger risks and strike out more often. This is an approach you cannot afford. Contrary to what most other people think, I am very happy to step up to the plate and hit a single. Guess what? With this approach I have never struck out!

   For the past few years or so, in many parts of the United States it's seemed as if every deal is a home run. At business organizations and investment clubs I hear from people who've made $20,000, $30,000, $50,000 or more on their very first deal. This home-run mentality has been built up in the media, to the point where people either (1) feel certain they can't lose in the real estate market or (2) are terrified to invest because they think the bubble is going to burst at any moment. But in my experience, the greatest danger in real estate is when you create your own bubble by failing to follow the formula of the Maverick approach. If you pay too much to acquire the property, if you overimprove, if you don't market or sell your property well, then you run the risk of having too much invested to make the profit margin you wanted, or worse—having more in the property than anyone is willing to pay for it. You can't count on being able to hit home runs in real estate, but you *can* do your best to make a profit with every deal. To this day I don't think we've ever aimed to hit a home run with any of our properties. We've based all our deals on an investment formula (which you learn in Chapter 7) that contains a sizeable margin to accommodate any challenges we might encounter.

If a baseball player swings for the fences and strikes out, he knows there'll be another at-bat in this game or the next. In real estate, with anywhere from tens of thousands to millions of dollars on the line, most of us can't afford to strike out even once. In the Maverick approach, home runs aren't as important as getting on base every time, meaning that every deal makes you a profit. If you can keep doing deals that make you small yet consistent profits, eventually you may hit a few more doubles and even triples, where you exceed your estimates and expectations. But in the game of real estate, getting on base every time is your most important goal.

Remember, the Maverick approach is like a first-class stamp that will work no matter how many properties you buy and sell, or at what price points. But until you've received a piece of mail that's been delivered with that postage, your confidence level may need some boosting. Your first deal should be delivered "certified mail, return receipt requested," that is, you should take your time, choose carefully, run your numbers again and again, build in good-sized margins for time and cost overruns due to inexperience, negotiation, closing costs, and so on, and make sure your profit margin is adequate to make the deal reasonably profitable even if your numbers don't work as well as you thought they would. Once you've gotten one deal under your belt, you will be able to use this approach as many times as you desire, building your net worth along with your success.

In short form, here are the four steps of the Maverick approach.

STEP ONE: LOCATE
(LOCATION, LOCATION, LOCATION—OR IS IT?)

A real Maverick believes in *making* the location rather than following one. While we'll talk a good deal about choosing your neighborhoods and areas, ultimately you'll be making the location by raising the values in the neighborhood. Finding properties where you can take the entire surrounding marketplace to a new level is the key. A Maverick knows that many times the property is more important than the location because upgrading a property will often upgrade the neighborhood and in turn, the location. At the same time, a Maverick evaluates properties based on their ultimate sale-ability and possible return on the investment of time and money. In this step you'll learn how to evaluate properties first and location second, and how to determine the property and neighborhood that are your best possible choices.

STEP TWO: NEGOTIATE/BUY
(YOU MAKE YOUR MONEY THE DAY YOU SELL, OR DO YOU?)

You make your money the day you buy, not the day you sell, and a Maverick knows that buying right is a lot easier when you focus on what buyers and sellers *really* want from a deal. In this step you'll learn secrets for calculating returns, working with banks and sellers to negotiate based on their needs and wants, structuring deals to your advantage (time, money, budget, financing, etc.), and closing the deal to fit your requirements. You will learn how to buy right.

STEP THREE: IMPROVE
(SOLID GOLD OR GOLD-PLATED?)

You can lose all potential profit in a deal if you don't approach this step correctly. Unfortunately, many people renovate based on what *they* think is important rather than discovering what the potential buyer may truly want and dream about. You need to know what improvements are most important in your particular market. Are you in the wood, aluminum, nickel, silver, gold-plated, or solid gold category, and where's the best place to put your dollars? In this chapter you'll learn to make improvements that will cause your target buyer to lust after your property.

STEP FOUR: MARKET AND
SELL, SELL, SELL!

From the time you see a property until the time you turn the keys over to the new owner, you must be marketing and selling. Our marketing has always focused on heightening the five senses to the state of subliminal euphoria: Every part of the buying experience is designed to move clients subliminally to the point where they make the decision to buy almost without realizing they've done so, and they'll do whatever it takes to make the home their own. In this chapter you'll learn the secrets that help a Maverick sell properties at every price point to every kind of client.

Remember, the Maverick approach is not a get rich quick solution. You must be willing to put in the work, follow the system as closely as possible, learn from your mistakes, and then do another deal. If you're not willing to apply yourself every day, to stick with the system, take the risks and make it happen, then you've wasted the money you spent on this book. However, I believe you're ready to learn how to step up to the plate, and I'm willing to be your coach, mentor, guide, goad, and ally. Remember: the human cell is 1/1,000th of an inch across, yet it contains DNA instructions that would fill a thousand books at 600 pages apiece! So believe me when I say that you have a Maverick within you; it's time for you to put him or her to work.

Our $20 million Manalapan estate—sold in 62 days.

6

The Maverick Approach, Step One: Locate (Location, Location, Location—or Is It?)

Most real estate gurus will tell you that location is at least half of the value of your property. But as Donald Trump writes, "I've seen a lot of idiots ruin good locations and a lot of geniuses make incredible investments out of horrible locations." A Maverick believes he or she can make the location rather than the location making the property. I began my career buying properties in neighborhoods where no one else would, and improving those properties to sell to people who never thought home ownership was an option. I've taken beachfront communities in Palm Beach County that were considered backwater and down market and turned them into the newest fashionable addresses for billionaires. A Maverick knows that the property is more important than the location, because upgrading a property will often upgrade the neighborhood. At the same time, a Maverick evaluates properties based on their ultimate sale-ability and possible return on the investment of both time and money. Your job is to locate properties at the right price and then improve the property to the point where it can set new benchmarks for the neighborhood. You, not the location, are the ultimate determiner of property value.

Creating value is possible in two ways. First, you can go into a good neighborhood and find a house that you can improve and sell for a significant profit. But in many areas the chances of that are slim, especially in markets and neighborhoods where property is fully valued and margins will be too narrow to make it worthwhile. You won't locate a great deal in a great neighborhood unless you're very lucky or on the inside track, and that probably won't happen often enough. While it may seem harder at first, it's actually easier to go in and create value. It takes a little more time, but the proactive approach to value creation can expedite your results. But this also means you can't spend a lot of time looking in established neighborhoods. Yes, keep them on your radar because you never know when the perfect house will show up, and you want to be first in line if it does. Otherwise, you're going to have to go where others won't because you can see value where they cannot.

Your search for property begins with the vision and passion statement and objective plan we spoke about in Chapter 2. Those who lose money on properties usually do so because they don't have a clear plan. You can't just rush out to acquire anything that's in your price range. Each property has its own unique set of opportunities, and to take advantage of them you must fit those opportunities into your overall investment plan, which should include the following: (1) your chosen investment strategy: renovating/improving, building new, wholesaling/flipping, short sales, pre-construction, lease-optioning, and so on; (2) the type of property: single-family home, condo, townhouse; (3) the price point and targeted buyers of the properties you want to consider (starter, midlevel, upper echelon); and (4) your projected timeline (two months, six months, a year or more). With that information, you can start your location search by defining the geographical area where you will concentrate your efforts.

DEFINE YOUR AREA

In elementary school, did you ever use a compass for drawing circles? I suggest you use one to define your area of focus. With your own home as the center point, put the sharp end of the compass on a map and then use the pencil end to draw a circle. Start small, with a radius of five miles; that's the area you'll explore for potential investment opportunities. List all the neighborhoods and communities within that circle, and start researching. You're looking for *undervalued neighborhoods*, where home prices or general price appreciation hasn't kept pace with others in the area. Examine every neighborhood within your radius for undervaluation, even if you feel it's not a likely candidate due to the cost of property or condition of the neighborhood. If you don't find something within 5 miles, go 10 miles out, then 15, then 25, at most 50 miles. Every city, town, and county will have neighborhoods within a radius of about 25 to 50 miles that will fit your investment profile.

Once you have some possibilities, there are five main topics you'll want to research.

1. Look at the *prices of the homes in the area, both highs and lows*. To identify undervalued neighborhoods you need to know the entry-level or lowest price, and the highest price a house there has sold for. Local realtors, the county property appraiser's office, private appraisers, and other experts can help you find these numbers. Some local newspapers will list property values by ZIP code, and you can check public records in the county assessor's office for property sales in the area. A comparative market analysis search (done through your realtor or by you if you have your real estate license) will indicate exactly what is selling, at what price, and with what amenities, in your area. I suggest you track market values for the previous two to three years to determine trends in valuation. You're unlikely to see declining prices, as real estate holds and increases its value better than any other asset. Instead, you're looking for prices that have held steady or appreciated slightly, which indicates a neighborhood in stagnation. Most important, find out if there are any events on the horizon—municipal rebuilding, private business investment, rezoning, infrastructure changes, bond issues, and so on—that might increase the value of the neighborhood in the near term.

2. Research the *inventory in the area*: *what's available, what's selling, what's not, and why.* You want to know the average time a property in the area is on the market, and at what price point. A neighborhood with low turnover can mean two things: First, the area is fully valued and people aren't selling, or second, the neighborhood is undervalued and people aren't buying. You can get much of this information either from your local broker or the Multiple Listing Service. Look up number of sales, average asking price, size of the average house, number of bedrooms, bathrooms, and so on. As a Maverick you can certainly buck prevailing trends, but it's better to be in front of trends instead of trying to swim against them. If houses in the neighborhood all have pools except yours, you'd better plan on adding a pool unless you have a good reason not to or you're willing to lower your price.

3. Look at the *available pool of buyers*. If you're planning to buy starter homes, know where the apartment complexes are in your area, as renters may be your best clients. If you're targeting mid-level buyers, look where families already live in the area. (Remember, families don't want their children to change schools if they can help it, so they'll stay within school district boundaries. Even when kids are in private school, families want to avoid longer bus rides or school drop-off commutes than they already have.) Working with realtors and the MLS will help you attract buyers from all over, but it's still useful to know the people who might be driving or walking by the properties in the area.

4. Find out *any political or zoning considerations*. Your local newspaper is a great source for this information, but I suggest attending meetings of local government and various neighborhood associations. Join the Chamber of Commerce, Kiwanis, or other social and service-oriented groups. Know the area's city councilperson, Congressperson, and state representative, and let them get to know you. Keep tabs on local government activities, as everything from streetlights to potholes to potential zoning changes to the Wal-Mart that's

moving in down the road will have an impact on property values.

You also want to know any current information about the neighborhood. This includes police reports on violence, robberies, drug busts, and so on. Because undervalued neighborhoods may be underdeveloped or even marginal, you may find higher levels of violence and drug use than you would like, but this should not stop you from considering the neighborhood. Many marginal areas can be turned around through municipal investment and/or private projects, businesses, sporting venues, and so on, that are being built nearby. More important, your buying and improving a property in the neighborhood can create a ripple effect that uplifts the entire area.

5. Look up *any local building codes or restrictions*. If you're planning improvements, you'll need to know any restrictions on design, amount of property between houses (set backs), garages, guest houses, second stories, and so on. Different municipalities have varying regulations, and there may be different rules for new construction than for renovation. You have to go into each municipality and learn the code of ordinances that relates to residential construction. If you're building on the coast, or on other bodies of water like lakes or rivers, often there are much stricter regulations on both design and environmental impact. In Gulf Stream, where I've built three properties, a house must not look too dissimilar from others in the area as mandated through an architectural review process. If you're buying townhouses or condominiums, there may be regulations that will restrict the improvements you can make, the construction you can do, even the paint colors you can use. Know the rules as well as who will approve your plans, as both will affect your ability to improve your investment purchase.

Much of your research on all five topics can be done online, at realty and government web sites, at the property tax office itself, through local publications including newspapers, realtor magazines, other local magazines, and, of course, the MLS. Read your local real estate listings. Utilize realtors to find the public records of property sales in the area. (Nowadays much of this can be accessed online.) Based on the information you gather, there will be neighborhoods in your area that you can eliminate (although you might find deals everywhere, so keep your eyes open). You'll also end up with a good idea of the neighborhoods you wish to target for your next step: ground-level research.

PROFILE THE NEIGHBORHOODS
WHERE YOU THINK YOU MIGHT INVEST

When you select neighborhoods for investment, there is no substitute for driving and walking around. I advocate starting with your own neighborhood first; you might be surprised at what's available. In Delray Beach, I know every single owner of an oceanfront home as well as many other properties in the community. I know when something's going on the market often before the realtors are called in. You, too, might turn a conversation with a neighbor who's being transferred to another state into a private party sale where you both get a great deal and avoid paying commissions.

After you get to know your own neighborhood, expand your research throughout that five-mile-or-greater radius. Walk and drive the streets. Talk with the people who live there. Where do they work? What kind of people are they? What do they have in common? The more you know the neighborhood, the easier it will be for you to (1) evaluate its potential, and (2) find properties in the area. Research the neighborhood in your local newspaper. Look at things that may raise housing values—a new store that's going in, projected improvements, and so on—as well as things that cause the values to drop—crime rates, community centers closing, infrastructure problems, and so on. Some real estate investment clubs will conduct tours of neighborhoods as part of their educational efforts. Of course you must do your own research, but these tours can be great for anyone who's just getting started.

While I recommend you keep your geographic circle tight, if you're in a fully-valued market you might have to adjust your search. I'd rather go farther out and get to know an entirely new area than try to buy something in a fully-valued neighborhood and eke out a minor profit for all my work. A Maverick's goal is to find undervalued property, usually in undervalued neighborhoods, and today that means going where others are not. If I were new to investing or to an area, the first thing I would do is go to a respectable broker and ask, "Where *shouldn't* I be? Where would you suggest that I stay away from?" and that's the first place I'd look. It's in the less desirable neighborhoods that your greatest potential for value is often found.

In researching these neighborhoods, I suggest you check the trends in violence and crime in an area. If violence and crime are growing, you might want to stay away. If the level of crime is either flat or declining, the neighborhood might offer a good opportunity. When surveying a less than good neighborhood with the idea of bringing it up, I always relied on my seat-of-the-pants feeling on the amount of time the neighborhood would take to turn around. If I felt it was a two- to three-year horizon, I'd consider investing. If it would take longer than that, I'd pass. That doesn't mean I didn't guess wrong every now and then. I once bought a fixer-upper in a poor Palm Beach County community, improved it, and sold it quickly, but within a year the house was boarded up again. Some neighborhoods will take more time and money to bring up than you are willing to spend. Before you invest you should sense from your discussions with the municipality and viewing other respectable houses in the neighborhood that this area might turn around within the next couple of years.

Almost every major municipality will have something in the works for its disadvantaged neighborhoods, and you can help lift them up with your properties. One of the smartest things you can do is to get to know the long-range revitalization plans of your town or city. When upgrading marginal neighborhoods, most municipalities will start at the fringes and work inward. If you know their target areas, you can actually partner with the city or town in their gentrification efforts. When I was first looking to acquire property in

Delray Beach, for instance, every day I walked by a building site not too far from the houses I wanted to buy. I talked to some of my contacts in local government, who told me the town was converting a boarded up old school into a performing arts center. This major addition to Delray Beach was within walking distance of the houses I was thinking of acquiring. You'd better believe I moved ahead with the purchase with a lot more confidence. But a Maverick doesn't wait for a city to revitalize, because he or she can make the rise in values happen first. You can increase the value of your properties through improving the physical structure of your houses, while you also improve the infrastructure that supports that value with or without municipal support. In Delray Beach we helped improve Bankers Row not only by upgrading the houses but also by getting the zoning changed to accommodate a combined commercial and residential use. This allowed our renovated properties to accommodate lawyers' and accountants' offices in the single-family homes. People could run home-based businesses, and this increased property values even more.

To find an undervalued market, you may need to look for areas that possess features of markets that are hot already. For example, today oceanfront property in Palm Beach County is almost completely fully valued. A couple of years ago I would have two to three properties I'd be developing, but now it's almost impossible to find even one property a year. I've been asked to look at properties in several different parts of the country but I have resisted, simply because I believe in my philosophy of local market focus. However, recently a broker asked me to look at the Vero Beach area, about 100 miles north of my historical target market. Vero Beach has many of the advantages that Palm Beach possessed about 15 years ago. It's on the coast, and land on any coast (or near water, for that matter) has greater value than inland property. There's only so much beachfront in existence, after all, and it will always be in greater demand. Three years ago you could buy land in the Vero Beach area for around $5,000 a front foot. Today it's probably five times that or more. It's a quiet community, populated with retirees. The restaurants and shopping are good. Its cultural and civic amenities are either established or in the development stage. Building restrictions are not overly burdensome; you can still build a good-sized house without problems. Vero Beach is an example of a market that has a scarce commodity (oceanfront real estate) but is still undervalued and underappreciated. If it weren't for my purchase of the 8.78-acre, ocean-to-Intracoastal parcel in Palm Beach County, I would probably be up there right now. As it is, it's becoming a popular area for investment.

Based on your research, you should be able to come up with a neighborhood that feels right for your focus. You also should have a number in mind that you will be able to pay for a house or vacant lot and the amount of improvements you can put into it and still sell with a good profit margin. Remember, you can buy a house in almost any neighborhood and add value to it, as long as it's currently undervalued. A property that you pay $300,000 for in a neighborhood where you can establish a new benchmark of $500,000–$550,000 when you sell is an undervalued property. When I bought the oceanfront property in Ocean Ridge for $1.1 million—more than triple the highest price any property in the area had ever sold for—I knew that, given the location of the property and its beautiful oceanfront land, it was undervalued even at that price. I also knew, based on my numbers, that I would ask $7 million for the home I would build there. That home sold in 84 days, and now the neighborhood of Ocean Ridge will never be the same.

FINDING PROPERTIES TO CONSIDER

As part of your search for properties, you should avail yourself of institutional sources such as banks (through the REO officer, as we discussed in Chapter 3), the county and the IRS (for property sold to pay back taxes), and sheriff sales (for property seized due to illegal activities). In most cities and counties there are regular sales of these "distressed" properties, as they are known. These courthouse step sales were one of my primary sources of deals when I first started. Each week I would pick up the listing of upward of 40 properties being sold for foreclosures and taxes the following week. In my first six months studying real estate, I went to the auctions every week and bid on properties in my head, but never actually raised my hand. I

learned the process, the area, the kinds of things to look for in foreclosures, which banks were dealing in these kinds of properties, and
so on. When I actually started putting in offers, I averaged one deal
for every 120 or so properties I looked at. Of course, I also got smart
and started going directly to the REO officers to make deals on properties before they went to the courthouse step sales (nowadays these
are called short sales). But I always did my due diligence on every
property: I drove by, inspected it, figured my margins, and then put
in my offer.

Twenty years ago there were maybe five of us bidding against
each other in those early foreclosure sales. Now there are hundreds
of would-be investors competing for the same starter properties. Depending on your market, by the time you discover a potential investment property you probably will have a lot of competition. So you
must get there first—hopefully before the property ever gets to the
foreclosure or tax sale stage. I recommend you drive through your
target neighborhoods looking for signs of a distressed property that
may not yet be on the market. Most real estate gurus will tell you to
look for unkempt grass, cracked windows, torn screen doors, trash in
the yard, and general dilapidation of the house and grounds. But in
today's market, you need to get to the owner of those properties before the grass gets out of control. You want to be in there first with
the best offer. And that takes driving, looking, and getting to know
not just the properties but also the people in the neighborhoods.

Locating property that is not yet on the market can be done in
many ways. When you're just getting started, I recommend trying
anything and everything so you can discover what works best in
your market. Put ads in newspapers. Join neighborhood associations.
Offer seminars, like I did. Write letters to home owners letting them
know you're looking to buy. Many people get mail lists of home
owners in their target neighborhoods. This is kind of a "smart bomb"
way of finding properties. The letters range from impersonal flyers,
the WE BUY HOUSES FOR CA$H! kind of thing, to more personalized ap-
proaches that make the buyer look like someone who needs a home
for themselves rather than an investor.

Whatever approach you use, nothing beats personal contact and
establishing relationships in the community. Drive through neigh-

borhoods and if any house looks less than pristine, talk to the owners and let them know you're looking for properties in the area. Chat with the neighbors; often they'll know whether someone on the street has had a change in their situation and might be thinking about selling (or might consider selling if the offer was right). Get to know the people and properties in your 5- or 10- or 25-mile radius. The seeds that you plant today might not come to fruition for years, but remember, you're in this for the long term. In my own area I've spent a lot of time meeting with and maintaining relationships with owners of oceanfront property, and as a result they call me first when they're ready to sell. Sometimes the deal works out, sometimes it doesn't, but I'm still offered the opportunity before anyone else. And that opportunity is gold as far as a Maverick is concerned.

WHEN TO SAY YES—AND NO

When you're first starting out, I advocate taking a look at everything, even if it's fire damaged, termite ravaged, with a cracked foundation, whatever. If it's in your target neighborhood and you can acquire it at a great price, most of the time you can improve it or even tear it down and build new and make a great profit. The key is to acquire it at the right price. In Chapter 7 we talk about looking at specific properties and deciding whether the numbers make sense for you to put in offers on them.

A Maverick knows that a house you purchase for investment is different from the house you purchase for yourself. You're not looking for something you like; instead, you must view every property according to one and only one criteria: the perceived value of the house in the marketplace. The goal is to make a profit from buying and selling at the right price, not to own real estate for its own sake. Therefore, you must never let your personal preferences get in the way. You may be a mid-century modern fan but everyone in your area wants brick Colonials. In that case, you'd better be buying and renovating brick Colonials unless you feel mid-century modern is the next wave in housing preference. I've created houses of many different styles, from Italianate to French Riviera to Old Florida to Contemporary. Could I have lived in any of them? Probably. Did I build them based on my own taste? Only to the degree that I believed my taste conformed to the tastes of my ultra-wealthy clients. I choose my properties and build my houses based on how I believe my clients would like to live. I learn this by listening to them and by keeping up to date on the finest materials and the latest trends in ultra-high-end real estate. I'm designing and building a nine-figure mansion because I believe it will be on the forefront of a growing trend, and the property I will be creating—on a piece of land that I owned many years ago and have just repurchased (more on that later)—will be the trendsetter, the finest of its kind in the world.

Eventually, when you've done several deals, you will develop enough knowledge and experience in your particular area that people will begin to present you with other opportunities—a commercial property or a small apartment building. Or perhaps someone will bring you a property at a higher price than you've ever considered. Once you've mastered the basics of the Maverick approach, I encourage you to listen to any offer that comes your way. There isn't anything I won't listen to at this point, especially if I feel it will help me make a new market. That doesn't mean I'll take every opportunity offered; I still adhere to the credo of concentrating my focus in South Florida's multimillion-dollar spec estates. But I've listened to proposals for property in locations from Nova Scotia to Vero Beach to Indiana. You, too, should listen to proposals that others bring you, as well as actively seeking out opportunities on your own. But first you must master the basics of the Maverick approach. I worked on small, fixer-upper properties for six years before I built up enough equity and stretched my risk tolerance enough to make the move to the oceanfront. And I thought about making the move for a year while I searched for my first oceanfront property and accumulated the capital. While six years is a relatively short time, it represented hundreds of smaller deals, a lot of looking, and years in the trenches, learning and applying the Maverick approach every day. That's one of the most important aspects of daily application: Not only will you get good at finding and making deals, but you also will increase your confidence level. You'll need this confidence to move up the ladder from your first fixer-upper to the million-dollar and multimillion-dollar price range. You must become comfortable enough to pull the trigger in high-priced marketplaces.

Every day the newspapers and MLS are filled with properties for sale; every day you should be searching for undervalued properties in undervalued neighborhoods. I don't believe in sitting and waiting. You've got to get out there; you want to be closer to first than last when investing in undervalued neighborhoods. However, your most important tool as a Maverick investor will be your ability to know when to say yes and when to say no. You must not be tempted to step outside the parameters you set for yourself. In your vision and passion statement and objective plan, you set out your goals for the kinds of real estate deals you wish to focus on. Staying within those guidelines can be difficult, but it is essential for your success. You may need to adjust your price point; you may need to move your compass circle outward to consider more neighborhoods; you may need to go into areas that might feel somewhat uncomfortable; you may need to take a lot more time than you want to locate the properties that meet your criteria for undervalue. But stick with the basics of the Maverick approach. Even in the hottest markets, like South Florida, coastal California, New York, Las Vegas, and so on, there will always be enclaves that are undervalued and underdeveloped. Eventually you'll find the spot where the amount of untapped value meets your desire for profit potential, and when that happens you will have succeeded at the Maverick approach.

One of our oceanfront dream kitchens.

Photo credit Corey Weiner/Red Square Photography

7

The Maverick Approach, Step Two: Negotiate/Buy (You Make Your Profit the Day You Sell, or Do You?)

In 20 years of real estate I have never lost money in a for-profit deal because I have always paid strict attention to the buy side of the transaction. Whether you're buying distressed properties below market value or putting everything into a multimillion-dollar oceanfront lot, you must be sure that your acquisition price will ensure a good profit. It all starts with the purchase. You can decrease your expenditures on improvements, raise your asking price when you sell, even take advantage of increases in property values. None of these will have the same impact on your bottom line as buying at the right price with the right terms.

Throughout my career I have attempted to apply the same formula for calculating the finances for any deal:

Acquisition + Improvement = 50–60 Percent of Retail Selling Price

Acquisition = your cost to buy the property, including deposit, purchase price, loan amount, points, closing costs, and so on.

Improvement = what you do to add value, from a coat of paint to building a new house from the ground up. Acquisition + improvement = 50 percent to 60 percent of the retail or asking price of the house when you complete renovations. Retail selling price = typically 10 percent to 20 percent above current retail in the neighborhood, as your goal is always to create new highs in your marketplace. By applying this formula you will realize between 50 percent and 100 percent profit on your investment.

   Here's an example. Suppose you find a property you can purchase for $75,000. Improvements will cost around $35,000, for a total investment of $110,000. Based on the formula, your selling price should be about $220,000, which should set a new level for the neighborhood while being realistic; you're not going to sell a $300,000 house in a $200,000 neighborhood, but with the right improvements you can sell a $220,000 house.

   I use this calculation as a rough estimate whenever I'm looking at a property. I don't believe in overanalyzing a deal; I've seen people who have lost out because they spent too much time calculating their returns. If I can look at a property's acquisition price and say, "If I acquire this property at X, and I know I can do the renovations or new construction for Y, that means I have to sell it for Z. Do I feel confident I can make a new market at that price?" It takes me a very short time to make those calculations and decide if I want to put in an offer or pass.

   Sounds easy, right? It is and it isn't. When you first begin using the Maverick approach, I suggest you find potential properties and run the numbers simply for practice. You can learn a lot by testing the formula on different properties at different price points. You'll also learn about any contingencies that could affect your bottom line on your first property. Your acquisition costs and improvement costs will be easier to determine because they're known. What's unknown is your ability to make a new market. You must have confidence in the possibility of increased values not only for this property but also for the neighborhood. Is there a chance you won't achieve your profit goals? Naturally. This acquisition formula is designed to be an estimate, and the selling price will flex depending on circumstances. But there's enough profit potential to handle most situations and still give you a nice profit.

Once you're familiar with the calculations of this formula and have used it with properties on paper, I suggest you start putting in offers, using what I call the Maverick Equation for Acquisition Success.

The Maverick Equation for Acquisition Success

Current condition and future retail value of the property
+ your ability and options to finance the deal
+ seller's psychology =
An acceptable offer at a price that will allow
you an excellent level of profit

To make a qualified offer and to have it accepted, you need (1) an accurate assessment of the condition of the property and its current and future value in the marketplace, (2) the financial resources to acquire and improve the property, and (3) an idea of the seller's psychology—what he or she needs most from the deal. You must do your research, find properties that meet your requirements, gather your financial resources, and then negotiate with both the seller and financial institutions to ensure the deal will provide the profit you desire.

KNOW THE CONDITION AND VALUE OF THE PROPERTY

Now we get down to the nitty-gritty of choosing properties. In Chapter 6 we discussed knowing the neighborhood and areas in which you want to invest. Based on your research, you should know:

- High and low prices of houses in the area currently on the market.
- Potential municipal improvements scheduled within the next year.
- Current inventory: what's available, what's selling, what's not, and why.

■ Average time a property is on the market, asking price, size, bedrooms, bathrooms, and amenities.

■ Historical relation of asking price to selling price.

I recommend considering anything that is even remotely possible in your target neighborhood. Cast your net wide, because you never know who will bring you a great deal. When you find a property that you believe has potential, research it thoroughly to establish whether it represents good value, meaning you can acquire it for 30 percent to 50 percent below current prices in the neighborhood. Look for external factors that could lower the selling price—zoning problems, liens, tax issues, and so on. Check the property's sales history: Has it changed hands frequently? Talk with the neighbors about the property and the owners. Assess the neighborhood for appearance and upkeep. Remember, you're not focused on whether this will be a great place for you to live, but a great property to buy, improve, and sell for 10 percent to 20 percent above current market values.

You must evaluate three things before you make an offer.

1. *Condition of the property.* To buy right and budget right for renovations, you need to know what you're getting into, so get a professional inspection if possible. I consider the fees for inspections some of the best money a Maverick can spend. Now, a bad inspection report needn't keep you from acquiring the property. Even if termites have eaten the roof supports, the house can still represent a great value. But (1) you need to budget for those repairs and (2) you may be able to use the damage as leverage in your negotiations.

2. *Timeline for improvements and sale.* Are you looking at a couple of months or years before you can bring the property to market? If you're counting on the neighborhood turning around, how quickly will it improve? You've got to feel that things will come up to the level you need within the next two years. If not, you may need a backup plan—lease-optioning, renting, moving in, lowering your price, auctioning your property, and so on.

3. *State of the current real estate market.* Are prices rising, falling, or stagnating? One of the benefits of real estate is its ability to hold its value and appreciate steadily through the years. But you can't count on a real estate appreciation to make you a profit if you pay too much. As I said earlier, the only real estate bubble you have to worry about is the one you create yourself by overpaying for a property and not applying the Maverick approach. You don't want to invest in a neighborhood where values have run up for the past few years and now they're hitting a plateau. If you do, you've just lost money, because you may improve, market, and carry the property and still not be able to sell at 10 percent to 20 percent above current values.

When you're examining a property you might wish to acquire, I suggest you run through at least five different scenarios. First is your best-case scenario, which is represented by the acquisition formula. If you acquire the property at X, and you put Y improvements into it, your selling price must be twice X plus Y. Once you have that number, look at a worst-case scenario: For instance, you have to hold on to the property for a few years, paying for marketing, insurance, maintenance, the interest on the loan and other unforeseen carrying costs. Or there's a hurricane, or the local industry moves out of town, or you can't get crews to do the work and your renovation costs explode as a result. Or the bottom drops out of real estate in your area and you can't get 10 percent to 20 percent above current market price. Does this deal still make sense in those cases?

Once you calculate the best- and worst-case scenarios, come up with at least four options to make money with this particular property. The more options you have for the property, the more likely you are to realize a profit. Can you resell the property as-is? Lease-option it? Sell it with minimal improvements? Rent it for positive cash flow? Move into the house yourself and sell or rent your current home? Renovate it for mixed use, putting in an office? Sell part of the land or the entire lot? Your most profitable option may be to stick with your vision of buying, adding value, and selling, but being aware of other possibilities will help you make the most of opportunities and mitigate potential setbacks.

Nothing in life is certain, and circumstances change quickly. You may need access to your capital for an emergency or for another opportunity. Or the situation with this particular property may change: The local government may deny your permits, or the neighborhood may be rezoned. While real estate is not as liquid a commodity as stocks, you still can sell any asset if you're willing to reduce your price or give favorable terms to the buyer. You want to have that worst-case contingency plan to sell the property and recoup your investment plus a small amount of profit if possible. And if you buy at the right price, you should be able to realize a profit at almost any point.

If you're in a market that is currently at the top of its value range, don't be discouraged. There are still properties to be found that will meet your desired profit goals. You may have to take longer and look harder to find them, but they're out there. My sister, Martie, lives in San Diego, California, which has been one of the hottest real estate markets in the country for several years. Not long ago she and her husband Jeff bought a two-bedroom townhouse as an investment property. The purchase price was in the low $300,000s, and the property had a sliver of an ocean view. She put 20 percent down and financed the rest of the purchase price and improvement costs. She put in a new kitchen and bathroom, and put the townhouse on the market. It sold almost immediately, netting her a $50,000 profit. You, too, can locate undervalued properties even in a hot market. You'll need persistence and patience, and a willingness to move quickly when a property becomes available. You'll also need an accurate evaluation of the property's condition, a good idea of the amount of renovations needed and the time they will take, and a general sense of market trends. Only after you have considered all of that should you start negotiating the price at which you will buy the property, and use the Maverick acquisition formula to determine if the deal makes sense. That's when you will need to have your financing ready to go.

NEGOTIATING WITH LENDERS

Unless (and if) you decide to use cash for your purchases, banks and/or other lenders will be your partners in every real estate deal.

However, at the beginning you should be cautious about the amount of debt you take on. This may be an unconventional and unpopular statement, because one of the great attractions of real estate is its ability to be highly leveraged. I don't believe in the "no money down" school of investing. To me, debt is a meter that's always spinning, and every spin adds to my costs and reduces my profit. Remember, while you are building/renovating and marketing the property there may be no income to counteract the debt meter, and it could take months or even years for you to sell. Until you reach a point where you can dictate terms to your lenders rather than having them set for you, keep your debt levels low.

If you already own your own home but you're purchasing your first investment property you may be in for a shock, as you're going to pay more interest and points on your investment loans than you did for your home mortgage. (Since most loans are designed with primary residences in mind, and the terms are far more advantageous, you may want to consider living in your investment property while you renovate it. You also can shelter the capital gains from the sale if you live in a property for two years and roll the profits into a property of equal or greater value.) You'll also need to put down a larger deposit for investment property. If you have a decent credit score, banks will require a minimum down payment of 20 percent. I suggest you put down *at least* 20 percent to 30 percent, and cover improvement costs yourself rather than factoring them into your loan. This will increase your chances of a profitable deal when you sell, because you won't end up giving a large percentage of your profits to the bank.

How can you find the money for your down payment? First, obviously, is savings. Second, you can pull equity out of any asset you have—your home, stocks, bonds, cars, and so on. Third, you could sell household goods that you're not using or no longer enjoy. Fourth, you could get a second job. Fifth, you could reduce your lifestyle temporarily. Yes, sacrifice today for a better tomorrow! If you still don't have the money, see if you can borrow cash from friends and family on a short-term basis. In a pinch, you can use credit cards (although this must be your last resort, as credit card interest rates are almost always higher than loan rates on real estate).

Once you've accumulated your down payment and found your property, you need to find a lender for the balance of the investment. There are several sources of real estate loans.

Your Bank

The most conventional source of financing is your bank. This is where the relationships you've developed with the bank loan officer and REO officer will come in handy. (In fact, you should go to the REO officer when you begin your property search, to see if anything the bank has in foreclosure or pre-foreclosure meets your criteria. With the cooperation of the homeowner in foreclosure, you then can pay off the mortgage on the property, usually for less than the face value of the loan—a short sale.)

In today's lending environment, bank practices are changing because they have to keep up with a wide variety of other lending institutions. Therefore, you may have greater wiggle room when it comes to terms. However, don't count on that flexibility for your first deal unless you've already established relationships with the bank. It also means you have to negotiate. Your negotiation skills will put money in your pocket, yet you'd be surprised at how few people use them when it comes to loans. You should be prepared to ask for better terms on every aspect of a deal, including:

- *Amount of the loan.* Ask for more than you think you'll need to help cover contingencies.
- *Interest rates.* Because you don't know how long you will have to hold the property, interest rates are probably the most important variable to negotiate.
- *Points or loan origination fees.* Sometimes banks will try to compensate for low interest rates by raising the points or loan origination fees. Certainly a bank needs to make money and you should expect to pay something for the loan, but negotiate to keep fees low; start from zero and go up gradually.
- *Tenure.* How long the loan is for. Time can be your friend when it comes to creating value. Especially if you're building from scratch or planning to do extensive renovations, you need a

longer tenure to give you the time required to complete the improvements and sell.

- *Loan-to-value (LTV) ratio.* Typically banks will loan up to 70 percent of a property's value for investment real estate. Always seek to establish a line of credit rather than an outright loan where you have to draw down the full amount at closing. If you can get the bank to 75 percent LTV and then put down a larger-than-required deposit, you can use the additional loan funds on your renovations. For example, say you're looking to acquire an investment property for $1 million. You can get a loan for $700,000, which means you have to put down a $300,000 deposit. If you put down $500,000 instead, you can instantly have access to a line of credit worth $200,000, which you can use to make improvements on your investment and build your creditworthiness at the same time. This will come in very handy later in your real estate career.

- *Other terms.* You want a lot of flexibility as to where and how you'll use the funds. Designate the loan for "business purposes" or "real estate," and leave it at that. The deal you're working on may fall through or you may find another property that provides a better opportunity, and you'll want to apply the loan to that purchase.

Remember, banks are in the business of making loans and collecting interest. They lend money against cash flow or future loan payouts. They don't want to know about the value of your property other than to assess how much money they will loan against it. They certainly don't want to take the property back and sell it themselves, regardless of the LTV! All they care about is your ability to service your debt, so they'll want to see the kind of track record you have as a borrower. If you don't yet own a home, that should be your first purchase, even if you treat it as an investment property, renovating it and selling it two years later. If you do own a home, the equity you've built up plus the income from your employment will be factored into your viability as a loan candidate. Certainly the deal you bring to the bank will have some effect on your ability to take out the loan; even the most conservative loan officer may be willing to give you a mortgage on a property that you're buying for 50 percent of assessed value. But until you have a track record of borrowing and repaying loans, you can expect to pay more for the privilege of using the bank's money.

A Secured Line of Credit on Your Own Home or Other Asset

You do this with the bank that holds the mortgage on your property, or you can go to any number of other lenders. With a line of credit you pay interest only when you actually use the money, and you can use the funds for pretty much anything. However, a line of credit is easy to abuse. Don't be tempted to use it for a vacation, a car, or improvements for your residence (unless you are planning to sell in the near future). Any line of credit must be used only for *opportunity* and *insurance*. It allows you to seize opportunities without worrying whether you have enough cash for the down payment. It also insures that you have accessible funds for renovations and carrying costs should you need extra money until the property sells. Lines of credit typically are for three years, with the possibility of an extension. Just remember to repay your line of credit as soon as you realize your profits so the money will be available for your next deal.

Mortgage Broker

If your bank won't give you the loan or you don't like the terms, a mortgage broker can be your next best source for capital. When I first started investing in real estate, my mortgage broker was my pipeline; I did several deals with her assistance. Mortgage brokers get paid only if they put together a deal for you, so they're highly motivated. They will be up to speed on all the different mortgage loans with different interest rates, terms, loan-to-value, tenures, and so on.

Hard-Money Lenders

Depending on your situation, your mortgage broker may refer you to one of many "hard-money lenders," typically individuals or smaller finance companies that lend based upon the future value of the property. These loans carry significantly higher rates and points, but they may be a good option until you can replace them with bank money or sell the property. Although ultimately bank money is cheapest, if you don't have a track record or access to home equity you may have to use a hard-money lender. You'll pay a higher cost of funds—typically 12 percent to 15 percent plus 2 to 3 points, depending on your credit—but you'll also find them more willing to take a chance on your deals. While banks look 80 percent at debt service and 20 percent at value, hard-money lenders are typically the exact opposite. And since you'll be dealing in properties with great potential value, you may find it easier to obtain financing through this alternative source.

Hard-money lenders also will tend to be more proactive and involved in the loan process. Whereas getting a bank loan can take weeks, some hard-money lenders will drive by the property, assess it, do the comps (comparable research), and close a deal within days. Especially if you haven't been able to set up a line of credit with your bank in advance, hard-money lenders will allow you to jump in and snap up a deal before it goes to someone else. If you can make tens of thousands on a deal with hard-money loans versus missing out because the bank took too long, an extra $2,000 or $3,000 in interest and points might be worth it in the short run.

Hard-money lenders advertise on TV, radio, the Internet, magazines, newspapers, bus signs, billboards, yellow pages, and so on. Many real estate investment clubs maintain lists of hard-money lenders in the area, and there are national hard-money lenders as well. Typical terms for a hard-money loan include 65 percent to 70 percent loan-to-value based on the property's future value (so if you buy the property right using the Maverick acquisition formula, you may not have to put down any money), terms of a year or more, some prepayment penalty, a lax minimum credit score requirement, and prompt closing. Your terms will depend on your individual situation, and just as with the bank you must negotiate to get the best deal possible. You'd also better be sure that you're buying your property at 70 percent or less of market value and you can get in and out of the deal within a year. *Note:* This is certainly NOT your preferred source of funding. Bank money is your best option, should it be available to you.

Seller Financing

Some motivated sellers will hold the note on the property. This is a great option if you can get it, as you can then put all your available cash into improvements and other costs. However, most sellers are interested in cash in hand. If you need seller financing and you're willing to live in the property, you might offer the owner a lease-option, where they hold the note and a portion of your rental payments goes toward paying down the mortgage. You can make improvements, put the house on the market, sell it, use the proceeds to pay off the owner's note, and then take the profits.

Individual Investors

Private investors can give you great flexibility, as you don't have to worry about the approval process of a lending institution. Lack of credit and/or experience may not count against you as much, either. However, you may have to give up some control and a larger part of your profits. As long as the deal will pay off your investors while leaving enough profit to make the project worth your time and effort, private investors can be a good choice.

A variation on private investors is a partnership. A partner can be actively involved in the project or simply provide the money in exchange for a larger share of the profits. If you need to bring in a partner, I suggest you build a general partner's fee of 20 percent or more into the agreement. You would receive 20 percent off the top of net profits, and then split the rest 50/50 with your partner. The general partner's fee would be your additional compensation for the work involved in creating and executing the project.

When you bring in a partner or other investors, you'd better (1) know your investors well, and (2) make sure any agreements are legally binding and in writing. In today's litigious society, you and your investors need to be protected, with procedures for settling disputes clearly spelled out. I also suggest that your partners agree to be silent and absent. Many cash-rich investors have nothing better to do than come down to the property site and offer advice. You're going to be a demanding enough taskmaster for yourself; you don't need anyone looking over your shoulder telling you what color to paint the trim.

If you wish, you can factor your improvement/construction costs into your loan. A hard-money lender will do that for you in one step, but again, you'll probably pay a higher interest rate for the convenience. A bank won't loan you money for improvements until you have acquired the property (with the bank as the lender). Then they'll require an appraisal that confirms the property will be worth more than you paid for it once the improvements are implemented. If so, you can get a home equity loan or line of credit to cover the construction/improvement costs. Your best bet is to cover any improvement costs with home equity loan money, because interest on a home equity loan is tax-deductible. Remember, when you sell the property, you will pay off both the mortgage and any home equity loans before you calculate and take any profit. And always budget more for improvements than you think you'll need. There are sure to be surprises as you renovate or build, and having a financial cushion is essential to your success.

When deciding upon which lender to use for your loan, always run the numbers. A bank loan at 6 percent or 7 percent will save you thousands over a hard-money loan at 12 percent or 15 percent. But always go back to your bank for your next property. Eventually you'll have enough of a track record that the bank will take a chance on you, and because interest rates are better through a bank, you'll make more money in the long run. And make sure your financing is in place before you approach the seller. Nothing makes a seller more nervous than having to wait for a buyer's loan to be approved. A financing contingency in a contract will get in the way of your presenting an offer that is lower because it's "all-cash." Settled financing will be a huge point in your favor when you sit down to negotiate with the owner of the property.

NEGOTIATING WITH SELLERS

If a property is on the market, the owners want to sell. Whether it's sold to you will depend on the amount you offer, but equally important can be the relationship you create. You've got to get to know the owners, understand what they want from the sale, and do whatever you can to fulfill their needs. Before entering into any negotiation, you must learn what the other side needs, desires, or wants. Do your homework on the seller's stage in life and health. Stage in life is defined by (1) age, (2) business (their current involvement in the business world), and (3) circumstances: Are they retired and looking to move to a place with lower taxes and maintenance, do they need to move into a managed care facility, or have they just added to their family and need more space?

You also need to research the property: how long it's been on the market, any price reductions, what the owner bought it for, how long they've owned it, any outstanding liens, loans, tax bills, and so on, and how much total debt is currently held on the property. These factors will affect what the owner wants from the deal. For instance, the current mortgage payoff will have a large bearing on how much the owners will accept. It's rare that you can offer much less than what's owed on the mortgage, unless you negotiate a short sale directly with the bank. In some cases, however, you'll make your best deals with owners before the bank takes possession. That's why you should get to know your bank's REO officer and whoever records foreclosures in your city or county government. There's a gap between the time the notice of foreclosure is filed and the foreclosure date. During that period you can contact the owners and see if you can assume the loan or pay it off. This is a win for the owners, who gain some money from the sale, a win for you, as you acquire the property usually at a great price, and a win for the bank, which gets its money without having to take possession of the property.

I always try to find out as much as I can about the owner. I'll Google the name to see if there's anything on public record. I'll also try to find out from the agent and, if possible, the owner, why this property is on the market. If it's an older owner, you also may need to contact the heirs or anyone else who has a financial interest in the property. (Usually heirs will want cash, so they have an even greater interest in selling the property quickly.) You may need to negotiate with heirs directly if they are handling the affairs of the owner, even though the older person remains the owner of record.

Based on my research, I try to determine what the owner's greatest need is and how my offer can fill it. Perhaps the owners have been transferred to another city and need to sell quickly; they may take less than asking price in exchange for an immediate payout. Perhaps the tax bill's gotten too big for the owners but they don't want to leave. If the deal's good enough, I've let people stay in their homes for up to a year. If they're fixed on getting a certain price, I may ask the seller to finance the deal at an interest rate below bank rates, so my final cost is within my parameters. I craft my offer based on my acquisition formula, the terms I'm willing to offer, and the way I believe the terms will be perceived by the seller. I always do my best to make sure both sides of the transaction feel good about the result. Very few people want just money. Some want to get out quickly, others are sorry to leave their homes. Fulfilling the seller's true needs gives me a greater chance of acquiring the property at a price that works for us both.

CREATING THE DEAL

I used to be very detailed in my offers to owners; I'd specify every single lighting fixture that was to remain. Now even with multimillion-dollar properties, I've found that the simpler and clearer the offer, the greater chance of the owner accepting my terms with less haggling. Let me be clear: I never make an offer without doing my research and running my numbers. But once I have a number that meets my acquisition formula, I put it out there to the owner, see if I've got a deal, and then I fill in the details.

To give your deal a greater chance of being accepted, do the following.

- ■ Don't be greedy. If any party in the transaction gets too greedy—the bank insists on that extra quarter-point interest, or the buyer won't pay for inspections, or the seller insists on squeezing every penny out of an offer—the other parties can just walk away. You have to know when to stand pat, of course, but more important is to know when to give a little to get a lot. Greed will doom more deals than anything else.

- Make your offers and contracts clean, simple, straightforward, and able to be executed quickly. The longer the time between signing the contract and closing, the more time the deal has to fall apart.

- Offer a good-sized deposit; this shows the sellers you're for real, and gives them the incentive of cash in their pockets.

- Purchase "as-is with right to inspect." I get inspectors in within a few days, but the deal isn't contingent upon their findings. This clause gives me a free look and allows me to cancel the contract for any reason within a short period of time. Another conditional clause I put into my contracts is "subject to a satisfactory survey." Banks and title insurance companies require an updated boundary survey, which measures the size of the lot and the position of the house. The survey allows us to do a personal inspection of the house and grounds, and to get out of the deal if there are any problems with encroachment, property easement, or any other reason whatsoever. This gives me enough "wiggle room" in case I find something unexpected that would have a serious impact on the deal.

    An "as-is with right to inspect" contract benefits both you and the seller. You take the property off the market while you have a 20 to 30 day free look at it, and the seller has an "as-is" offer they can count on once the 20 to 30 days pass. If you find something substantially wrong, you can use these clauses to get out of the contract. But if you've done your due diligence, you already should know about anything that might decrease the value of the property (and you will have factored it into your offer). You shouldn't be looking to get out of the deal anyway. For the most part if we've gone to contract, I want the deal to go through, and I'll fix whatever the problem is afterward.

Even with the multimillion-dollar deals I do today, my initial purchase offers consist of no more than five key terms.

1. *The dollar amount.* That's where the owner's eyes will go first.

2. *The fact that it's a cash offer, with no financing contingency.* The closer you can get to representing to the owner that you are offering cash, the better. That means you've already gone to your lender with the deal, and they've given you the go-ahead for any financing you require.

3. *The deposit amount.* Make it sizable enough that the owner knows you're for real.

4. *The closing date.* Most mega-transactions take 60 to 90 days, but I will offer 30 days or less, since I know it will take the bank that long to complete the paperwork.

5. *A statement that the sale is "as is,"* subject to the contingencies just referenced (my back door out of the deal). Once the seller agrees to the more significant terms and they have "bought into" the deal, we then will negotiate that the seller pays for most of the closing costs (which are typically paid for by the seller). We also always try to get our own attorney, Scott Elk, to write the title insurance.

Once you move into higher-end properties, I suggest you include a confidentiality clause, requiring all parties not to discuss the deal or its terms until after closing. I've had situations where I've offered a contract and the seller has shopped it around to get a better deal. I've also heard of brokers who will do the same, telling the seller, "I can get you more money." I won't tell anybody about a contract until the sale becomes a matter of public record. I want to close deals quickly when I make them; I don't place roadblocks in front of a deal. I tell the owner that if there are any other terms, the lawyers can work it out, but we have a deal when they sign the agreement. I also prefer to deal with owners, not lawyers or brokers. To my mind, lawyers are there to draft terms, not make them. I believe you succeed when you create a deal that's fair to both sides, keep contingencies to a minimum, and move swiftly.

The timing of your offer can be critical. That's one of the reasons you want to be able to make an offer quickly. Other times, however, you may want to hang back and wait for the right moment. When I bought back the $50 million property, for instance, I had driven by that house for two years before I decided to make my offer of $19 million. Had I gone in too early, the owner would have thought the offer insulting and ridiculous; had I been too late, he could have sold to someone else. My timing is far from infallible; Donald Trump outbid me on a property in Palm Beach probably because I waited too long to counter his offer. But having the flexibility to put in an offer quickly, and to know enough about the seller to calculate the best time to make the offer, has helped me close a lot of great deals.

Successful deals should be wrapped up within a day or two: the initial offer and then the response the following day. With the Maverick Acquisition Formula, you shouldn't have to spend hours analyzing a particular purchase. In short order you should see whether the deal's going to work for you. It's a common human tendency to procrastinate a little bit, but in real estate delay is not your friend. Agree on the big things and sign the contract; leave the haggling over the smaller details to the lawyers.

Conversely, to be successful with your deals you may need patience. Many people make a mistake of feeling that they have to be in the game no matter what. But you don't want to make foolish decisions and overpay on the acquisition side. You always need to be willing to walk away from a deal. In fact, some of my best deals are the ones I didn't make because the numbers didn't work. For the past year I've been coaching a couple from Rhode Island, the great Bob Lindo and his wife, Valerie. They'd done several small deals and wanted to make the jump into higher-priced properties. Six months into our relationship they called me, concerned that they hadn't made a purchase yet. "We made an offer on this and went up to X, but at that point we walked away," they said. I told them, "There's no point to a deal where the margins won't reflect the amount of work you put into the project. It's okay to wait, knowing that when you do buy, you will have made your money already."

If you don't get the terms you want, you have to be willing to let the deal go. For instance, in 2004 I was bidding on a property in Palm

Beach, but due to the investment in the property—$40 million—every eighth of a point of interest the bank charged would cost me $50,000 a year. The bank wouldn't give me the terms I felt I needed, so I walked away. My bank was shocked, and there were days I regretted my decision. But because my funds weren't tied up in that deal, I was able to seize upon a much better opportunity, which is a great story of the Maverick approach in action.

In 1998 I bought a property in Manalapan for $17 million. This was a huge plot—8.78 acres, with more than 820 feet of direct oceanfront. I had a vision of building one of the most beautiful, expansive, extravagant properties in the United States: a 70,000-square-foot Italianate villa. I hired an architect and had a model built of the property; then we worked on the design and permitting for the property for over a year. But at that point, in early 1999, I received an offer of $27 million to sell the land. I would reap a reasonable profit, but I'd have to give up my dream estate. I ran the numbers over and over, and I called a client to whom I had sold a $12 million property to ask his advice. He said, "Take the offer and move on, Frank." I did and was glad, as it allowed me to build several other magnificent properties—but I kept the model of that villa in one of our storage units.

In late 2004, I had just sold three properties, one worth $7 million, one worth $17 million, and the $50 million estate. Except for a small project in Indiana, I essentially had no inventory for the first time in years. I was getting ready for the Badwater 135-mile Ultramarathon (you'll read about that in Chapter 10) while looking around for other properties in South Florida. Then I heard that the 8.78 acre Manalapan property I had sold in 1999 might be available. I started dreaming of building an even larger house that I had once envisioned for that site. Based on my acquisition formula, I knew that if I sold off two 150-foot lots and developed the rest of the property as one estate, the remaining 5.5 acres, with a mansion approximately 70,000 square feet in size, would have a value between $100 and $125 million. Now, *that* excited me. I would be creating a whole new level of luxury and shattering market price points at the same time, building the first new nine-figure spec home in the United States. I felt that $40 million was a good value for the land, and I knew I could meet my acquisition formula numbers with the project. If nothing else, I could sell the land in a year or so for $85 million, either as one large lot, two lots, or five smaller lots that would still net me a healthy profit. Or I could divide the lot into two parcels, sell one and build a beautiful, somewhat smaller mansion on the other that would still set new levels of luxury. I felt comfortable with all these possibilities (even if my heart was set on building the $125-million-plus estate).

So I offered an all-cash deal for $40 million with a $4 million deposit. The offer was accepted, but then things hit a snag, with the seller asking for changes to the contract, the lawyers getting involved, and so on. I felt something was wrong but didn't have any solid information. Then, in February 2005, I went into the hospital with a ruptured appendix. When I came out, the seller called and said, "I've gotten a better offer, so the deal's off." I was not at the top of my game at that point, so I didn't fight him on it, but in my heart I believed that the owner's representative had shopped my offer around to get better terms from someone else.

I've been doing this long enough not to take things personally, but I was disappointed. I did some research and found out who the new buyer of the property was. I knew there would be a due diligence period, and I kept looking to see if the sale had been recorded. After 60 days there was nothing. Now, even with high-ticket deals such as this one, everything should be wrapped up in 60 days, so I asked around and heard that the buyer was having second thoughts. Meanwhile I had taken an option to buy another oceanfront property in Boca Raton. But after 90 days the pending Manalapan deal still had not been recorded. So I called the owner, who lives in England. We had maintained our relationship ever since 1999; he's a supporter of my Caring House Project Foundation, and I also knew he was a runner. We chatted about the Foundation and my preparation to run the Badwater Ultramarathon. Then I said, "I just put a piece of property under contract in Boca Raton, but I have a few more days before the contract is binding. I heard that your deal with Mr. (and I used the last name of the other buyer) is not going to work out. Excuse me for being presumptive, but if that's the case, I would rather own your land than the property in Boca. So if I'm right and your deal is dead, I'd like to start negotiating again. And I'll pay 5 percent above what I had offered the first time."

He said, "You have a deal."

I was excited but cautious. I said, "You told me that before. I respectfully request that we put our agreement in writing. By tomorrow at five o'clock, which is the time I have to accept or cancel the deal in Boca, I require a signed contract." And that's what happened. Within 24 hours we signed the agreement, and within 30 days we closed on the property.

This negotiation was a result of never giving up, fostering relationships long after the sale, knowing what the seller wanted, and being willing to be flexible as long as the numbers fit within my acquisition formula. This same approach works with properties at any price point. If you stick with the acquisition formula, locate properties in your chosen area, determine their value and their acquisition price, get your finances in place, and understand the seller's psychology, then you will make offers that will be accepted by the owners and acceptable to you. And like an annuity, you'll have made your money up front because you will have bought the property right (as a Maverick always does), right from the start!

The library in one of our $18 million estates.

8

The Maverick Approach, Step Three: Improve (Solid Gold or Gold-Plated?)

W hen you're preparing to improve or build your house, you've got to stop thinking of it as a property or an investment that just sits there on a piece of ground. Instead, think of it as your art, your craft. This step is where you take on the identity of not just an investor but an artist, and your vision and creative abilities will come into play.

There are three keys to choosing and completing the improvements your house will require.

1. *Know your target buyer and neighborhood.* Ultimately the only opinion that matters is that of your target buyer, and you must improve based on their preferences and aspirations. Make your design choices subtle enough for the general market, with a splash of the pizzazz that you believe your market will enjoy. Your goal is to put your improvement dollars where they'll do the most good, and also to choose improvements that will create the "wow" factor without raising the price of the house beyond the level of the market you are creating (current market plus 10 percent to 20 percent). Putting

solid gold improvements into a $50,000 starter home will only raise the asking price beyond what the market will bear, while not necessarily meeting the needs of your buyers—a classic case of overimprovement. Conversely, if you put gold-plated improvements in a multimillion-dollar mansion, highly discriminating buyers will simply walk away and take what is left of your reputation with them. You must decide if you are in the wood, aluminum, nickel, silver, gold-plated, or solid gold marketplace, and improve accordingly.

You also must realize that tastes and desires change, so you need to keep abreast of current trends. For instance, we used to put elaborate dedicated home theaters in our high-end properties. These beautiful rooms enhanced the value of a home while allowing for a healthy dose of creativity. However, except for use by movie buffs, we found that these rooms remained dark for all but a few times a month. We wanted to incorporate more everyday use into such a room—for example, turning it into a very masculine home office or media room that, with the touch of a button, could convert to a home theater complete with large drop-down screen, casual couches, and a Hollywood-style projector. Such rooms are used almost daily in our creations. Your ability to know your buyers and provide them with the amenities they want at a level higher than they ever thought they could afford will make marketing and selling your property easier than you ever dreamed.

2. *You must have a plan and a budget.* The Golden Rule of new construction and renovations is to know what you're getting into. No matter what you think you're going to spend there will be unexpected costs, and you need to have the resources available to handle them. As the investor, you must be the driving force on the project, both creatively and organizationally, and you must keep both the vision and the budget firmly in mind as you proceed through this very important stage of the Maverick approach.

While most of this chapter is targeted toward improvements, its lessons also can be applied to building from scratch. When I build new, I enjoy having the ability to create on a blank canvas. In some ways building new is more predictable: With renovations you don't know what you're facing until you start swinging the hammer. When you build new, you can plan costs and timelines more easily. On the downside, building new usually will take longer before you can bring the property to market, due to the time needed for planning and designing. When deciding between building new and renovating, ask yourself, "Given my investment objectives, what will create the greatest amount of value and bring the greatest return?" Then remember to (1) budget more time and money than you think you will need, (2) be prepared for as many contingencies as you can, and (3) be flexible while adhering to your overall plan.

3. *Put your improvement dollars toward elements that will give you the biggest bang for your buck.* Your property needs to possess something that other houses don't, and the easiest way to do that is with creativity and quality. For instance, where I grew up many houses had white picket fences to greet you as you came home. So I put white picket fences around each of my starter houses, because I believed that first-time home buyers had the same vision of the American dream. Little touches like white picket fences, frilly draperies at the kitchen windows, and brand-new appliances deliver more than most entry-level buyers expect. When it comes to ultra-high-end buyers, you also must exceed their expectations, which is far more difficult and requires greater creativity. Your goal must be to provide an experience of subliminal euphoria, with touches that make the buyers feel at home while providing more luxury, convenience, beauty, and "wow" factor than they realized was possible. There are specific renovations you can make in any property that will increase its value more than others; we discuss these later in this chapter. Your entire goal must be to improve in such a way that your house will appeal to your target buyers by offering them great design at a price that represents increased levels of value, so your house will sell quickly for the price you want. That's a Maverick's first, last, and most important goal.

YOUR "PROGRESSION TO CLOSING" PLAN

Before you begin any level of improvements, from putting on a coat of paint to razing and building from scratch, you must have a plan. As soon as I acquire a property, after writing the vision statement I create a "progression to closing" plan, covering every stage of renovations until the sale closes and the new owner takes possession. A progression to closing plan allows you to "begin with the end in mind," as Stephen Covey says, and to work backward from there. Your progression to closing plan also allows the people working with you to understand what you're asking them to do.

Your plan must include objectives, tasks, responsible parties, and timelines. For instance, your objective might be to "clear all debris from yard." Tasks might include "removing rusted lawn mower," "cutting grass," "pulling out dead plants," "demolishing shack in back of house," and so on. Responsible parties might be you, a cleaning crew, a landscaping outfit, your teenage son (whom you're paying to cut the grass), and a hauling company. Your timeline might be two days to a week. We use a scheduling program that charts every task from the first to last day of the job. These kinds of systems will eliminate brainless tasks that can sap your time and energy. The sooner you can get on a system, the more stress- and hassle-free your career will be.

When you start investing, I suggest that you work on only one property at a time rather than spreading yourself too thin. Once you've made some progress on your improvements, you can start looking around for other properties. Eventually you may find yourself acquiring a new property while you're completing another, and then your progression to closing plans become absolutely critical. Only when you feel you're ready should you try two at a time, and then if that works out, expand to three.

Your progression to closing plan should include three areas.

1. *Appearance.* What do you need to do immediately to make the property look good enough for someone to consider buying it? (Your options for a piece of property can change through time. As soon as we close on a property, it's for sale as-is to

any potential buyer. If we're getting ready to build new, we'll sell the lot while we're demolishing and clearing the land. Once the foundation is poured, however, I'm committed. At some point when you are nearing completion you may want to take your house off the market until the improvements are done and the house is completely ready to be sold. We talk more about this "build-up of suspense" in Chapter 9.) Appearance would include clean-up, some minimal landscaping, and fixing any broken windows or obvious defects that can be seen from the street—think immediate curb appeal.

2. *Marketing.* You can't wait until renovations are finished to start planning the sale. You need to create your marketing plan right away. For instance, if you're in a hot market you could have a hardhat open house, showing buyers the progress you've made and supplying drawings and color swatches to give them an idea of the finished product. We talk extensively about your marketing plan in Chapter 9.

3. *Renovations.* The work on your property must follow a sequence: demolition, new construction or reconstruction, electricians, plumbers, drywall, floors, paint, and final touches. All of this needs to be laid out on a schedule with a clear timeline. Every day your house is being renovated or built is another day of costs you must carry, so make sure that the time is used as efficiently as possible. I believe that for most small improvement projects, a four- to six-month timeline from acquisition to sale is realistic. You (1) create your plan while you're waiting for the closing, (2) clean the site the first day you own it, and (3) have your contractors, handymen, and subcontractors ready to go in the right order and sequence. If the renovations required by the job are fairly basic, you should be able to complete work in about a month. If the property needs major renovations due to fire damage, roof damage, or structural problems, you'll need to push the timeline back. A basic timeline formula is a month to a month and a half per thousand square feet of interior space for basic renovations, and two months per thousand square

feet for more elaborate jobs. I prefer to spend a little more money to get the job done on time rather than delay bringing my properties to market, because every day my house isn't for sale is an unrecoverable cost.

Any renovation or construction is going to take longer than you think, so I suggest you build a 10 percent to 15 percent "fudge factor" into your timeline up front, and check frequently to evaluate your progress. If one area is falling behind, you can put more resources into fixing the problem. For instance, if your electrician has found a problem and can't finish the wiring, you can (1) bring in more help, and (2) tell the drywallers not to come until the afternoon instead of the morning. But *you* must be on site every day in order to make these kinds of decisions. Checking your plan often will allow you to stay on top of your project and provide for the most efficient use of resources, while ensuring that your project is finished on time, on budget, and with the quality you desire.

CREATING A REALISTIC BUDGET

When getting ready to purchase a property, you must have the resources ready to (1) start work immediately, (2) finish the job with some fudge factor in time and money, and (3) carry the property until it sells. Setting a budget and keeping to it is the difference between a Maverick investor and a real estate hobbyist.

Remember our formula from Chapter 7: Acquisition plus improvements equals 50 to 60 percent of the retail price. If your retail price is commonly 10 percent to 20 percent above current market levels, you can easily determine the amount you can afford to spend for renovations. Let's use the example from Chapter 7. You acquire a property to renovate for $75,000. Comparable houses in the neighborhood are selling for $150,000, so the projected retail price for your property will be $165,000 (10 percent above $150,000) to $180,000 (20 percent above $150,000). Your final cost for acquisition plus improvements should be no more than 60 percent of retail. Therefore, the most you can spend acquiring and improving the property will be $99,000 (60 percent of the lower retail price of $165,000) to $108,000 (60 percent of the higher retail price of $180,000). Subtracting your acquisition cost of $75,000, this means you can afford to spend between $24,000 and $33,000 on renovations. (Remember, don't lose a deal over a few thousand dollars. This example is meant to show you how much flexibility you have on either side of the acquisition and improvement costs.)

You also must base your budget on your goals for the property. For instance, if you're thinking of reselling quickly with very little improvements (wholesaling), you may have to budget only for clean-up and carrying costs. If you want to renovate, you must prioritize expenditures based on the desires of your target buyers. If you're uncertain of what priorities will bring you the most return, go with the basics as described later in this chapter.

Create your budget for your big-ticket areas first. Any structural changes, such as adding a room or repairing a foundation, will be a big ticket. Your kitchen will always be a big ticket. Carpet and flooring will probably be less of an expense but you need to budget for them nonetheless. When preparing budgets, I use estimates from contractors, my own experience, and research I've done on the elements I want to include in a house. I always round costs up rather than down, and I try to chart a course between best-case and worst-case scenarios. I also build in a 5 percent to 10 percent "miscellaneous" category to cover any unexpected costs that will undoubtedly arise, many of them being elective in nature. In general, my overrun tolerance in any overall budget is 4 percent to 5 percent maximum. (Of course, when you're building a $20 million house, that's $800,000 to $1 million.) I have to admit we have never come in under budget, and the more elaborate our estates become, the more I must pay close attention to cost overruns.

Discretionary decisions can cost a lot, therefore you must evaluate each choice based on your budget. Nowadays more categories in your budget may involve discretionary decisions. Drywall comes in a dozen finishes. Foundations can be made of different kinds of concrete, waterproofing materials, and so on. Costs of materials also can fluctuate depending on demand. In 2004 four different hurricanes hit Florida within a period of two months, and the cost of construction materials and labor went sky high. Did that have an effect on my budget? Of course. The same will hold true for the hurricanes of 2005 and beyond. Your goal is to do your planning up front, decide what level of materials and finishes your renovation dollars will support, and then stick to your decisions along the way.

One expense to include in your budget is a small amount of insurance to cover major disasters only. I carry high deductible insurance for major losses during construction. A policy with a 20 percent deductible can save you thousands of dollars per project. I also suggest that you fix some of the smaller things yourself rather than putting in a claim, so your premium will remain low. I've used my insurance only a few times over 20 years. I was glad I had it, but I'm even more pleased that my rates continue to be low because I have a high deductible and handle the smaller things myself.

The demands of a tight budget can make it tempting to cut corners on your renovations, but cutting corners is a mistake, as I discovered early in my own career. In one house I had to rip out thousands of dollars of landscaping and driveway material because several potential buyers complained that there wasn't enough room for their cars to turn around due to the size of the driveway. There's a difference between being budget conscious and being cheap, and people will see it as soon as they walk in the door. So use the best carpet in your price range. Buy brand-new appliances. Put in a tub with Jacuzzi jets instead of a plain tub. Go for the nicest materials you can afford, and your "wow" factor will increase significantly. Again, think of yourself as an artist whose canvas is your property. True artists never look for ways to do the job cheaper; they're trying to do things better and more beautifully. I believe that's the passionate mindset a Maverick must take into the improvement process, because without that, your results will be ordinary.

However, the other potential mistake is to overimprove and forget the bottom line. Beware the temptation to put solid gold improvements in a house in a silver-plated neighborhood. You have to balance the artist and the businessperson, the creator and the budgeter, and choose your renovations based on that balance. After each job, make sure you do a quality, budget, and schedule postmortem. You must review where your estimates were accurate, where they were off, where your gains and losses occurred, and how you can do better the next time.

FINDING AND DEALING WITH CONTRACTORS

For some people deciding to use a contractor is a no-brainer, because they don't have the skills to do any of the renovations themselves. In the beginning of my career, I hired handymen who had skills I didn't, and I would act as their unpaid labor. But unless you want to learn building skills on your own property, your first task will be to find a quality contractor who holds a general contracting license.

I define a quality contractor by (1) their talent to do the work, (2) the timeliness and quality with which the work is done, (3) their ability to stay on budget, and (4) the honesty with which they approach the job. I've found some great contractors by driving around, seeing what people were building or renovating in the area, and walking up and asking to speak to the guys in charge of the job. I'd have them show me their work, and if I thought it was a good job I'd ask for their references, and check them out with the Better Business Bureau. Personal recommendations and actually seeing someone's work are better ways to choose a contractor than the Yellow Pages or any other advertising.

I strongly suggest you use only contractors who are licensed and have both liability and workermen's compensation insurance. This is for your own protection and peace of mind. The last thing you want is for someone to be hurt on your job and have to cover the expense yourself. Unless you're protected, just one accident can wipe out not only your profit but all your personal assets. Every person on my projects is required to carry insurance.

Early in my career when I hired a contractor, I looked for a jack-of-all-trades rather than a specialist, because of the nature of renovations. Especially with your first few projects, you don't want to have to hire a carpenter, drywaller, and so on, if one general contractor who has a wide range of skills can do all the work for you and do it well. A versatile general contractor also will troubleshoot and handle the unexpected situations that come up in any renovation. (Even with a great general contractor, you should build into your plan and budget the use of a licensed electrician and plumber, simply because of their specific skills and licensing requirements.) Your general contractors will hire the subcontractors for your project and then run the project—under your close supervision.

When you're first starting out, I suggest you work alongside the general contractor or handyman. You can paint, perhaps do some minor repairs and clean-up, re-sod the lawn, and so on. You can learn a lot about renovating properties that you can use in future projects. If you can do some of the small fixes on your house without calling anyone to help you, you'll save both time and money. You'll also learn what questions to ask, what materials are needed for a job, how a general contractor operates, and so on. Eventually you can supervise carpet layers, landscapers, and other skilled workers. You'll become a far more intelligent employer and you can shield yourself from getting ripped off by people who may want to make a little on the side from your project.

Today it seems that everyone is improving their homes, and therefore great contractors and subcontractors are very busy. When real estate is hot, it's a contractor's market, so you have to treat your subcontractors well. This can be as simple as arranging to pay them every two weeks instead of at the end of the month, which can make a big difference in a worker's cash flow. Nowadays we employ so many contractors that this is often impractical, but if your renovation will take only a few months, paying a subcontractor or contractor more frequently may keep them on your job instead of someone else's. Also, always pay those who are counting on you on time and without excuse—honor your commitments to them and they'll be more likely to keep their commitments to you.

How a bid is written will tell you a lot about a contractor. If it's organized and put together well, that's often an indication of how the contractor will do the work. I usually get at least two to three bids for any job, and meet with the contractors prior to choosing one. I also make sure that I'm meeting the person who will actually do the work, not just a salesperson. I always check references, either by calling the customers or going out to inspect the contractor's previous work. Then I decide based on work quality as well as the bid amount. Don't be tempted to always go with the lowest bid; I find it's better to select reputable contractors and subcontractors even if it costs a little more.

Contractors always worry about underbidding. If they overbid, the worst that can happen is they won't get the job. If they underbid, they stand the chance of taking money out of their own pockets to pay for their miscalculation. (Some contractors will just walk off a job they've underbid, to keep from losing money.) Every contractor builds a "what-if" factor into a bid, to cover contingencies that he can't know about up front. The more expensive the job, the higher the what-if factor. If the bid is high, I try to get the contractor to itemize materials and labor in terms of an hourly rate. By having them think about the job in terms of time (hourly), you are more apt to have the bid reduced. If your contractor passes the honesty test you also can consider having him price the job on a cost-plus-a-fee basis or by the hour, thus eliminating some of the what-if factor in the job. This approach must be handled with a great deal of caution, as a portion of the incentive has been removed from the contractor to finish on time. (With ultra-high-end properties, I prefer to use larger contractors who have what I call a "seller's mentality." They are able to think of me as the seller and realize that if I don't sell on time, on budget, and for the price we are asking, there will be no future work. With a little patience you can train your contractors to think like this.)

I provide one-year warranties on any of my brand-new properties, so I try to negotiate that the warranties offered by my contractors and subcontractors start the day the house sells rather than the day work is completed. If this is too open-ended for some of my contractors, then I may build in language that allows for the warranty to commence "when the house sells or two years from the issuance of the Certificate of Occupancy, whichever occurs first." At the least, you should try to get extended warranties for the roof, electrical, plumbing, air-conditioning systems and windows, as these can be problem areas.

One of the most painful things you must do as an investor is to get rid of a contractor or worker. On your side, you must set clear expectations for time, budget, and quality. Confirm the plan with them: "Mr. Contractor, you're going to be putting in all new kitchen cabinets, moving the electric, putting in air conditioning, and finishing everything off to be ready to show, and you say you can do that in a month. Is that correct?" When you repeat it back to them, you may help them realize what they're promising is not realistic so they can change their timeline. You set the expectations going in, the communication is there, and the contract language speaks for itself. If they default and come up with excuses, let them go—immediately.

IMPROVEMENTS THAT GIVE YOU THE MOST VALUE

Your goal in improving your property is to make it stand out from all other properties at your particular price. Your competition will be other properties that have been previously owned, and production-built homes that are what I call "vanilla boxes." Any improvement or feature, small or large, that (1) sets your house apart in terms of quality and style and (2) seems to provide greater value than the other houses in the area, will help your house sell faster and at a higher price.

There's a show on HGTV called *Designed to Sell*, where couples who want to sell their homes have a realtor walk through the house while commenting on what needs to change. If you don't have an eye for design, you might want to enlist the help of a realtor, professional designer, or appraiser to look over your property and make recommendations. Make sure they know your target buyer, and don't feel you have to take their advice, but listen to their perspective and suggestions as you plan your renovations.

When building new, you must start from the foundation up; with renovations I've found it's best to start from the top down. Begin with any renovations that are safety- and structure-related. Your roof, wiring, plumbing, and so on must comply with local codes. None of these repairs, while essential, will add to the "wow" factor of your house, but if you've been following the Maverick system, you should have factored these replacement and repair costs into your (lowered) acquisition price. Once your property is up to code, then you can start work on the rooms that will take the most time and money and provide the most value.

Inside the House

Even in our ultra-high-end homes, on a per-square-foot basis more money is spent in the kitchen, master bedroom, and master bathroom than anywhere else. That's because these rooms are the most important to almost every single buyer.

Kitchen: No matter what the property's price point, every family will spend a large amount of time in or around the kitchen, so this room should get the majority of your renovation dollars. In my experience, every $1.00 spent on renovating the kitchen will return an average of $1.40 to $1.50 when you sell. For starter homes, your kitchen will need to appeal mostly to women, as they will be more likely to see themselves doing more of the food preparation. Do what you can to make the kitchen large enough to allow for family congregation. This room must be functional and easy to use, a place where the family will be happy to spend mealtimes.

Upgrading the kitchen can be relatively simple and, if you don't have a lot of money, relatively cost effective. For instance, you don't have to put in new cabinets if your budget won't allow for it; reface them instead. Countertops are one of the primary ways a kitchen shows wear and tear, so I suggest you replace the countertops unless the current ones are in immaculate condition. You also may want to add a double stainless steel sink—a relatively inexpensive upgrade that will enhance value. Until you move into mid-level and higher homes, your plumbing fixtures can be basic, as long as they are new and nice. A kitchen island also tends to add value. It doesn't need to have a sink or even power; it can be a freestanding butcher block in the center of the kitchen, space permitting.

Because the kitchen will be one of the main selling features of your house, proper lighting is essential. Get rid of fluorescent overhead lights, as they look old and harsh. It's relatively inexpensive to put recessed lighting fixtures ("high hats") over the sink, the island, and any important food preparation/eating areas. Putting in lights under the cabinets (the one place you can use fluorescents) costs very little money but will accentuate the appearance of your countertops. I also like to put a nice chandelier over the island or the eating area (if you have one in the kitchen).

I love using hardwood floors in a kitchen. Wood is not that expensive, and while we don't use them in our estate homes, there are also some great wood laminate and manufactured wood materials that also work well. The other feature I feel adds great value to a kitchen is an eating area. In my smaller houses I usually knocked out part of the wall that divided the kitchen from the dining or living or family room to create an informal eat-in dining area. (I like to use half-walls, counters, aquariums, and freestanding wet bars to separate spaces. When a house isn't chopped up into small rooms but one space flows into another, the entire house seems bigger.) I'd put a countertop on the kitchen side to create knee space, and underneath would be barstool-type chairs. During open houses I'd have a couple of place settings on the counter, so buyers could see themselves in the morning, on the way to school or work, pulling up a stool and eating their cereal. By adding seating at the countertop, and with a nice, sizable island in the kitchen with plenty of room to walk around, even our starter kitchens became the true hub and heart of the home.

New appliances are key to any kitchen renovation, so make sure your dishwasher, microwave, stove, and refrigerator are new or in mint condition. A nice stainless steel range hood, perhaps trimmed in wood, adds style for very little money. And put in refrigerators with icemakers. You'll need to run a plumbing line, but this particular addition provides a lot of "wow" factor to a starter home. A few inexpensive small appliances, like an under-the-cabinet coffeemaker, will make the kitchen more homey without cluttering up the counter space. Depending on budget, I'll also put a small TV in the kitchen. (In mid-level or higher-end properties, it'll be a plasma or flat screen LCD TV that flips down from under the cabinet.) However, I won't put in toasters or can openers as I feel they add clutter.

In ultra-high-end properties the kitchen is one of the most important elements when it comes to perceived value. Everyone goes into the kitchen at some point—for a midnight snack or early morning breakfast if nothing else—and having a great space will always help sell your property. In our estate homes I put in a main kitchen and a separate catering kitchen or two for parties. Our main kitchens are outfitted with every convenience and luxury you can imagine—warming drawers to keep plates and food hot, convection ovens or Viking or Wolf nine-burner ranges, Sub-Zero freezers, and so on. Most often we will put in gas ranges because the ultra-wealthy who cook are hobbyists, and they take their food seriously.

Master Bedroom: This is where your home buyer will likely spend the greatest amount of time, so the bedroom should have a romantic and intimate feel. It should be a grown-up's cocoon, removed from the children, a small piece of Shangri-La where parents go to be with each other. If you get the master bedroom and bath right, selling the rest of the house will be much easier. The master bedrooms of our mansions are truly the ultimate in romance, luxury, comfort, and relaxation. First, the room itself is always quite large. In the current $125-million-plus spec home we are designing, the master bedroom will be more than 5,000 square feet, twice the size of the average home in America. The master bedroom in another estate was on the first floor, but the room was two stories tall, with floor-to-ceiling windows overlooking the beautiful Florida beachfront and ocean. We used silk upholstery on the walls with sound-deadening materials behind it, and mahogany wood wainscoting. The carpet cost $250 per yard and was imported from Holland; many clients commented they wouldn't need a mattress because the carpet was so plush!

You, too, can create a sense of luxury in your master bedroom.

Make the carpet in that room the nicest quality you can afford. (You can use the same color carpet throughout other carpeted rooms in the house to save money and make the house look bigger, but put the nicest quality carpet in the master.) At the very least, put a thicker padding under the carpet to give the feeling of greater luxury. A fireplace in the master bedroom can create a warm, welcoming atmosphere that will truly set your house apart. I also suggest putting window treatments in your master bedroom. While we use beautiful silk damask in our high-end properties, you can find very elegant drapes or roman shades at discount linen and bedding stores, and nice drapery hardware at Home Depot and Lowe's.

Master Bath: This should be considered a part of the master bedroom suite, so everything should be upgraded. For instance, there are production sinks that look hand-painted; one of these will help create a great look. The bathroom countertop also must be the best your renovation dollars will buy. Upgrade your plumbing fixtures, including the showerhead. Put ceramic tile in the shower enclosure and around the bathroom counter. (We use onyx, quartz, or marble in our high-end homes, and there are some nice composite materials to use in mid-level homes.) Replace or repaint the tub if needed. (I've repainted tubs even in some of my high-level houses, where the tub was old and cast iron, and I liked the antiquity represented by its unique look.) I also love using wood for bathroom flooring. The wood floors in the bathroom in my home in Florida have been there since 1935. You can't let water run on it for hours, but otherwise a wood floor will stand up to the water and humidity in a bathroom without trouble.

Family Rooms: This is the one part of the house where a man will put a lot of attention, because this is where the television and audio system usually reside. For starter houses, I'd put a TV (for mid-level homes, an LCD or plasma TV) in the family room, along with a comfortable sofa, to allow the man of the family to imagine settling in and watching the big game with all his friends. Good flooring in this room (wood, nicer carpet, or a combination of both) will help to create the sense of comfort and a place for friends and family to gather.

Other Bedrooms and Baths: In a home's second, third, even fourth bedrooms you can do the basics—painting, replacing carpet, perhaps putting in baseboard, making sure everything is fresh and clean. One nice touch is to paint each bedroom a different color, so children can pick their rooms. In the second and third bathrooms, you can put in basic countertops, plumbing fixtures, single vanities, medicine cabinets, and so on.

For the rest of the house, here are some other general areas that you want to upgrade whenever possible, depending on your budget.

Trim: Putting baseboard and crown moulding throughout the house is an inexpensive upgrade that will add a great finish. If your dollars are running low, put baseboard and crown moulding in the master bedroom and kitchen, and just baseboard in the other rooms.

Ceilings: Popcorn or "knock down" ceilings date a property, and they're relatively easy to replace. If your house has popcorn ceilings, scrape them off and go with a smooth finish with very little texture, or a flat finish.

Lighting: In starter homes, most recessed lighting fixtures won't need to be changed. However, you should replace any hanging fixture that doesn't look good or is dated. Use fluorescent bulbs only for your under-the-cabinet lighting in the kitchen or in closets. Throughout the rest of the house, swapping regular lightbulbs for halogens or colored lights can make a big difference. Halogen lightbulbs give off a different, warmer light than regular bulbs. Replacing only one lightbulb in each room with a halogen light can give your house a warm glow. Bulbs with a pink or light lavender color can create a very flattering light in the bedroom. Also, for your showings you should overwattage your lights. If the light fixture calls for a range of 60 to 75 watts, put in 75; the additional light will make the house look great.

Appliances: Putting a washer and dryer in your starter homes is a relatively small investment that will create a lot of perceived value. The last thing a first-time home buyer wants to do after purchasing a house is to spend more money on appliances. Put in a basic washer and dryer, hook them up and leave the tags on them, and your first-time buyers will love your house even more.

Flooring: I advocate using hardwood or manufactured wood flooring in the dining room at a minimum, and perhaps also in the kitchen, living, and family room. (You can economize by putting carpeting throughout the rest of the house.) You can move up to marble as you move up in price.

Especially in starter homes, you want to put your renovation dollars where they will have the most impact. You can set yourself apart from other homes in the area through your use of granite countertops, hand-painted sinks, nice lighting, and so on. When you put in touches that are out of the ordinary, such as an island in the kitchen or a particular kind of ceramic tile in the bath, your buyers will feel your house has been designed and refitted with them in mind.

Outside the House

The first thing a buyer will see is the outside of your house, so make sure you take care of its appearance. Start from the roof and work down.

Roof: Hopefully you won't have to replace the roof, but you should make sure it's repaired and clean. Pressure-cleaning will get rid of any moss, mildew, or dirt that may have accumulated. Many roofs can be painted to give the appearance of a newer roof.

Outside Walls: You should almost always paint these, as nothing says "new" like a few fresh coats of paint.

Front Door: This is one of the most important elements of the visual impact of your house, so make sure it stands out. (For the $17 million property I sold in 2004, we had a huge front door custom-built at a cost of $25,000. There was actually a smaller door inside a larger door. The overall door was five inches thick, and inset into the smaller door was a porthole—85 pounds of sold brass—reclaimed from a 1912 sunken yacht.) Your front door can create the "wow" factor to draw the buyer inside. At the very least, paint it a different color from the rest of the house, perhaps to match the shutters.

Entry: Make sure the house numbers are visible and attractive (either metal, or a plaque with numbers on it). There always should be a nice lighting fixture at the front door. Changing exterior lighting fixtures on a house will update its look with very little expense. And don't put a screen or security door on the front, as it will detract from the impact of your beautiful new front door. If you feel a screen or security door is essential, it should be at least as nice as your front door.

Outside Windows: I believe that shutters add immensely to the value and visual impact of a house. Along with the white picket fences I used on each of my starter properties, I almost always put decorative shutters around the front windows. To this day, my high-end properties feature custom-built shutters made of materials like mahogany, with designs like palm trees or sailboats cut into the tops. The shutters and front door can be painted a complementary yet contrasting color from the house. Flower boxes can add even more visual interest. If you don't want to tend real flowers, put silk ones in for your showings; they look nice and never need watering or deadheadi g, only periodic replacement when the color begins to fade.

Driveway and Walkways: Make sure the driveway and walkways leading up to the house are in good condition. Don't spend a lot of money, however. I knew someone who put a stone driveway into a mid-level house; it was gorgeous, but it cost a fortune. Even if you simply patch the driveway and put down a coat of new blacktop, it will help the house look new and fresh. Always spruce up the walkway to the front door; you want to create a sense of arrival that draws the buyer to the house. The walkway should be repaired and free of weeds or grass. At the very least, line the walkway with annual plants like impatiens or other flowering varieties, and make sure there are nice lights along the path.

Mailbox: A beautiful new mailbox is a low-cost item that will add a high-class touch. And check it regularly, because nothing says "uncared-for house" like accumulated junk mail. Whenever I visit one of our properties, I always check the mailbox and remove the junk mail.

Front Yard: Landscaping dollars go a long way toward increasing the value of your property. Make sure the lawn looks great. If you're doing a quick turnaround, I suggest putting down sod for an instant lawn. Hedges around the edges of the property are a nice touch and add to privacy while showing the buyer the extent of the lot. And remember that white picket fence, especially for starter homes!

Showing the buyer the lot boundaries is critical, as buyers will be paying for every square inch of ground. I always do what's called a "staked survey," where a professional surveyor defines the boundaries of the lot and puts stakes all around the outside property line. I also trim back all the foliage along the boundary. If tree branches from the neighbor's yard are hanging over your property, cut them back.

Back Yard: Part of the American dream is to sit in your own back yard, invite your friends over, and have a barbecue while you watch your kids and the dog play. A nicely finished back yard is like having another room in the house and will add significant value to both starter and mid-level homes. Usually the only renovations you will need to do to the back yard is to clean it up, trim the foliage, put in grass seed or sod, and make sure that any feature already there—patio, barbecue pit, screened-in porch, and so on—is repaired and tidy. Don't spend a lot adding features to the back yard, as most people prefer to add their own. Depending upon the part of the country in which your property is located, putting in a sprinkler system is a nice touch for mid-level and above houses. And in Florida, where I live, for anything but a starter home a pool is considered an essential selling point. Anywhere the summers are hot, adding a pool will return approximately $1.30 to $1.40 for every dollar you spend.

If the houses on either side of your property are in bad repair, one of your best investments may be to help improve their exteriors. For my first properties, I would go to the neighbors and offer to paint their houses while I was painting mine, or to break up the dirt and plant grass seed in their front yards. Upgrading the exteriors of your neighbors' homes may cost you $500 in materials and another $1,000 in labor, but it can significantly improve the value of your property while cutting down on its time on market. Sometimes if people see you renovating your home, their pride of ownership begins to reappear. Neighbors may paint their houses themselves, or trim the bushes and trees on their side, or plant grass. Remember, Mavericks don't just sit and wait for the neighborhood to come up to the level of their properties; they take an active role in reshaping the area to make it more livable and valuable.

Where Not To Spend Too Much Money

With most improvement projects, you want to put your improvement dollars into the things that are most important to buyers, and put less (or no) focus on the rest. Here are a few areas where you won't need to spend too much money. (Obviously, if these items are nonfunctioning or broken, you must take care of them, but your fixes should be simple and inexpensive.)

Back Door: If you need to replace the back door, go for the basics— a simple wood door will suffice. If the back yard is important, a slightly more upscale door with a window might work. In most climates, it's also important to have a screen door so people can keep the back door open in hot weather.

Windows: Replacing windows can get extremely expensive. When you replace one, you must replace them all, so it's better to repair than to replace. One exception: Some older properties have jalousie windows, which are a security concern. I always replaced jalousie windows with safer options. In more upscale houses in Florida, hurricane-rated windows are a great selling point.

Laundry Rooms/Garages/Attics/Secondary Rooms: Unless your property is high-end, do not overspend on these rooms. Put basic appliances in the laundry. Clean the garage but don't put in a lot of storage. (If you put in the wrong storage, it can make your garage look smaller.) However, when you move into high-end properties, your attention to detail will show up in these secondary spaces. Our garages are magnificent, with mahogany-framed windows, marble floors, and room for over a dozen cars. (One appraiser said that we spent more on the garage than most people do on an average home.) Our mechanical rooms, which contain all the electrical and mechanical controls of the house, are carpeted or have marble floors. They're air-conditioned and double-insulated so no sound leaks out into the rest of the house. The wires for the entire property (more than 11 miles of wire in a recent home) are tied perfectly, organized, and labeled. A built-in wooden cabinet contains the warranty books of every appliance and system in the house, along with architectural drawings, elevations, and blueprints, in case the owner ever needs them. I believe buyers will look at these hidden rooms and think, "If Frank took that much care in here, I know he did right by the rest of the house, too." Even with starter homes, your attention to detail will help convince your buyer of the value of the house.

FURNISHING AND ACCESSORIZING YOUR HOUSE

It's far easier for your buyers to imagine themselves living in your house if you have furniture and accessories placed strategically throughout. While this can add to your budget, especially if you're just starting out, it's well worth it. There are professional "stagers" who will come in and set the stage using properly placed accessories for your showings. Depending on your own artistic eye or design ability, bringing in a professional stager might be a great investment. If nothing else, they can give you some decor and design ideas that will increase the property's appeal at a relatively low cost. (After all these years, I've developed a pretty good eye for design elements in a house, but I've been fortunate to have one of the best stagers and interior designers in my own family—my wife, Nilsa. She is masterful at the details that make our mansions into homes.)

There are several strategies you can use for furnishings. First, if you can't afford much, take anything that's nice from your own home that you can do without and put it in your property. These items can range from little-used furniture to small accessories. Second, you can rent furniture and then spend a little money for accessorizing with drapes, small appliances, and so on. Third, go to a furniture store in your area and propose a deal: They allow you to put their furniture in your house as a sort of "remote furniture showroom." You'll have the brochures for their store placed strategically throughout the house. "After all," you'll tell them, "more people can afford your furniture than can afford my house, and there'll be a lot of people walking through my open houses." If the buyer purchases the house fully furnished, you will have an agreed-upon price with the furniture company for all the stock. If the house sells unfurnished, you'll pay the store a restocking charge (essentially, rent on the pieces you've used during the sales period). You may need to do some persuading with the furniture company, but if you can get an agreement once and prove that the practice works, you have a source for furniture for your future projects as well.

Fourth, you can buy a small amount of furnishings yourself. Luckily, nowadays there are some great resources for inexpensive decor. Stores like Wal-Mart and Target can provide you with very nice bedding, towels, accessories, small furnishings, and so on. For instance, silk/fabric plants will add a very rich touch to even a starter home. They cost relatively little and take no care.

If you're on a strict budget, put your money into furnishing the rooms where you have put the most effort: the kitchen, master bedroom, and master bath. Put a table in the kitchen, with place mats and place settings on it. Set a little scale on the island, and maybe a couple of canisters and a bottle of olive oil on the counters. (Nilsa might add a faux cake in a glass-covered cake plate and an open cookbook next to it.) In the master bedroom, accessorize for that intimate feeling. Put scented candles on a side table to help create a romantic mood. In the bathroom, buy some towels and hang them on a nice towel rack. Buy a bathrobe and hang it on the back of the door. Put out small scented soaps on the sink and the tub. And have soft toilet paper in all the bathrooms. It's a small touch but it will say luxury to your potential buyers. Then as you show the house, plan to hit those rooms first.

In Chapter 3 we talked about the ways Disney and Ritz-Carlton immerse their customers in environments designed to touch all the senses. The Ritz in particular creates an atmosphere that says to guests, "You deserve the best. You've arrived." That's the kind of experience you should endeavor to provide the buyers for your properties. Think about the amenities provided by the Ritz—the luxurious white robes, the slippers, the 500-thread-count sheets, the special toiletries in the bathrooms, the chocolates on the turned-down bed sheets at night. What could you do at your showings to duplicate this kind of upscale experience and make your prospects feel that, if they buy your house, they, too, will be moving up? For example, I would follow the Ritz's lead and put fine soaps and other toiletries in the master bath. I'd also put in the most luxurious towels and rugs, and have a couple of candles burning as well. "Bathroom as spa" is a huge trend in homes today, and for a very small investment you can make a bathroom feel absolutely sybaritic.

Remember that the Maverick approach to improvements is like that first-class stamp: exactly the same no matter whether your house is entry-level, mid-range, or ultra-luxurious. If your budget dictates that you reface the cabinets and put composite wood flooring in the kitchen, or, as I did in one $30 million estate, you're knocking out walls to combine the old kitchen, butler's pantry, sitting room, and breakfast room into a 1,500-square-foot culinary retreat that even the most upscale chef would be thrilled to use, you're still (1) targeting your improvements to suit your target buyers, (2) spending money where you will get the most "wow" factor, and (3) setting your renovation/building budget based on the formula of acquisition price plus improvements equals 50 percent to 60 percent of retail. Your goal is simple: to raise the standards of the market enough to set new price levels while you provide more luxury and value than your buyers could ever expect. That's the very essence of the Maverick approach.

We created this "coming attractions" poster for our $15 million estate in Gulf Stream, Florida. We mounted it and hung it at the entrance to the mansion's home theater. The buyer loved it so much that he kept it. The estate sold in 25 days.

9

The Maverick Approach, Step Four: Market and SELL, SELL, SELL! P.T. Barnum Meets Willy Wonka

When it comes to marketing and selling properties, a Maverick has to combine the showmanship and business acumen of P.T. Barnum with the enthusiasm of Willy Wonka. Your goal is to set new standards, and that will come from your ability to sell what you have created. Most people compartmentalize or put into phases their involvement with a particular project, and it's certainly appropriate to put more emphasis on creating and renovation at a certain point. But from the first moment that you own a property you must be marketing and selling it. Whether your property is selling for $50,000 or $100 million, you can use the same principles to attract buyers, trigger their desire, and then close the deal quickly and at your desired profit.

We always have a vision and passion statement (see Chapter 2) that helps us stay excited about the opportunity this property represents. The vision and passion statement describes the product, what it will represent for us, why we have acquired it, and what we are going to do with it. A good vision and passion statement will turn even

> 1370 South Ocean represents an extremely rare opportunity to redefine a world marketplace we continue to create and dominate. 1370 South Ocean shall be considered a breathtaking work of art, the crown jewel of all multimillion-dollar oceanfront estate homes. It will shatter the standards set by us and other properties that dare to compete. Those standards include creativity, functionality, quality, price, and total sensory experience. Simply put, the eventual owner will experience a lifestyle where all five senses are heightened to a state of subliminal euphoria, where, upon arrival, the state of mind is altered as one anticipates peaceful relaxation, re-creation, renewal, and family fun.

the most rudimentary starter home renovation into a living, breathing entity whose destiny you control. It will shape the marketing and selling of your property, the experience of your buyer, and the deal you will be able to make. At the top of the page is the vision statement for the $50 million property we bought and sold in late 2004.

Whether you renovate or build new, the only way you're going to make top dollar is to satisfy the desires of your buyers. With first-time buyers, need may drive their decision to look for something to buy, but desire will drive them to buy your property and pay above market price for it. You must understand the psychology of your target market—get inside their minds and emotions so you know what will turn lookers into buyers. Your property must satisfy their conscious and unconscious preferences, nuances, and practices. The quicker you can learn and sense how deep their desire runs when it comes to this decision-making process, the more money you will make from any transaction.

I've developed the sense of what buyers want through years of showings, open houses, feedback, mistakes, and talking with buyers and brokers, asking, "Why did you buy this house? What set this one apart from the others?" I've found that when you ask a premium price, you must provide a premium experience. For starter homes, this may mean simple things like a new carpet (with that new carpet smell), a nice backyard, and a kitchen and master bath that have quality countertops and fixtures.

In the ultra-high-end market, buyers are all about desire and (dare I say it) lust. They can have whatever they want, so for them to choose one of my properties, they have to feel almost a physical sensation of wanting. The key to awakening their desires is to heighten the experience they have through their five senses to a state of subliminal euphoria. We must magnify the emotional return they will receive from the home, let them feel how much they would enjoy living here. Every part of the buying experience must be designed to move clients to the point where they make the decision to buy almost without realizing they've done so.

Let me take you through a typical showing at one of our high-end properties. When a broker and client pull up to the house, often I'll put a traffic cone at the end of the driveway and meet them there. I want them to stop, get out of the car, take in the scenery around the gate and property wall, and then walk up the rest of the driveway so they can hear the waterfall, see the lush tropical foliage, feel the light mist that cools everything 10 degrees immediately, experience the richness of the marble paver driveway, and hear the sound of their feet on the wood of the bridge. As they walk, I'm narrating: "This lot is a full five and a half acres with 520 feet of oceanfront. Did you notice the dock on the Intracoastal Waterway? It can accommodate a yacht of any size. The tennis court on your left doubles as a sports court; you can rollerblade, play basketball on it, whatever you want. It's lit at night, too. Over there are the two guest houses: Each is two stories, with two bedrooms and two baths. Each has its own kitchen and balcony, facing the water."

By now we're at the top of the motor court, and I have them turn back and look over what we've just walked through. Then I'll tell them about some of the structural elements that they won't see. "The house was built using more than 500 concrete and steel pilings that go 40 feet down into the coral shelf. The whole house is built of concrete; there's no wood used except for the trusses. The handmade barrel tiles are screwed down, glued down, nailed down, and foamed down. The windows and doors are hurricane proof." While I talk I'm reading the buyers' body language to see if it's time to go inside.

We pause again at the $50,000 front door. This will be the entry to the next several years of the buyers' lives, so it deserves a moment.

Then I open the door and let the clients take a breath and feel the house as they get their first glimpse of the magnificent interior. I give them a general overview of the layout, referring to the floor plan in the brochure they're holding, or I hand them a simple, one-page floor plan so they can orient themselves to the house. (Every room on the floor plan has a succinct but descriptive name: "oceanfront grand master suite" instead of "master bedroom," for example.) "The entertainment wing is there, the master suite is up those stairs, the kitchen and dining area are that way, the family area is down there, and the entry to the deck is through those doors," I say, directing their experience before they take another step into the house.

Then we start the tour. Our walkthrough is very slow and deliberate, and I'm narrating much of the time. There's a specific pattern for showing each part of the house in a particular order. However, our houses are so big and there are so many exquisite details that it's impossible for clients to take in everything in one walkthrough, so I make sure to double back through certain rooms at least once. Some people will say, "I don't want to hear about the house, just let me look around." In that case, I sit back and give them free rein. If I find them looking at a particular feature for a while, I walk up and say, "I noticed you looking at the wood floors. This wood was salvaged from an old church that was built in the late 1700s in York, Pennsylvania." I give them their space and then step in with a little description to enrich their experience.

Once we've walked through the entire house, no matter how slow or fast the tour was I say, "You know, this house is big and we went through it quickly. If you've got the time, why don't you just show yourselves around? I'll be down here if you need me." (They're not going to talk to each other about the house while I'm there, so I give them the space to do so.) Then, as they're getting ready to leave, I say, "Might I suggest you see this house at night? It's completely different: The landscape lighting is beautiful, the lights on the seawall show the marine life in the ocean, the subtle lighting enhances the draperies in the master bedroom, the media room/theater rivals what you would find in Hollywood, and the fireplaces—it's exquisite." I turn to the broker and say, "I don't need to be here. Here's the key; if you want to come back, just let me know, and I'll leave the alarm off." (Why am I talking to the broker? I want him or her to sell the property when I'm not there.)

When the clients come back at night, I arrive early, put out wine and cheese, light a fire in the fireplace, and set the home automation to evening mode to show off the house at its best. I also vacuum the carpet in such a way that I'll know exactly where the clients walk. When they open the gate using the security code, drive across the wooden bridge and past the waterfall, park the car in the motor court, walk up to the entry, take out the front door key, put it into the lock and turn the handle, they have just performed the same routine the owner of the home will. I've created an emotional experience of ownership that is worth millions of dollars, and it's usually just a matter of time before they call with an offer.

PREPARING FOR THE SALE

For all but the highest-end estates, one of your first tasks is to get an appraisal that establishes the increased value of your property. First, get a comparative market analysis through your realtor, or by utilizing one of my favorite resources, the county property assessors web site. (Many county government records are now accessible online.) Second, you can hire an appraiser—but make sure he or she is evaluating your property accurately. An appraiser will look beyond the neighborhood for a comparable property if you draw his attention to it. You also should point out the improvements you've made, and any increase in value in the area over the past few years. When we were just starting out with our first-time home buyer homes we usually did a pre-appraisal report, literally taking an appraiser's form and filling it in based on properties we would consider comparable but which the appraiser may or may not consider.

You also must bring your brokers on board with your increased price. Even with the $7 million Ocean Ridge mansion I sold in late 2004, I had brokers question whether I was being realistic in my asking price. These price points are not due to overconfidence or ego; they're based on studying the market, my acquisition formula, and my instincts about what buyers will want. I may look like a risk taker, but in truth I believe in taking only intelligent risks, backed up with a lot of preparation and cold, hard facts.

YOUR MARKETING PLAN OF ATTACK

Our marketing plans are drawn up with military precision and all aspects of the campaign mapped out to the last detail, because I believe that planning will result in a successful sale at a top price. We draw up the first marketing plan for a property before we close. Our marketing plans are one or two pages at most, very simple, yet they are the plans of attack that allow us to sell our properties so quickly. Each plan starts with a clear outcome, which is always the sale of the property at a specific price, and below are listed the different marketing avenues used to achieve it. On the next page is a marketing plan for one of our properties. This version was an update of our initial marketing plan after the grand unveiling for this estate in May 2004. This property sold for nearly full asking price 47 days after this plan was drafted.

Your sales and marketing approach should be multitiered and dictated by certain time milestones. Every single moment you own a property you must be evaluating and reevaluating its greatest potential for a profitable sale. For example, if you buy a piece of vacant land, you can put the land up for sale immediately, in the size you bought it or broken up into smaller pieces that are sold separately. (We have done this very thing with the $85 million, 8.78-acre direct oceanfront property we are marketing as vacant land in Manalapan, Florida.) If you buy with the idea of renovating, you should put the property on the market as-is at a price that guarantees you a respectable profit. Then you should evaluate every offer you receive before you start renovations by asking, "Is it going to be in my best interest to consider taking a short-term profit? Or have I bought the property so right that my ability to improve the property represents an exponentially greater upside? Would it be better to resist the temptation to be taken out early and follow through with the plan?" Part of the reason to have a marketing plan and vision statement is to be able to judge the merits of any early offers against the ultimate goal of your construction or renovation plans.

Post-Completion Marketing Plan
July 1, 2004 – September 30, 2004

OUR PRIMARY OBJECTIVE: Sell our 11,387+/– sq. ft., 6-bedroom, 8.5 baths (including 1-bed/2-bath guest house) Spanish/Mediterranean ocean-to-Intracoastal estate for $17,000,000.

Frank McKinney & Company (FMC) will undertake the following in an effort to compliment the overall marketing plan being implemented by FMC and Christie's/Premier Estate Properties. We have now fully transitioned into the most important phase of any FMC project, Presentation and Sale. It is now time to properly Present and Sell what we have all worked so hard to create.

1. Preparation & Presentation: Routinely implement the QR (quality review) checklist and proactively update and complete the work list so the home reflects the very essence of the FMC way, every day, every showing until sold.

2. Showings: All to partake in setting the home up for a showing & participate in a mock showing. All to have complete knowledge of the home and call Frank immediately when we have an inquiry.

3. Signage: Make temporary sign for beach using new brochures. Brochure boxes (3) *always* full. Signs always clean and neat (especially ocean).

4. Brochures: Home stocked with new brochures in acrylic display on table by front door and randomly throughout the house. Binder and portfolio of past projects in same location.

5. Open Houses: Prepare for "Brokers Only" Open House.

6. Web: Scan our final aerial photos (one set laminated; post others in binder) onto our web site. Schedule professional video tour. Frank to continue to monitor and update both ours and Premier's web site (new brochures).

7. Merchandising/display: Clean and repair model in garage. Display monthly progress photos on south wall in garage. All other material in garage storage loft (blow-up of model photos, brochure floor plans, color renderings of front & rear elevations, site plan).

8. Meet quarterly with Premier to discuss the overall marketing efforts & assist Premier in any way.

As before, we must adapt our marketing strategy to a marketplace we continue to create. We continue to establish the plan, formula, and format for this new marketplace. Consequently we must apply the utmost creativity and a deep committed focus to our always-proactive marketing approach. If we diligently endeavor to accomplish the above and with the Christie's/Premier Estate Properties marketing plan, the sale of this world-class property is only a matter of time.

Our marketing plans are drawn up from day one and are modified every three months, but they really kick into gear six months before completion. That's when the blitz of advertisements begin, brokers need to be on board so we can educate them about our latest masterpiece, and we ramp up our efforts on the web site, direct mail, and so on. Each quarter our marketing plans are assessed based on one question: Have we achieved our goal of selling the property at a price that shatters previous records? We evaluate current market conditions and make adjustments as needed. We reassess everything—advertising, showings, client contacts, and so on. Our web site is updated regularly, and we check with the brokerage to make sure they're on track with advertising placement in newspapers, magazines, and online. I believe you must check in quarterly to proactively and creatively reevaluate your results, and change your approach as needed.

Depending on your resources, your marketing plan should include the following elements at a minimum:

Real estate brokerage	Web site
Brochures	Direct mail and flyers
Signage and on-property displays	Print/TV media
Public relations	Grand unveilings
Open houses	Showings

Real Estate Brokerage

Up until our most recent $100-million-plus home, our properties have been listed with Christie's/Premier Estate Properties, firms that deal exclusively with ultra-high-end properties. However, even with a great brokerage, you must be prepared to put your own time, money, and efforts into marketing. While the brokerage pays for all advertising, I write the copy and make sure the ads are placed in the right magazines and positioned on the pages I want. I'm also very involved in the brokerage's marketing plan, which is only one part of our overall marketing campaign.

Always put into your listing agreement that you will be notified prior to any showing so you can either (1) help the broker sell or (2) sell the property yourself with the broker's assistance. (If you're not great at selling, this chapter teaches you some of the basics, so you should find it easy to take clients through a house and trigger their desire to buy. If you would rather leave selling to the broker, give him or her a copy of this book—or make them buy their own—and insist they follow its suggestions.) Some brokers seem to believe they're doing their job if they unlock the front door and tell their clients, "Go ahead and look around. I'll be here when you're done." As a Maverick you must not tolerate that approach. Work with your broker and teach him or her how you want your property shown—and attend every showing yourself.

Web Site

Nowadays with the click of a mouse and without the hassle of contacting a realtor or getting into their car, prospective home buyers can take a pictorial or video/virtual tour of any property online. They can eliminate homes that don't have the features they need: bedrooms on the ground floor, a back yard for the dogs, a big enough kitchen, and so on. Before you put an ad into a newspaper or magazine, I would put your property on a current, easy-to-navigate, informational web site—preferably your own, and at the very least on your listing broker's site and any other participating web sites that feed into it. I've had my own web site for more than 11 years, and I also have my properties featured on Premier Estate Properties' web site, which is linked to dozens of other global high-end real estate sites. All of these are also linked to my own site, www.frank-mckinney.com.

I suggest you write into your listing agreement all the different sites on which your property will be displayed. You should have display space on your realtor's site, your own site (if you have one), any national site that is connected with your realtor's office (coldwell banker.com, remax.com, and so on), as well as global real estate web sites like realtor.com. Depending on your property, you also should negotiate with your realtor where your listing will be placed on their web site. If you're selling a starter home, you need to realize that other, more expensive properties will probably take precedence, but you can insist upon having input on the ad copy and the photos of your property on the site.

I strongly suggest getting your own web site. It's not that expensive either to set up or maintain, and it will give you a valuable ongoing marketing presence. You can ask the person who sets up your web site to provide you with passwords that will allow you to update the site yourself. You or your web master can put up photos of renovations in progress, announce your property acquisitions, and essentially maintain a selling presence in cyberspace every hour of every single day you own a property.

I also suggest you add a virtual and/or video tour as part of your web site. There are companies that will create virtual or video tours of your property for less than $500, or if you're technologically savvy, you can put one together yourself. But this is a place you should spend some money, as a quality video tour will sell your house to people from all over the world before they ever set foot on the property. In a virtual tour, a stationary camera takes 360-degree shots of your property. A basic virtual tour will display one front and one rear elevation, and a couple of interior rooms (ideally the kitchen and master bedroom/bath, where you've put your money). A video tour is a narrated, moving walkthrough of the house; it's almost like having an open house on your web site, and to my mind it's much better. In addition to posting the virtual or video tour on your web site, you can put it on CD or DVD, to use in your direct mail or information packets at showings.

Brochures

Even at the entry level, you should have a brochure, which can be a double-sided 8½-by-11 color copy with photos and a brief description of the highlights of your house. If you're in the middle of renovations, I also suggest you have one-sheets (single color copies, printed one-sided) with photos of the work that's being done—a new roof, kitchen cabinets, tile in the bathroom, and so on. You always should have ready for potential buyers a packet of marketing materials, including a brochure with floor plan and a one-sheet with the realtor's information.

For the higher-end market, brochures become more elaborate. Our current brochures are 4 to 12 pages long, glossy, custom-made and beautiful. We tell the story of the property using photos that are works of art, illustrating the ultimate in manmade luxury combined with natural beauty. (Sunrise and sunset can be great times to shoot brochure photographs, as there's a quality to the light then that makes the house look even more warm and inviting.) The text is evocative and designed to kindle the five senses experience in the reader. I write the copy and always proofread the brochures myself before they go to print. On many of the pages in this book you will see photos drawn from some of our past brochures.

Flyers and Direct Mail

When I was selling starter homes I printed up flyers, which I distributed in rental communities and throughout the neighborhood. Flyers are still a great way to tell people about your entry-level property. You can put the details of your house and any open-house dates on a nice-looking flyer with color photos—the color will set it apart and make your property look even better. Post flyers in grocery stores, dry cleaners, fitness centers, local community bulletin boards, and so on.

A few important things to remember:

1. Distribute flyers within a few miles of your property. People like to stay within the same general area (school district, work, church, recreation, etc.) if possible, so this will be your primary market. Put special focus on any rental complexes in the area if your property is a starter home.

2. Make sure the flyer has a shelf life. Don't just advertise one open house; hold open houses every weekend until the house is sold.

3. Make sure your flyer is informational and that it stands out. Have a nice color photo of the outside of the house and maybe one inside room, and then list the features and amenities of the property. Any open house information should be

emphasized and set apart with type, color, or some other device. Put the asking price at the bottom, along with your phone number and web site address.

4. Post your flyers wherever and whenever you can, and distribute them in as many ways as possible. This will pay off in more traffic for your open houses and a greater pool of potential buyers.

These same flyers also can be used as part of a direct mail campaign. Many realtors will do their own direct mail targeted toward people who can afford your property. For my estates we mail a full package, including brochure, to Fortune 500 CEOs, clients of Sotheby's or Christie's auction houses, and clients who have already bought homes in this price range. Mailings are also sent to targeted affluent people in ZIP codes throughout the United States. You can purchase mailing lists based on demographics, income, or location— lists of renters in the area, or people with children, and so on—for your own direct mail campaign.

Print and TV Media: Ads in Newspapers, Magazines, and TV

If you're selling your property yourself, the first place you'll commonly go for advertising is your local newspaper. To reach as many buyers as possible, however, I suggest you place ads in everything: citywide papers, local community papers, free newspapers, and so on. Your ad doesn't need to be big, but it does need to have something that sets it apart. Spend a few days or even weeks reading the classifieds and see what ads will catch the eye of your target buyer. Pick a few words or phrases you like and then put your own spin on them. The first line of copy should be in boldface type and emphasize whatever will attract your buyer. Since affordability is often the most important aspect of a first-time home purchase, headlines like OWN WITH DOWN PAYMENTS LESS THAN FIRST, LAST, AND SECURITY! BUY FOR LESS THAN RENT! usually work. (Remember, most first-time buyers will be thinking of what they must pay each month rather than the overall cost of the property.) If your realtor places ads in newspapers for you, insist on reviewing and approving all ad copy. Ask about placement of your property in their listings in the newspaper, and which papers they will be advertising in. If you feel they're missing certain community papers that could provide valuable leads, invest a little of your own money and take out an ad.

Working with a realtor gives you access to local realty magazines. These are usually glossy publications that consist of nothing but property listings, photographs of properties, and advertising by realtors of their services. Realtors use these magazines to find properties for their customers who are looking to buy, so placing ads here will help drive both realtors and buyers to your door. However, in these magazines you have to work even harder to make sure your property stands out from the others. If possible, ask to see where your ad will be placed in the magazine. Placement toward the front of the magazine is preferable, and an ad on the cover, inside cover, back cover, or back inside cover is better than in the regular pages. If your ad is on an interior page, ask that it be placed on the right-hand page rather than the left. Of course, if you're selling a starter home you're less likely to be able to choose your position in the magazine, but you still should be able to make sure the copy and photos in the ad show off your property to its best advantage while appealing to your target buyers.

I've seen a ton of ads in glossy realty magazines, and most of the text, type, and visuals are really dull. Your ad needs to draw the buyers' attention. Ask if you can have a bigger ad in the magazine than the standard size. Anything larger will stand out more and make the house seem of higher value to the reader. (Your broker will be the one paying for this advertising and so you may run into some resistance to your request, but a bigger ad will help the house sell more quickly.) Even if you're selling your property yourself, you can take out ads in the local realty magazines like *Homes and Land* as a FOR SALE BY OWNER listing. If you're buying the ads, spend the money for a half-page or even a full-page space. The amount of display you will gain will more than make up for the cost. Many magazines also have web sites, so make sure your advertisement appears in both. I also insist that my web site address is on all advertising, even that which is placed by the realty company. I want every reader to be driven directly to my site rather than having to go through anywhere else. If the realty company wants their web site address on the ad as well, fine, but mine must be listed, preferably first.

As we get closer to showings and open houses, I increase the number and size of advertisements in both newspapers and magazines. Again, do whatever you can to make your open house listing stand out from the others. You can accomplish this with something as simple as a special headline or unusual open house time (12 to 5 instead of 1 to 4). Anything that drives buyers into your showings will mean more potential clients and possibly a quicker sale.

Signage and On-Property Displays

Your signage helps create a unique identity for your property. If you're selling the house yourself, don't just go to the hardware store and buy a FOR SALE BY OWNER 12-inch-square sign with a space for you to write your phone number. Go to a sign company and have a couple of nice metal signs made with your phone number and web site address on them. It's a small investment that will reap big rewards.

Let's assume you have a nice sign in the front yard of your property. Next to the sign, attach an information box into which you put your flyers or brochures. Check your information box every day (or at the least every other day) to make sure it's clean, neat, well maintained, and fully stocked. Throw away any damaged flyers or brochures and replace them with fresh ones.

I have visual displays of the house construction posted in one location at the property. For instance, I have a helicopter fly over the project and take pictures of our progress every month. We then mat these photos and display them to tell the story of the house's construction without saying a word. You, too, can use photos as a selling point for your property. If you're renovating a house that used to be the neighborhood eyesore, take photos as you clean up, upgrade, and improve, and display them somewhere in the house during showings. Let the photos show how your lump of coal has now become the neighborhood diamond.

Public Relations

Publicity is one of the best ways to drive buyers to your property. Of course, unless your house is remarkable or you have a great story, getting publicity is tough. We have a public relations firm on retainer to help us get coverage for all our projects and continue the development of the Frank McKinney brand. Even as a beginning investor, publicity is a valuable addition to your marketing plan. Do you have any charitable endeavor that you could tie to your property? Is there something interesting about you or someone who helped with the project that local newspapers or media outlets could report on? We talk more about public relations in Chapter 10 when we discuss branding.

Showings and Open Houses

Open houses are gold to a Maverick who wants to learn to sell. There are so many opportunities to (1) hone your sales skills, (2) get to learn your product better, and (3) understand the reaction of your target buyers to your product. For my early properties I never relied on brokers to sell at the open houses. Every weekend I would kiss Nilsa good-bye, say, "I'll be back at the end of the day," and go out to my properties myself. Every afternoon I would set up signs and tie balloons to the tops of my houses, clean the grounds, and put out food. Then, as people arrived, I would show them around and practice my sales skills. It was selling in its most pure form, because I had to deal with so many different kinds of people. I learned about my houses; I learned what buyers really wanted; I learned how to work with brokers; I learned how to close deals. I learned to listen to feedback about my houses and implement suggestions for the next time. (I even discovered that letting people think you were someone other than the owner got you more honest feedback.) Those open house weekends were some of the most valuable training I could have received, and I use what I learned at them to this day.

Before you hold your first open house, I suggest you do market research by going to open houses for properties in your neighborhood, as well as properties at your price point and above. First, you'll see the houses that are your direct competition. Second, you'll see how your competition markets. Third, and most important, you'll get a real sense of your potential customers. You can listen to their comments, see what excites them and what they criticize, so you can make sure your property thrills your target buyers.

The goal of an open house is to get buyers in the door so they will be "wowed" by your property and then make an offer. Only if your property touches them at a visceral level will they cross over from looker to buyer. Your objective is to heighten the experience of their five senses to a state of subliminal euphoria. You also must deliver the unexpected—for first-time buyers, something they thought they would never see in a house at their price point, or for high-end buyers, something that takes luxury and convenience to new heights. Remember, people are buying not merely a piece of property, but an emotional experience of "home." Your primary objective is to tap into those emotions and get them to start imagining your property as the place they will spend the next several years.

Getting Buyers to the Door: You've done your advertising, contacted the brokers, and distributed flyers in the area; you've gotten the word out. But now you need to create a path that will lead buyers to your property. Here are a few key elements to make it easy for people.

Broker Open Houses: In most communities there are recurring open houses for the general public; these usually happen on Saturdays or Sundays. Then there are open houses for brokers held at other times, often on weekdays. If you are selling your property yourself, find out when the broker-only open houses are held and hold an open house at the same time, complete with advertising, signage, and so on. It's a great way to bring brokers to your door, who will then bring their clients. When you get to a higher price point, the only open houses you'll schedule will be for brokers, who will bring you their clients for showings. For our brokers-only open houses we send out nice invitations for an afternoon event.

Hours: I always suggest that you hold open houses on both Saturday and Sunday, every single weekend, until the property sells. If there are any big events scheduled in your area, plan your open houses to take advantage of them. For instance, there's a big festival called the Delray Affair in Delray Beach, close to many of my properties. It brings around 250,000 people into the town. You'd better believe I scheduled open houses that weekend!

Also, start your open houses earlier and end later than regular hours. If most open houses are 1:00 to 4:00 P.M., then yours should start at noon and go until 5 P.M. This will help you capture more potential buyers over the course of a day. If your open house starts at noon, you must get there at 11:00, because people will start arriving by 11:30! At 11:00 A.M. you'll have a little time to walk through the house, set out the food, do your final inspection, and be ready to welcome buyers.

Signs: Whenever I held open houses I would put directional signs several miles away, guiding buyers to my front door. Unless your property is on a main thoroughfare, choose the most traveled highway in the area and start your directional signs from that point. At every intersection put another sign, leading buyers straight to your property's driveway.

Decoration: Create some kind of visual decoration above the house so people will be able to tell immediately which property is for sale. Originally I put Mylar air-tunnel balloons, like you see at used car lots, in front of the house. I'd also tie helium balloons to the mailbox, chimney, and rooftop. I even hired a guy to put on a pink gorilla outfit, stand on the main thoroughfare, and hold an OPEN HOUSE sign with an arrow pointing to my property. Obvious? Yes—but people knew which house was for sale. You may not want a guy in a gorilla suit, but could you perhaps hire a teenager or two to hold OPEN HOUSE signs at the closest main intersection and wave people toward your street?

Your Quality Review (QR) Maintenance Checklist: During the showing period, one of your main jobs will be quality control and maintenance, to ensure your property is ready for a buyer. I'm obsessive about maintenance. I do a maintenance walkthrough midweek for every property we have on the market, and on the day of a showing I walk through again to handle any last-minute cleanups and fixes. Even in the starter homes I built in the 1980s, before a showing or open house I would go into every bathroom with a rag and a bottle of cleaner and clean the toilet seat, and fold the end of the toilet paper to a perfect diamond tip. I still check the bathrooms before a client walks through to make sure that diamond tip is on every toilet paper roll.

For each property we have weekly and monthly QR (Quality Review) checklists, which combine ongoing interior and exterior maintenance plus whatever is needed to prepare the house for a showing. While there are crews of people that do weekly and monthly maintenance on our properties, I'm still out there every week making sure things are immaculate. Cleanliness costs you nothing, yet this attention to detail will set your property apart almost as much as $250 per yard carpet and honey onyx countertops.

Here are a few of the tasks you'd see on a typical QR checklist.

Interior QR: Weekly

- Vacuum all carpet to show perfect lines; carry chem-dry spot remover as you vacuum.
- Vacuum wood floors, then light mop w/wood floor cleaner.
- Mop stone floors w/suggested cleaning solution.
- Wipe down countertops with Windex (kitchens, baths, bars).
- Clean all brass, nickel, stainless, etc., fixtures & hardware.
- Dust all rooms (furniture, picture frames, window sills, etc.).
- Clean all sinks.
- Windex all mirrors and interior glass.
- Clean toilets & fold toilet paper neatly to a diamond point.
- Remove streaks from hardwood floors, if any.
- Keep all storage cabinets or storage rooms neatly organized, labels forward.
- Have ample supply of shoe booties (floor protection) by front door.

Exterior QR: Weekly

- Rinse & squeegee exterior window glass & frames (including light fixture glass, camera lenses, brochure box glass, etc.).
- Pick up all trash by street and on entire property (neighboring properties also).
- Sweep or blow off, then rinse exterior decks/drives/railings.
- Wipe down outside counter tops, sinks, and barbecue (check cabinets for bugs, trash, etc.).
- Seal & protect stainless in sinks, barbecue, refrigerators, gate entry keypad, exterior shower fixtures, and all metal and stainless.
- Water plants in pots on decks and check sprinkler coverage.
- T-9 all door hardware, hinges, A/C units, pool equip, all exterior metal that is not part of the mandatory monthly T-9 treatment. (T-9 is a lubricant used in aerospace—it's the best you can buy.)
- Check exterior lightbulbs, clean & trim away leaves & branches to allow ample light.
- Clean out waterfalls and ponds and make sure fountain by front door is clear.
- Freshen up mulch in high visibility areas that need it; keep some mulch on hand.

Mechanical QR

- Weekly—walk entire property (inside and out) to change burnt-out lightbulbs.
- Weekly—clean filter in pool, waterfalls, and fountain.
- Monthly—change all air-conditioning filters.
- Monthly—T-9/lube: window cranks & parts, shutter tracks, door locks, throw bolts, cabinet hardware & hinges, canvas curtain track, pool, spa, winch, front gate operable swing arms, auto garage door chains, exterior a/c units, light fixtures & all exterior metal.

- Monthly—remove dirt/dust from all central vacuum canisters.
- Monthly—remove and clean silt, dirt, and mulch from fabric covering all drainage grates.
- Monthly—start generator.
- First few months—clean faucet aerators.
- First few months—test all appliances, toilets, faucets, fireplaces, etc.—"run the house."

To bring top dollar, your property must always appear new and/or fresh; anything that's the least bit dirty or broken will stand out to your potential buyer. Even a burnt-out lightbulb or a pile of clippings in the yard sends a negative message. For example, at one of our properties, in the master suite there was a 60-inch plasma TV hidden behind a beautiful painting especially commissioned for the space. At the touch of a button the painting was supposed to rise slowly to reveal the TV screen behind it. It was a great effect—only at one showing when I pushed the button the painting stayed put. Now before every showing we check to ensure everything—sound system, theater system, cooling system, gates, alarms, appliances, and so on—works as it should.

I suggest you go through every part of your property weekly, making notes and fixing things as you go along. Carry a little cleaning/repair kit with you—Windex, carpet stain remover, touch-up paint, a rag, a screwdriver. Put yourself in the mindset of your potential buyers. What are they likely to see? What will distract them from the experience you want them to have? What wouldn't they notice unless it's broken or not up to par? Start at the road and go through the front yard, back yard, and entry. Look at the neighbors' yards and see if there's anything that will affect the impact of your property, and clean it up. Check the mailbox for any junk mail. Then go inside and walk through every room in the house. Check all the operating systems. Do any spot-cleaning that's required. Turn on all the lightbulbs and dust them if needed. I even check the electrical plates of the light switches, to see if the grooves in the screws are aligned north-south. Sit down on the closed toilet seat so you can see what someone will have in their vision if they use the bathroom. (This is a great way to spot dirt and disorder that is often overlooked.) Fold the toilet paper ends into those little diamond points. Check the operating systems of the house—air-conditioning, heating, water heaters, and all appliances—to make sure they're plugged in and working. (Early on I made the mistake of thinking, "I don't want to use this stuff because I don't want to break it," but appliances will seize up and not function properly if you *don't* use them.) Run water through the pipes. Flush all the toilets. Take the ice out of the icemaker and let it fill up again.

Once a month go into the spaces where buyers typically won't venture—the hot water heater closet, mechanical rooms, attics, and crawl spaces. Your buyers may never see them, but if an inspector goes through the property and finds them neglected he won't be happy, and neither will the buyer. (In between showings and open houses, you can unplug water heaters, water recirculating systems, and so on. This will reduce both your carrying costs and wear and tear. I also draw the drapes to keep out the heat or cold and block UV rays that might fade carpets and wood.)

Each showing or open house is show time—the curtain's going up and you must be ready. Your attention to detail and maintenance helps to create the "wow" factor that demonstrates the value of your property and its exceptional quality.

Running a Winning Open House and/or Showing: The goal of every open house or showing is to get people to your door so they will be impressed by your masterpiece. Here are eleven points to remember.

1. You are the best showperson for the property, therefore you should do your best to be the one who takes prospective buyers through. (At open houses, it's a little harder as you have no control over the number of people who show up at any given time.) For every 10 scheduled showings you'll probably be able to direct 8, and the other two groups are going to show themselves through. But your goal should still be to guide the experience of potential buyers so you can shape their perceptions of the house.

2. Dress nicely, professionally, and neatly. Your appearance will reflect on the house, as will your enthusiasm. Let people see

how proud you are of what you've created, and how much you love the results.

3. Learn to read prospective buyers. Part of your learning curve will be to discern whom to spend time with, who's just looking, who wants to be left alone to walk through the house, who will appreciate a guided tour, and who is truly in the market and ready to buy. Meet people at the door and listen to what they have to say. "We're just looking," "We were driving by on the way back from church," "I'm curious about what you've done with this house"—such responses will usually indicate a general interest but not a lot of motivation. "We've just moved to this area," "We're having a baby and need more space," "We saw your flyer and want to get out of renting and move into buying"—these people have a need for a house, and it might very well be yours. Spend the time necessary with these buyers.

You can never tell at first sight who's going to buy your house. I've had guys wearing jeans, T-shirts, and baseball caps make full-price, all-cash offers for multimillion-dollar homes, and I've seen people who didn't have the money to buy a hamburger, much less their first house, drive up in rented Bentleys. (What's the difference between an eccentric and a lunatic? The eccentric has money.) You'll learn which are your potential buyers by listening to their comments, not by judging their appearance. After you've held a few open houses and sold a property or two, you'll have more of an instinct for separating buyers from lookers.

4. Create a showing path through the house. Meet people at the door or in the front yard, show them the outside of the house first, and then move inside, guiding them through the rooms on a predetermined path. Runners over carpet and hardwood floors help provide a road map, showing potential buyers exactly what rooms to see in what order. You can use runners made from the house carpeting, or clear plastic. (Be careful of leaving runners on top of hardwood floors too long, as they will cause discoloration.) Double back frequently so clients will go through the rooms more than once.

End up by the front door or in the kitchen, or in our case, by the ocean, and have a contract handy in case they're ready to make an offer right away.

5. Make sure your house appeals to all the buyers' senses. Draw up a list of the five senses, and next to each one write down what you've done to enhance the experience of that particular sense. How can you create a subliminal, euphoric experience that engenders extreme desire? Here are some suggestions for heightening the five senses experience.

Sight: Make sure the front yard, driveway, and walkway of the house are green, trimmed, and landscaped. Put a decorative plate around the doorbell and a nice lighting fixture at the entryway. Replace the house numbers so they're visible and attractive. Have silk plants in the flowerboxes under the windows. When people arrive, encourage them to walk around the outside of the house first. Take them through the back yard, show them the beautiful grass (people love green yards), and let them see the property boundaries of their new home. Put patio furniture in the back yard—this essentially adds a room to the house, as it provides additional living space.

Inside, dress your house as if it's ready to move in, with plants, place settings in the kitchen, candles in the bedroom, towels in the bath, as many furnishings as you can afford, and so on. Above all, cleanliness and order are essential. Use drapes or curtains in your kitchen, living room, and master bedroom. One touch that impresses buyers is to use wooden hangers in the master bedroom closet. Place stacks of brochures throughout the house, so buyers may pick up and read them at any point.

Sound: I use sound throughout a property to create atmosphere. In the early days I would hide a CD player behind the living room curtains, and play calypso music or Jimmy Buffett. I'd have another CD player with romantic instrumental music in the bedroom. I tend to stay away from classical music; you want to wake your buyers up, not lull them. Choose music that's current, snappy, happy, something suited to the mood you want to create.

Get rid of any sounds that detract from the buyers' experience. Check your appliances for rattles and eliminate them. If you have fans that make noise, replace or fix them. (Here in Florida a lot of properties have ceiling fans, and the knob at the end of the fan cord can hit the fan blades, so I would remove the cord.) If the street is noisy, keep the windows closed. On the other hand, should your property be situated close to nature and it's a nice day, let the outside provide your soundtrack. I've turned off sound systems that cost hundreds of thousands of dollars to let buyers hear the ocean waves. If your property is close to woods, let people hear the wind in the trees, or the beautiful birds that nest in the trees on the property.

Smell: Smells are our strongest memory triggers. Outside, fragrance from fresh-cut grass or flowers along a walkway is wonderful. Inside, the house must smell clean first and foremost. Potpourri plugged into a heating unit can add a nice touch. (Nilsa puts potpourri into the containers for the silk plants.) You also can dab scent on the lightbulbs. Think "homey" when choosing the scents for your rooms: lavender or vanilla in the bedrooms, apple pie in the kitchen. And chocolate chip cookie dough, sliced, put on a cookie sheet, and placed in the oven at 150 degrees will create a wonderful atmosphere in your kitchen during showings.

Taste: My open houses always had snacks—early on, I put a bowl of chips in the kitchen and sodas or waters in the refrigerator, simple food for people to munch on as they walked through the house. I like to put a little bowl of chocolates right by the front door to encourage people to stay and talk a little longer. If you can't afford Ferrero Rocher chocolates, Hershey's Kisses are just fine.

Touch: If you've put new stucco, wood railings, or shutters on the outside of your house, have people feel the textures or knock on the wood. Any special wall finishes on the inside, drapes, kitchen cabinets, countertops—have your buyers run their hands over the materials. In my high-end properties, I'll ask people to remove their shoes and put on paper booties before entering the house. This accomplishes three things: First, it keeps the carpets and floors clean. Second, it allows people to feel the luxury of the carpet and flooring beneath their feet. Third, it makes them take a moment before they enter the house to get ready for the experience—perhaps the same experience home owners have as they comfortably walk in their home with their shoes off. Even in starter homes, having potential buyers take off their shoes will save you a tremendous amount of clean-up while creating a sensation of a special event.

6. Learn to tell the story of your house without making it sound like a sales pitch. Think of yourself as an artist describing your work. Point out all the amenities. Call the buyers' attention to the high quality of improvements you've made. Mention the great kitchen cabinets, the new flooring, the lighting fixtures, carpet, and so on. Talk about the things they won't necessarily notice, like a new roof or sprinkler system, upgraded plumbing or wiring, or a new central air system. Your goal is to give them just enough information and then let the house speak for itself. Don't just pay attention to the obvious rooms: Show them a closet or mechanical room if you've made renovations in there. I try to create one "wow" feature in every room of every property, something that will impress buyers with its beauty and luxury. This could be anything from a great hobby room to the tub in the master bath. In one property it was a wet bar that was also an aquarium: You could set your martini glass down and see exotic $500 tropical fish swimming inside the glass-topped bar. After a very small number of showings or one or two open houses, you'll start to recognize the selling points of your house according to your buyers' tastes.

7. Sell buyers on the area, neighborhood, and community. With my starter homes I knew where the closest schools were, all the major churches, supermarkets, dry cleaners, and so on. I'd provide a list of babysitters, veterinarians, doctors, dentists, and other services people need. I'd also mention any civic or business improvements in the works.

8. Allow enough time to show the house. If people say, "We only have a half-hour," tell them, "It takes at least an hour to see this house properly." Ask serious buyers to come back and see the house and the neighborhood at night. If the home is in an up-and-coming neighborhood, you want them to make sure they feel safe on the streets after dark. Offer to give the keys to the broker or to the potential buyer themselves (if they are people you can trust) and let the buyers come back on their own. Say, "Just let me know when you're coming so I can have the lights on." Then arrive beforehand and put out wine, cheese, and crackers, or beer and nachos, whatever is appropriate. You can watch the tour from a distance and see how much they love your house.

9. Train your listing broker to show the house the way you do, following the same pattern and emphasizing the same amenities. Many times the brokers can act as the client's sounding board. The client will say to the broker, "Okay, the owner obviously has a vested interest in this house, but as a professional, what do *you* think?" It's important for you and your broker to present a united front to the buyer as far as the house and the deal are concerned.

10. As I said earlier, most properties are sold through the buyer's broker rather than the listing broker, so I send thank-you notes to the brokers of everyone who comes to look at the property. If this client doesn't buy, perhaps one of the broker's other clients may. Use every client and showing as an opportunity to build another relationship.

11. Every showing is also an opportunity for me to learn more about my target buyers and their desires and needs. Not everyone is going to love my properties, and that's fine, but I do my best to learn as much as I can from each person who walks through the door. After a showing I'll contact the broker and say, "Tell me what you think I missed that we might add to our future properties." Early in my career, I am somewhat ashamed to say, I sat at my open houses and passed myself off as someone other than the owner; I was so eager to hear peo-

ple's unedited comments. I believe that when you first hear a comment it needs to be duly noted. When you hear the same comment twice, you'd better start to pay attention. When you hear it a third time, you'd better act immediately. Anything you can discover about your target buyers' likes and dislikes will help you as you acquire, improve, and sell your next property.

Grand Unveilings

For properties selling for less than $2 million, open houses work fine. For high-end properties of $2 million or more, special events and grand unveilings are better for drawing the VIP buyers, top brokers, and the media and publicity that will help sell the property. In truth, grand unveilings are simply a bigger version of the open houses we used to have for our starter homes 20 years ago. As our prices went up and the available pool of qualified buyers went down, the best way to attract our buyers was a big, theatrical event.

I believe that we do grand unveilings better than anybody else, probably because we have such a good time with them. With a grand unveiling, we build interest in the artwork we have been creating for years and now will reveal to the world. I always choose a theme or scene rather than simply having a black-tie reception. Granted, this appeals to the theatrical tendency of my personality, but it also gives more likelihood of media coverage and attendance by brokers. People know my unveilings are always spectacular and they attend for the show, but the *real* show starts when they walk inside the house for the first time.

Our guest list focuses on five groups.

1. Buyers—we send invitations to people in high-rent ZIP codes in the area, as well as our own qualified mailing list and that of the listing broker. We invite VIPs even if they're not currently looking for property, since they may know someone who is. We'll also arrange an early showing for VIPs. At one event, while people were gathering for the party I was inside showing the property to a client that just couldn't wait.

2. Brokers—we invite brokers who sell properties worth a million dollars and up. We find them by looking at advertising in high-end real estate magazines, and then going over the names with our listing broker. Brokers enjoy the food and drink and marvel at the theatrics, then go back to their clients and say, "It was the most outrageous party I've ever been to—but you should see the house."

3. The media—we employ a public relations firm that assembles a very targeted media list, which includes both print media and television. I also call my own media contacts personally. We employ our own film crew: In case some of the TV stations don't send cameras, we'll create a short tape to be able to give to any interested media outlets. To increase media interest, we always have a theme to our grand unveilings and raise funds for our Caring House Project Foundation as part of the event.

4. Community movers and shakers, city officials, Chamber of Commerce members—all the people I've been working hard to develop relationships with over the years.

5. Former clients and other guests who know my product and just want to come for the show.

Our grand unveilings usually benefit our charity. For one event I promised that if we raised $250,000 that night for the Caring House Project Foundation, I would cut my trademark shoulder-length blond hair. Hundreds took me up on the offer; we raised more than $250,000, and I got a haircut my father would be proud of, in front of the entire party.

The grand unveiling for our $17 million and $7 million properties was anything but typical. It was a Pirates of the Caribbean story, with me playing Jack Sparrow, the good pirate, versus Blackbeard. More than 500 invited guests were let onto the property at 6:00 P.M. but were kept on the other side of the waterfall and bridge leading up to the house. The house itself was completely covered with a custom-made veil, just like a priceless piece of art. (The ultra-wealthy always want what they can't have, and taking it away from them is a critical element of marketing. We had started the buzz about the house weeks before, with press releases describing the property as the most magnificent 12,000-square-foot oceanfront estate in the world. Then we completely covered the entire house three days before the party so no one could see it.) At 6:45 there was an enormous explosion, a "concussion" in pyrotechnic terms. Searchlights scanned the property and then focused on a figure teetering on the top of the roof, nearly 60 feet above sea level. "It's me, Frank McKinney, king of the ready-made dream home, and not even you, Blackbeard, will stop me from unveiling to the world the finest oceanfront estate ever built!" I announced. Blackbeard and I had a running gunfight on the top of the house, and then I leapt off the roof and shot down a concealed zip line to the guest house, 200 feet away. From there I "shot" Blackbeard, who, with his dying breath, fired at me, igniting a fuse that ran back up to the roof of the main house. Just as the spark reached the main house, fireworks exploded, the veil dropped, and the house was revealed, with me standing in front of it. I finished the performance by saying, "I've brought you all here for a wonderful party, to be entertained and to support our Caring House Project Foundation. Now go enjoy the house. There will be a special hydrofoil pirate ship waiting to ferry you to the other property at any time this evening."

The guests enjoyed delectable food and free-flowing alcohol (we usually create a special martini or other mixed drink to commemorate the event). Throughout the main house we had brokers from our listing agency in different rooms. Since I couldn't take all 500 guests on a personal tour of the property, I had the brokers do it. The brokers felt more of a part of the sales process, and they got a chance to enjoy the party.

Why go through all that trouble for an occasion that was, at its core, a glorified open house? (Even my mom asks me, "Mickey, why don't you just invite people over to see the house?") Simple: Grand unveilings attract the kind of people and media coverage that will reach the 50,000 or so people worldwide who can afford my properties. These folks are (1) hard to contact, (2) hard to attract, and (3) hard to impress. A grand unveiling allows me to do all three. Plus, grand unveilings build name recognition that is worth every penny spent.

No matter what the price point of your property, you can create a "special event" to attract more people. Even if you're doing a For Sale By Owner (FSBO) of a starter home, you can invite neighbors and local brokers to an open house that features food and a nice speech by you. If you're not theatrically inclined or uncomfortable with that amount of flash, do something more reserved. There's a gentleman by the name of Mark Pulte here in South Florida who also builds high-end properties on spec. Recently he had a black-tie reception to unveil his latest $20 million mansion. He served champagne and great hors d'oeuvres, and let the house do the talking. Mark builds beautiful homes, and the property sold within days.

If you want to hold an event to attract attention to your properties, here are some suggestions.

- Have a theme or story that will attract media attention.
- Choose a charity to benefit from the evening.
- Send out invitations to brokers who specialize in this kind of property. Collaborate with your listing broker as well as doing your own research.
- Find a way to tell the story of your property. Let's say you bought a crack house that was an eyesore in the neighborhood. Take some "before" pictures and mount them on a nice easel so people can see what you've done. Use the story in press releases sent out both in advance and after your grand opening.
- Make sure your property reflects the kind of quality and amenities that will excite the attendees even more than the party.

A Maverick isn't satisfied with the ordinary and mundane; instead of taking the passive approach to selling, we do whatever is necessary to bring our properties to the notice of as wide a group as possible. Ultimately, grand unveilings and open houses are all about the sale. Their purpose is to get buyers in the door, so they can be sold on the quality and amenities of your property. If one of my properties had sold prior to a scheduled grand unveiling, I happily would have stood at the end of the driveway telling guests, "Sorry, the house is sold; we're hosting a party at the Ritz-Carlton instead. See you there!" You have to be prepared for such an eventuality and keep your eye focused on the outcome you want: a quick sale at your desired price.

MAKING THE SALE

The decision to buy is a dance between need and desire. People pick up the newspaper or a magazine and see a notice of your open house or an advertisement for your property. "Three bedrooms, two baths, big lot—that's what we need," they'll say. Need is the first criterion buyers will use when deciding which homes to investigate. There is no emotion involved as yet. When buyers arrive at your house, however, your job throughout the showing process is to awaken and heighten their desire. When a buyer sees your property and that desire is engendered, that's your window of opportunity, the impulse window within which you can move the buyer from a maybe to a yes. That window is open only for a short period of time, so you must take advantage of it quickly. Once the impulse window closes, it's almost impossible to open it again, and you're better off expending your efforts with a new buyer.

Most buyers come in pairs—husband and wife, committed partners—each of whom will have their own needs and desires. You have to learn to read them individually and slant your presentation to satisfy their requirements. Is she the practical one who handles the couple's finances and just wants to know about the bottom line? Does he need to know whether there's enough room in the garage for his jet ski, and where he's going to put his big-screen TV? The key is to give them each an experience of subliminal euphoria as they define it. She might love seeing figures that prove the house is a great long-term investment, while he might be happy knowing that the sofa in the family room will be the absolutely perfect distance away from the 60-inch plasma TV he wants to buy. Sometimes your personality may fit with one member of a couple but not the other. In those cases, a really good broker can be very helpful. You can talk with the husband, for instance, while the broker gives the wife the personal attention she needs. And never let your ego get in the way of a sale. If for some reason there's a personality clash with a client, get out of the way and let someone else take them through the house.

Prequalifying Buyers

Before you enter negotiations with buyers for entry-level to mid-level homes, I suggest you or your broker make sure they're prequalified and, hopefully, pre-approved for a mortgage. ("Prequalified" means that, based on the opinion of a lending institution, the buyers' financial resources will allow them to purchase the house. "Pre-approved" means that the lending institution has already approved their loan up to a certain amount.) With most properties at mid-level or above, buyers will come in with financing in place, and you don't have to worry too much about them being qualified to purchase the house. (If they're working with a broker, the broker should be showing them only properties in their price range, anyway.) Nowadays most first-time home buyers know enough to call a bank or mortgage company and get prequalified for a mortgage. If a potential buyer says, "I really love this house but I don't know if I can afford it," that's your cue to prequalify them yourself. "Great!" you reply. "Have you been pre-approved for a mortgage?" If they answer "No, I've never bought a house before; I don't even know what that is," you say, "Okay, before you come out let me just ask you a few questions." You'll ask about income and job stability, credit history (and if it's okay for you to pull a credit report), savings, residence history (rental or owning), and so on. Based on their answers, you can tell them whether coming out to see your house is worth their time and yours.

First-time buyers can be intimidated by the idea of a home purchase; it's probably more money than they've ever spent, and they're assuming a large amount of debt. You need to help them understand that this is not just a significant expense but also an investment that can bring them long-term benefits. If bought right in the proper neighborhood, their home will provide a greater part of their net worth than any other investment. Your job as the seller is to help buyers understand the value of what they will be getting. That's why you provide comparative analysis of other properties in the neighborhood, show them historical appreciation figures for the area, lay out just how much equity they will be accumulating by owning rather than paying rent, how their net worth will grow, and so on. Since most people own a property for seven years or less, show them what their home might be worth in seven years' time when they sell and move into their next residence. All of this information was part of the Mortgage Qualifier Program I taught years ago, and I suggest you make the same information available to your potential buyers.

Everyone wants to feel they've gotten a good deal. Most buyers want concrete proof that they are getting good value and not over-paying. Even high-end buyers don't want to feel they've been taken advantage of; they want to know (1) if they're paying a lot more than their neighbors and (2) what their potential exit strategy will be. (Businesspeople are trained to look for exit strategies.) Since a Maverick's goal is to set new price levels for their marketplace, this means that you must educate your buyer as to the value you're pro-viding. Could they buy a cheaper house in the same area? Ab-solutely. Will that make it look like they're overpaying for your property? Possibly. Your job is to show them why your property rep-resents a true value based on actual numbers.

Let me give you an example. Assume you find a starter home that's on a property 100 feet by 100 feet, a fixer-upper that you can purchase for $100,000 (essentially the cost of the land). The house on the property is 2,500 square feet. To build that house from scratch, you'd spend around $100 per square foot (a relatively modest cost for construction—we spend over $1,000 per square foot in our estates), for a total cost of around $350,000 for a new home ($100,000 for the land, $250,000 for a 2,500-square-foot house). If your fixed-up starter home is priced below $350,000 (and in a neighborhood where you can buy a teardown for $100,000, your market price is probably quite a bit under $350,000), you've just demonstrated the value they'll be receiving. You're also saving them the year or more it would take to construct a new house, and for many people who want to get out of renting or need to relocate, this consideration is almost as im-portant. Of course, because you've followed the Maverick acquisition formula, you will have paid far less to acquire the land and to build or improve the house, but that doesn't change the fact that your prop-erty represents a great value. You just need to demonstrate it to the buyers' satisfaction.

Different Options for Selling

Now, suppose the market in your area slows down and your prop-erty doesn't sell as quickly as you want, or perhaps you're running out of cash to cover the carrying costs. There are a number of ways you can realize some cash immediately. First, you could reduce your price. If you've followed the acquisition formula, you should have a margin of 40 percent to 50 percent of your retail price to play with if you need to come down a little. Another choice is to do a lease-option deal. With a lease-option you get a certain amount of money up front. This is nonrefundable cash, paid directly to you. In return, you agree to sell the house at an agreed-upon price to the option holder within a certain amount of time, while he pays you monthly rent, part of which is applied to the purchase price of the property. If at the end of the option period the option holder either doesn't want or can't afford the property, you're free to put the house on the market again. As you can see, lease-options provide (1) immediate cash from the option payment; (2) a specific purchase price from a buyer; and (3) monthly rent to cover your carrying costs for the term of the option. Should the deal fall through, all you've lost is time, and you've been compensated for most of that anyway. The downside is that optioning/renting the house to anyone undoubtedly will produce wear and tear, and you don't know what the value of the house will be if the option expires and you have to put it back on the market. Plus, you will have to spend money on a new round of marketing, open houses, and so on. However, if your house isn't selling at the price you want, lease-options are a good way to realize some cash.

Another choice is simply to rent the property. You'll cover your monthly carrying costs and if you rent month-to-month you can keep the house on the market. You can also use the depreciation as a tax benefit. Or you could move into the investment property and put your own home up for sale. (If you sell a home in which you've lived for two of the last five years and put the profits of the sale into a house of equal or higher value, then you can avoid paying capital gains tax on the profits up to $250,000, or $500,000 if you are married.) Finally, you may simply need to increase or change your marketing to attract the right buyers to your property. I believe there's always a way to make money on a real estate transaction, as long as you've followed the Maverick acquisition formula.

The Offer/Selling Agreement

When I was selling starter homes, I'd always have a contract with me, completely filled out except for the price and the buyer's name. I'd say something like, "I'm not pushing this on you, but if you'd like to take a look at a contract . . ." While they may not take one, you're always wise to have a contract ready just in case. Even for high-end properties, the basic contract is fairly simple: It lists the buyer's name, the amount the property will be sold for, the terms (if any—most upper-level properties are cash deals with no financing), and the time to closing (very important—I like closings to occur as quickly as possible, having lived through several hurricanes and other contingencies that can sour a deal).

I prefer not to let the broker negotiate the deal. I will let them make the introduction (and I'll pay them very well for it), but then I want to deal principal to principal. If the deal does not go through or I don't read the person right, let it be on me. Out of every hundred signed deals I've probably had two go bad. Why? Because I believe in being thorough and diligent. I also anticipate as many contingencies as possible. Especially with first-time home buyers, a hundred things can go wrong on the financial side. You have to be willing to bring people along every step of the way. Remember those classes I taught for people who wanted to buy their first home? As part of those classes I had checklists of the financial information needed to qualify for a mortgage. When it came time for those people to put in an offer on one of my properties, I'd work with them on their mortgage application. I'd take the documents from their bank or mortgage underwriter and go over them with the buyer: "You need your W2 forms, your tax returns for the past two years, last week's paycheck stub verified," and so on. We'd run down the list together so when the buyer submitted the application to the bank, everything was correct. Then we'd work with the loan officers and mortgage brokers on finalizing the deal. As the seller, you should keep up-to-date with the different mortgage options that are available, as there are quite a few creative products today. And as we said in Chapter 4, the relationships you have with bankers, loan officers, and mortgage brokers may help your buyers as well as you when it comes to financing.

Negotiations

Negotiations usually happen in two or three stages: the initial offer, the response (either acceptance or counteroffer), and then any counteroffers after that. The most important aspect of negotiating is your buyers' psychology. Everyone has a different way of negotiating. Some people like dancing, back-and-forth, waltzing, and wasting time. However, most buyers for high-end properties are used to negotiating large deals in their businesses, and many of them are "cut to the chase" negotiators. They know quickly if the deal will work or not, and they either make it work or move on. On the other hand, first-time home buyers are making the biggest purchase of their lives, and many of them have only negotiated buying a car (rarely a pleasant experience). You may need to educate your first-time buyer as part of the negotiation process, or ask your broker (or their broker) to help you reach an understanding of what's appropriate in negotiations.

My basic premise with all realtors is, "Get me an offer and let me work with it." No matter how low the offer, I can try to convert it. For instance, if the asking price is $17 million and the buyer offers $13.5 million, depending on the strength of the market (which I as the seller know) I'll counter with an offer of $16.9 million and see if the response is more in line with what I consider a realistic price for the property. Remember, prices are market-driven, and you need to know the current ratio of asking price to selling price in your area. In a seller's market, you shouldn't have to come down too much from your asking price, as long as you've based your asking price on a 10 percent to 20 percent increase over current market values in the area. In a buyer's market, you may have to be prepared to negotiate a bit more.

Successful negotiations at almost any level should be wrapped up within about two days. Time is a deal's worst enemy; I've found the chances of a successful conclusion to a deal will diminish after day two. I've seen foolish buyers, sellers, or brokers talk too much or take too long, and the deal falls through because time has passed. People buy from emotion, and some of the strongest emotions that can come up around a home purchase are fear and remorse. The state of subliminal euphoria you've created with your showing can fade or be overshadowed in the short time it takes for the buyer's fears to materialize. Once negotiations start, get the deal closed quickly.

As part of negotiations you should try to get your buyer to assume as much of the closing costs, including commission, as you can. The buyer may try to do the same with you. If you're still too far apart, you've got to be realistic. Don't haggle for the sake of haggling. I never have a problem allowing buyers to feel as though they got the last word. Don't be greedy or hang on to the last nickel, or feel you have to beat someone for the sake of winning. If the deal's going to fall apart, you need to be honest; go to them and say, "Look, we all have to give a little bit here to get this to work." In the past when the deal was really close but there was no more margin on my side and the buyer seemed adamant, I've asked for both the listing and selling brokers to reduce their commissions slightly so we can make the numbers work. A good broker will recognize that a slightly reduced commission on a completed sale is better than no commission at all. When everyone gives a little, deals are closed faster.

If I feel a need to move the buyer from an on-the-fence status to making an offer, I won't hesitate to let them know that there are other people looking at the house and they may very well lose the deal if they walk away. This may be perceived as the oldest line in the book, but if I bring it up during negotiations, it's true. If I've created a great product and my showings are emphasizing the most positive aspects of the property, I feel it's my responsibility to let potential buyers know that their hesitation may lose them the opportunity. I've done the same thing with banks that don't offer me the terms I want, or with people whose properties I wish to buy. You create your own reality, and I believe firmly that there will always be another property, another bank, or another buyer that will help me meet my needs as far as my deal is concerned.

In negotiating, you have to balance ego with common sense, and be willing to hit a single instead of swinging for the fences. You should be happy with a reasonable profit within the parameters of your acquisition formula. But don't sell yourself or your property short. If a buyer tries to verbally depreciate your property as a negotiation technique, stand fast with the value you have created. You won't necessarily get everything you want from the deal, but you're likely to get more of what you want if you're confident about what you have to offer. Whether the house is $50,000 or $100 million, don't sell for less than what you think your property is worth. You should be very comfortable saying to a buyer, "I suggest you go down the street and buy the other three-bedroom, two-bath, updated ranch house with a big backyard and new appliances, because I can tell you, Sir, that that property will not compete with this one."

Ultimately, I don't care who buys the estates I create. I've created a beautiful work of art, and whoever pays me the sum that reflects the value of this masterpiece is privileged to do so. You, too, should make getting your price on mutually beneficial terms the primary goal of the negotiation process. Keep your eyes open for your next deal, and let the new owner enjoy the house you've created.

Now put on your best Maverick outfit, get out there, and market and sell, sell, sell!

PART THREE

ASSESSING A MAVERICK'S NET WORTH

Not too long ago I saw a very telling commercial on TV. A guy with a big smile on his face is sitting on a shiny new riding lawn mower, cutting the grass in the yard in back of his house that looks as if it would be worth close to a million dollars. He looks into the camera as he is bumping along and says: "I live in a great, gated neighborhood in a beautiful brand-new house. Look at my new car. I have all new furniture. I just joined the country club. I'm living the American dream!" Then you look a little closer and you see that his smile is not genuine, and there's desperation in his eyes as he says, "I'm in debt up to my eyeballs and can't afford any of this. Somebody, help me!"

You measure your net worth not by what you have but by what you own without the encumbrance of debt. And that goes for your personal life as well as your financial one. The goal of a Maverick is to build financial net worth while building character in the process. I learned about measuring net worth from my dad, who was a banker. While we were miles apart in outlook, attitude, and approach to life, and I spent my teenage years in complete rebellion against everything he stood for, he taught me the value of a healthy balance sheet. From the beginning of my real estate career and every year since, on December 31 I update the balance sheet for my business and my life. On the business balance sheet I list my assets and liabilities, subtract one from the other, and take a look at the result—my net worth. The goal, of course, is for my net worth to increase each year, and that must be your goal as well. Now, that doesn't always happen. Due to the nature of real estate, on December 31 I might be in the construction/renovation stage of a project (or projects) and my cash reserves could be low. In that case, however, I make sure that the value of the properties being created, when balanced against the liability of construction costs and any debt, represents a significant increase to my net worth upon their sale.

I do the same assessment for my personal life: I add up my accomplishments for the past year, the areas in which I have grown, the risks I have taken, and the progress I have made as a man, an entrepreneur, a sharer of God's blessings, a husband, and a father. Then I assess my liabilities honestly—where I have failed; where I have sinned; where I need to stretch and grow; the little and big areas of improvement where I must focus and persevere. While this evaluation is more subjective than the straightforward numbers of my financial balance sheet, assessing my personal net worth and determining what I must focus on for the coming year is fairly easy once I list my assets and liabilities side by side.

As you move ahead with the Maverick approach, I ask you to use both your personal and financial balance sheets as the means of evaluating your success. On the financial side, the net worth represented by your assets minus your liabilities is the most accurate measure of your entrepreneurial or business accomplishments. Many of those who buy into the no-money-down, quick turnaround/quick cash-out approach to real estate end up with very little to show for their efforts when they subtract their liabilities from their assets. They're overleveraged, often to the point of foolishness or danger. Worse, this get-rich-quick mentality all too often creates spend-it-quick debtors. If something should happen to these consumers—if interest rates rise rapidly, or a deal goes sour, or there's a personal crisis, or a temporary downturn in housing values—they're going to be in deep trouble. They'll be like the guy in the commercial, lifestyle-rich and cash-poor, saying, "Somebody, help me!"

Mavericks understand that getting rich is a long-term goal, and they must build net worth over time. They create value in undervalued assets, analyze the potential of every opportunity that comes their way, and do everything to maximize upside and minimize downside. Mavericks also know that, in order to build net worth, they constantly must be investing and reinvesting in both themselves and the undervalued properties they acquire and sell, for that's the only way to create greater value in the long run.

You've probably heard and read that more fortunes have been created with real estate than any other asset class. That's true, but those fortunes were amassed over decades and lifetimes, not a few paltry years of profits gained from flipping a house here and a condo there. I'm not saying that reselling quickly isn't a valid strategy when there's a quick profit to be had. However, true Mavericks understand that time and patience are their best allies in building a significant net worth throughout a lifetime of investing. What differentiates true wealth from the hit-or-miss, up-one-moment-and-down-the-next lifestyle is this focus on long-term accumulation of a significant net worth.

My father, the banker, knew about the importance of a long-term focus when working to accumulate the benefits of a personal and financial net worth. Only in his case, he first learned the lesson in the context of swimming. Day in and day out, as a child, teenager, and young man, he spent hour after hour in swimming pools all over the world, doing laps. He perfected his backstroke technique and built his endurance so he could be one of the best in the world in his chosen sport. As a result of decades of effort, practice, commitment, and drive, he won gold, silver, and bronze medals in the 1956 and 1960 Olympics. There are no shortcuts when it comes to athletics. As I myself discovered when I took up the grueling sport of ultramarathoning, you must put in unremitting work to achieve any level of success. In the same way, accumulating a significant net worth, either personally or financially, will require steady effort, long-term goals, and, more important, a willingness to *sacrifice today for a better tomorrow.*

Now I know that concept is contrary to what most people would like to believe. I'm also saying it from the perspective of someone who's worked hard for 20 years to ensure that his needs and the needs of his family are taken care of. But how many consumables does anyone *really* need? How many clothes, meals, houses, cars, boats, televisions, toys, trips, golf memberships, planes, or sports teams? How much of the money you've worked so hard to earn from your real estate deals do you want to squander? I'm not one of those guys who says, "So what if I lose it all? I can just make my fortune all over again." The *first* time through was hard enough. I'd rather take care of what I've made and avoid letting foolish mistakes tempt me into blowing what I've worked so hard for.

In Part 2 you learned the basics of how I buy and sell real estate, but what I have yet to share is the personal side of the Maverick approach—the secrets that will get you out there, every day, hungry for the right deal yet smart enough to take advantage of it only when it is right, enjoying yourself as you get into the game, playing as hard as you can, grateful for what you have achieved and who you have become in the process. In this section I want to teach you how to evaluate your net worth in terms of both the financial and the personal wealth you wish to accumulate during your Maverick real estate career. As you can tell, I'm not interested in giving up all my worldly possessions and living on a beach somewhere with nothing but the clothes on my back. I want to keep increasing my financial net worth yearly as much as I do my personal net worth. But both are equally important. And when you apply the Maverick approach consistently, measure your progress yearly and make adjustments based on your results, keep stretching your risk threshold, apply discipline, and be grateful for what you achieve, then you stand a good chance of succeeding in both business and in life.

As I said earlier, Nilsa and I have a beautiful little daughter, Laura, whom we call "Peek" (aka "Ppeekk," pronounced "Peekey"). Every day since she was four years old, I have walked her to school. Even on the day I got out of the hospital after an emergency appendectomy, she and I took that three-quarter-mile walk. Not too long ago they poured a new sidewalk along the road we usually travel, and Peek and I wrote our names in the cement—"Ppeekk & Dad." While most people would consider the multimillion-dollar properties I have built as the truest symbols of my success, that stretch of sidewalk where I walk every day with my daughter, and seeing our names inscribed next to each other, adds more to my personal balance sheet and makes me more grateful for my life than building the biggest, most luxurious estate on earth. I experience the same glow in my soul when we provide shelter to the world's most desperately homeless though our Caring House Project Foundation. I wish the same for you—that your personal net worth will always outdistance the significant financial net worth you will accumulate from applying the Maverick approach.

"The Maverick" outside our $20 million estate.

10

The Character of a Maverick

Many people would probably describe me as a "character" and not necessarily mean it in a positive way. However, I believe character is ultimately what sets a Maverick apart. It requires character to go against conventional wisdom, to take risks, evaluate your results, learn from your failures and triumphs, and make the changes needed to increase your success over the course of a career. If you truly want to go from a $50,000 fixer-upper to a $100 million mansion, it will take applying the Maverick approach in every aspect of your life, and that will require developing the character to accomplish your goals and accept the enlarged responsibilities that success will bring.

While there are many traits that go into the makeup of a Maverick, in this chapter we talk about three of the most important. First is a high tolerance for risk—the only characteristic that will allow you to accept the challenges that bring the high rewards you desire. Second is a willingness to establish a brand that will set you apart and make you the go-to player in your community. And finally is a commitment to share the blessings from the successful results of your enterprises with those less fortunate than yourself.

HIGH RISK MEANS HIGH REWARDS

Because you'll be going against the crowd and establishing value where little or no value existed before, the Maverick approach requires an ability to take on ever-increasing levels of risk. You've got to stretch and grow with each deal, not just in terms of the dollar amount you invest but also in the amount of human capital—the effort, courage, and determination—you put forth. This takes a concentrated focus on consistently building your risk muscle so it can adapt to the greater challenges you will face throughout your career.

I became acquainted with Robyn Thompson, the Rehab Queen, when she read my first book and invited me to appear at one of her boot camp weekends. Afterward she confessed that, while she wanted to move out of distressed fixer-uppers and start purchasing high-end properties, she was nervous about making the jump. I asked her to evaluate her threshold for risk using the following questions and continuum I developed years ago.

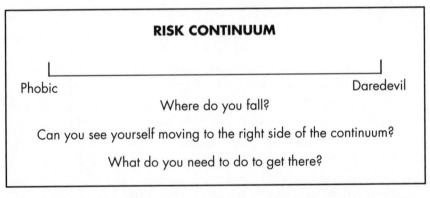

"Put a hash mark on this continuum, representing where you think you are currently in terms of your ability to handle risk," I told Robyn. "Then we'll figure out ways you can strengthen your risk tolerance, because the bigger the deal, the more risk you'll need to endure." Shortly afterward Robyn bought a $2 million property here in Florida. She recognized that to grow both her financial and personal net worth, she had to embrace greater levels of risk.

Not too long ago my brother Bob and I went on a personal planning retreat. Bob asked me, "Frank, you speak a lot to groups about success principles. What sets you apart from those people in the audience? What has made you so successful?"

"Two things, Bob," I answered. "First, I've constantly raised my risk threshold. I'm willing to put myself on the line every day, because doing so has made the difference between modest accomplishments and enormous success. Second, I use fear as a motivator rather than a brake. I'm not some daredevil who thinks everything's going to go his way and never feels any fear. I feel fear almost daily and listen to its warnings. But when I believe a decision is right, I will never let fear stop me from taking action."

To a true Maverick, risk is the ultimate performance-enhancing supplement. Risk increases the adrenaline while also increasing your opportunity for greater reward. To go from a $50,000 fixer-upper to a $100 million mansion successfully has taken 20 years of strengthening my risk tolerance on an almost daily basis. It's the one thing that will allow you to adopt the Maverick approach and use it successfully.

The first step in developing the character of a Maverick is to evaluate your current risk tolerance. Think back over the past few years and evaluate where your risk tolerance was for each year. Was there a point where you had to exercise your risk muscle strenuously? Maybe you got a new job, pursued a new relationship, or took on a physical challenge like a marathon or mountain climb. Perhaps there was a birth or death in the family, or a transition like graduating from school. Maybe it was your first real estate deal; how much risk tolerance did that require? Or perhaps you quit your job and decided to go into real estate investing full time. How did you feel while pursing an endeavor that caused you to experience greater risk?

Now, put a mark on the risk continuum where you think you are currently. If you're doing something new, you're probably feeling closer to the daredevil side, and that's great. But if it's been a while since you've taken a risk, you've probably moved further back toward phobic. This risk continuum is less of a line and more of a thermometer, because your risk tolerance will go up and down depending on the "weather" of your life. Once you've had your first successful deal, your risk tolerance will rise; a setback or failure can bring it down very quickly. You may even have gotten to the point that you wouldn't consider taking a risk unless you're absolutely certain things will work out in your favor.

Your risk tolerance can be lowered by an insidious yet pervasive factor: comfort. All of us have taken a risk and had it turn out well. In my case, going from distressed properties to oceanfront renovations was a huge risk that provided the foundations for my current success. Robyn Thompson went from working for IBM and waiting tables part-time at Denny's to investing in her first properties. That was a huge amount of risk, yet she did it and prospered. But then, like all of us, Robyn got comfortable. She was doing the same kind of deals again and again, and her risk tolerance went down because it wasn't being exercised. So when faced with the idea of million-dollar properties, she was fearful; her risk muscle had gotten flabby.

Just like every other muscle, our risk muscle operates on the "use it or lose it" principle. If you get comfortable sitting on the couch at home, your muscles will turn to jelly. If you get comfortable doing the same thing year after year, your risk tolerance will decrease. One of the advantages *and* disadvantages of the Maverick approach is its applicability to properties at all price points: Like that first-class stamp, you can use it again and again to produce great results. But that also can mean you get comfortable with it, and too much comfort leads to boredom. To keep your edge, you must find ways to break out of the comfort zone, and you do this by taking on greater risk.

Raising your risk tolerance requires a combination of four critical factors: (1) evaluation, (2) preparation, (3) courage, and (4) faith.

Evaluation

I'm not a "ready-fire-aim" businessman. While I love exercising my risk muscle, I want to do so when it's smart and the potential return is high. Therefore, I'm very careful to evaluate every opportunity that's presented to me for its risk versus return potential. I tend to be fiscally conservative even when I'm risking everything on my next big project. For instance, when I made the decision to move from distressed properties to the oceanfront, I was working on 20 houses at one time. I was spreading myself so thin I felt overstressed and overstretched. I said to Nilsa, "I'd rather risk more money on one piece of oceanfront property with a greater potential return than risk less on these smaller houses and work a lot harder for less profit."

When I made the move to the oceanfront, I began to invest in far more valuable property while eliminating 20 sets of carrying costs, plus the hassle of trying to manage 20 different building sites. Focusing on two to three large estate homes also has allowed me to create the kinds of masterpieces I truly want to build, with financial returns that more than justify the increased risk.

As you proceed with the Maverick approach you, too, may come to a point where you want greater returns. Instead of increasing the number of properties you're carrying, use your risk muscle and invest in fewer, more valuable properties instead. The difference between $100,000 and $1,000,000 is only one zero—and the enormous amount of fear that most people feel in making that leap. You must evaluate the risk versus return of every deal given your situation, resources, and investment goals. If the numbers make sense and all that's stopping you is fear, you know what you must do.

Preparation

The intelligent way to take risks is after an enormous amount of research, preparation, and forethought. I believe preparation takes two forms. First, strangely enough, is to minimize or mitigate as much risk as you can. As I said in Chapter 9, I'm always looking for as many ways as possible to profit from an investment. When I first considered repurchasing the 8.78-acre, $85 million oceanfront lot in Manalapan, I had sold my entire inventory the previous year and had had no project in hand for about nine months. That down time was great preparation, however, because it allowed me to clear my head and make decisions from a very different perspective. I ran the numbers on the Manalapan property for almost every option possible—reselling the entire plot of land, breaking it up into two to five lots and selling them separately, selling one or two lots and building on the remaining land, building five houses myself and selling them one at a time, or using the entire plot of land to build an elaborate oceanfront villa that would set new standards for luxury and price. I even considered an oceanfront hotel and casino (utilizing my Native American ancestry). I evaluated each option carefully based on risk versus return, and then asked myself the questions posed in Jim Collins' masterpiece, *Good to Great*, "What drives my economic engine? What am I deeply passionate about? And most important to me, what can I be the best in the world at?" I decided to do what had never been done before and build an estate with an asking price well into the nine figures. I believe in my heart that the risk versus return is well worth it.

The second part of preparation is to exercise your risk threshold in other environments. Take up a sport where you must push yourself—go skydiving, or run a marathon. If you're single, ask someone out for a date whom you think would be totally out of your league. Go to a seminar that will stretch you. Volunteer for an organization that requires you to get out of your comfortable lifestyle. Push yourself physically and emotionally. You'll find it not only increases your tolerance for risk, but it also makes you feel fully alive.

I had that kind of experience in September 2004, when Hurricane Frances was heading right for South Florida. We were getting ready to close on the $50 million property in Manalapan, and, going against an evacuation warning, I went out to the property and stayed there while the hurricane blew through, to make sure the house and grounds were protected from major damage. It was a very intense couple of days. I cleared trees with my chainsaw in 80 mph winds, wearing sunglasses because the rain was blowing horizontally and pelting my eyeballs. The power was out, and after my flashlight died I walked through the house using my laptop screen for light, inspecting and repairing any damage. But I felt more alive during those few days of the hurricane than I had the entire rest of the year. Better yet, when the buyer stopped by three days later, he said the words I wanted to hear: "Frank, it looks like this place was unscathed." Oceanfront houses all along A1A had had their roofs blown off and their trees decimated, but because I was there, this property looked immaculate. Fighting the battle to protect the house stretched my risk muscle thoroughly and helped prepare me for my next two big projects: the $125-million property, and the Badwater 135 Ultramarathon, which you'll hear about in Chapter 11.

Courage

You can prepare and evaluate until the cows come home; a mentor can coach you until you're blue in the face; but at some point you'll have to have the courage to take action, to push off from the pier and encounter the rough seas ahead. I've been doing this for 20 years, but it still takes courage for me to say, "I'm going to create the most expensive spec house ever built in the world." If you've never done even one deal and now you're contemplating putting all your savings into your first property, that $50,000 fixer-upper you purchase might take as much courage for you as the $125-million property does for me. Whatever the risk you want to take, you must gather your courage and make the decision to go for it. Often the decision itself requires the most courage, and things get a lot easier after that. I think you'll find that, once you're committed, you'll have the courage and resources to make your project work out as you have projected.

Faith

Stretching your risk tolerance requires a level of faith in yourself and your goals/projects. Faith is a belief in things not yet seen. You must have faith that you've chosen and planned well, and that by following the Maverick approach to its conclusion you will realize a healthy profit. I also believe faith requires active participation. Faith doesn't mean sitting back and waiting for God or your broker or the market or anyone else to make your deal work out right. I think it was St. Paul who wrote, "Faith without works is dead." In the Maverick approach, faith without works is nothing but wishful thinking, and it will never get you closer to your goals.

One of the times many people need faith is when they are deciding to leave their current careers and take up real estate investing full-time. I hope that somewhere along the way you're faced with this dilemma, as it means you've been applying the Maverick approach successfully. You must have faith in yourself, in your ability to shoulder risk, in your commitment to hard work, in your flexibility and adaptability, and in your perseverance and determination to make your living doing something you're obviously good at and enjoy. And remember, faith itself will diminish if you don't keep challenging yourself with new opportunities. So have faith in the Maverick approach and keep applying it to build an ever-greater net worth.

To keep your risk muscle in shape, check yourself on the risk continuum frequently, and as soon as you feel yourself regressing past the center point and moving toward fear, do something to stretch yourself. That doesn't mean that each time you have to swing for the fences and take uncalculated risks. Use the four factors—evaluation, preparation, courage, and faith—to assess each opportunity. But do *something*. You've got to get in the gym and exercise your risk muscle. You can start gradually, taking small risks frequently so that when the big opportunities come, you'll be ready. We talk about this more in Chapter 11, when you'll learn about the upward spiral of the Maverick approach.

BECOME YOUR OWN BRAND: BE THE GO-TO PLAYER IN YOUR COMMUNITY

A Maverick should never worry about being considered a character, because this designation can be part of establishing a unique brand in the marketplace. As you get to know your market, your market is getting to know you, so you must start to create your own unique brand early. In the television industry every proposed new show starts with a "treatment," which is a description of the show's proposed storyline in one or two paragraphs. You need to create a treatment for yourself, a brand that will give people a shorthand description of who you are and what you do.

When I first began buying properties, I had no thought about building a "brand" per se. All I knew was that I didn't want to approach my real estate career like everyone else. I developed a contrarian approach to real estate that I combined with my own natural inclination to be a Maverick, to go against what was expected and do things my own way. I started buying houses where no one had invested before—falling-down properties in crack neighborhoods. I said to myself, "I'm going to put material in there like nobody's seen before, and I'm going to market like nobody's done before." I quickly realized that in going against the ordinary and creating a better product, I was also creating a brand and a character. Taking a Maverick approach was building the brand of a Maverick, and it has made me the person I am today.

When I made the move to oceanfront properties, I realized how vital the brand was to my success. Florida oceanfront real estate is an exclusive market, both in terms of the number of properties available and the number of people who can afford them. To demand top dollar, my properties needed to stand out, and so did I. That's when I made a conscious decision to create the Frank McKinney brand, which combines outstanding quality with intriguing theatricality, backed up by the enormous value, beauty, and luxury of our properties. Today every high-end realtor in South Florida knows Frank McKinney & Company; we have become associated with the best in ultra-high-end real estate. My brand, built through 20 years of successful deals, helps me get financing, attracts buyers and sellers, and makes it easier to obtain exposure for my multimillion-dollar properties. If you choose, you, too, can take on the brand of a Maverick and then make it your own. You can become the go-to player in your community for undervalued real estate; and if you develop your brand correctly and consistently, people will bring you deals rather than your having to find them.

THE THREE COMPONENTS OF YOUR BRAND

Your brand is composed of three components. First are the *results* you create. I believe that a great brand is a combination of flash and substance. You can publicize your properties all you want, you can be the greatest at drawing a crowd and getting your name in front of the world, but ultimately your results will determine your brand. You can't cut corners; you've got to make the day-in and day-out effort that will create the results you desire. If you're following the Maverick approach, you can quickly establish a brand of building or renovating the nicest house on the block. Being the best and providing the most value is the most desirable brand, to my mind—far better than being the cheapest or fastest to market. As you embark on your journey as a Maverick, you must determine in advance what results you want to build your brand upon, and hold that standard for yourself with every property you acquire, improve, and sell.

Second is the *reputation* you build. Your results may speak for themselves, but not unless you speak out about them. Many excellent builders, designers, and creators of first-time home buyer homes or multimillion-dollar homes are struggling to sell their properties because they're weak when it comes to sharing with the world what they have created. You have to be your own town crier and public relations company rolled into one. When I met with Donald Trump in his

New York office a few years ago, he showed me an entire bin of his press clippings. Dozens of framed awards and acknowledgment letters were hung on the walls of his office. He was very proud of his accomplishments, and certainly he's one of the best at letting other people know about them. And look at the brand Donald has established!

Take a look in the newspaper on any given weekend and notice how much competition your properties have. How are you going to draw attention to your product? What do you want to be known for? You need to decide what you would like your reputation to be. If you're following the Maverick approach, your reputation will be based on creating greater value in every property you buy or sell. You must work to build not only great properties but also the reputation for building great properties.

Reputation is based on the quality you bring to the creation of your "art," the manner in which you share your greatness with the world, and your ability to close the deal—always with concrete results to back up your claims. People are naturally skeptical; you can't walk into your local newspaper and declare, "I'm the new king of rehabs!" and expect them to believe you. But suppose you walk into that same newspaper office and say, "I'd like you to take a look at the property I rehabbed over on 123 Sycamore. It used to be a crack den, and now it's going to be the nicest house on the block. I'm planning to do the same thing with the house around the corner. Drop by our open house this weekend and see for yourself." First, are they more likely to do a story on your property? Yes. Second, have you started to create a reputation? Yes—but only if you continue to produce outstanding results and let people know about them. Over time, you'll find you develop a reputation that will aid you in building a successful career.

Third is your *personality* or *ego*. Ego has gotten a bad rap in many circles, but I've found that a healthy dose of ego is essential when creating a brand. If you're going to become the go-to person in your industry, you need to cultivate a less-than-humble approach when it comes to what you do, especially when your representations are true. It's much easier and more common to be humble—that's the society in which we live. People who are perceived as having an ego are usually looked down upon. But if you want to create a brand, you've got to be willing to become the star of the show, yet know when to differentiate between the public brand and the private person. To paraphrase Eckhart Tolle, you must remember that you are not your ego.

Your personality is the extra dimension that will help drive sales of your properties, and you've got to be in love with the person whom you are or whom you've created. When I appear at a speaking engagement, my introduction consists of a three-minute video compilation of some of the grand unveilings, TV interviews, the trailer of our TV show, *The Maverick,* and other media I've done. Then the host gets on the microphone and says something like, "I give you the man, the myth, the maverick, Frank McKinney!" Bam! They start playing a heavy metal anthem, and I walk out as we set off fireworks that shoot sparks from the fingertips of special gloves I had made. People love it, and, truth be told, so do I. But then I talk to the audience very directly, as if we were sitting around a big campfire, about all the things they need to do to put the Maverick approach to use. I make my personality seem larger than life because that's what's expected of the Maverick; but I'm also true to the side of my personality that cares about people and wants them to understand how they can succeed in real estate doing exactly what I have done for the past 20 years. Promoting yourself should never be just for the sake of your ego, but always for the sake of building your brand.

It's possible my personality has a theatrical side to it; I certainly didn't start out that way, though. As a kid I was a very shy, insecure altar boy, creative but never assertive. But when I left home and went out on my own, I consciously decided to model myself after people I admired. The list was quite eclectic: Evel Kneivel, David Lee Roth, Willy Wonka, Mom, Rich DeVos, Donald Trump, Dad, Bono, Jimmy Connors, and John Adams, to name a few. It appears I took some of the outrageous parts of their personalities, combined them with a desire to be like Robin Hood (making money from rich clients and giving to the poor) and a dose of good business sense, and created the persona that's known as "Frank McKinney." Is this who I always was, or something I've created? It is who I *am,* and it's definitely helped me establish a strong and identifiable brand in the marketplace.

Your brand needs to be an accurate representation of your personality; otherwise, people will sense that you're trying to be someone you're not, and that will put them off. Whether you like Donald Trump or not, do you believe that his public persona represents at least part of who he is? Of course you want to set your product apart by what you do to it to improve and market it, but you also can use yourself and your own personality traits as an additional means of getting your properties noticed. When you create your own brand, you must accentuate the positive traits and qualities in your personality—ones that you'll be willing to live with over the long run and that represent your brand at its best. Everyone can find something in either themselves or their story that, when properly emphasized, will create a great brand.

Even though you're putting your ego into establishing your brand, don't let it go to your head. Ego in this circumstance must be combined with large servings of humility, humor, and common sense. Otherwise it will spin out of control and prevent you from seeing where you're going wrong. Just like a superhero costume, you should be able to put on your public persona, do great things, and then take it off. The Frank McKinney who loves dressing up like Jack Sparrow and sailing down zip lines while discharging a pistol at Blackbeard during a grand unveiling doesn't walk my daughter to school every day. Frank McKinney the "king of ready-made dream homes" doesn't sit at home at night in SpongeBob SquarePants pajamas with my daughter, Laura, watching cartoons or ESPN. Each day you're on the concert stage of life so you'd better make it rock, but you'd also better leave the rock star on the stage and come home as the loving family person that you are.

Enhancing Your Brand

Once you've built your brand with results, reputation, and personality, then you must enhance it. As you continue using the Maverick approach, each property has the potential to build your brand or tear it down. Building a reputation is kind of like construction: It takes months or years to build a house but only days to knock one down. One failure won't completely destroy a reputation, but it will harm it far more than one success will increase it. Take very good care to keep your reputation strong, as it will add immensely to the value of your properties and make your job as a Maverick investor a lot easier.

Unless tended, brands will diminish. Your brand may have some long-standing residual value, but as each day ticks by, that value erodes. A brand must be nurtured and fed with new projects, new information, and new exposure. Certainly you can take time off every now and then, but in the same way you can't make a career as a Maverick with one project every five years, you can't enhance a brand unless you keep your name and reputation in front of the public. You must always be marketing. Even if you have no properties currently in development, you can still be developing your brand name recognition. Get involved in your community. Keep the relationships you developed (as we discussed in Chapter 4) current and fresh. Do something that contributes to the welfare of others (a great way of building a brand and sharing your blessings—we talk about that later in this chapter). Keep your name in front of the public in positive ways, and when you're ready to do your next deal, the strength of the brand will be there to support you.

With a brand come expectations. When your brand is linked to you, people sometimes feel they are buying a piece of you when they buy one of your properties. They're making a purchase based upon some of the same feelings and passion that you had in creating the property, so an emotional attachment may develop. I've seen this happen with both first-time and high-end buyers. First-time homeowners are leaving a rental mindset, so they may think of you as their landlord and call you if the plumbing gets plugged up or the fuse blows. High-end buyers can think that, because they bought the house you designed, you should be responsible for anything that goes wrong.

While I believe part of any Maverick's brand should be great customer service, you have to draw the line. I put together warranty manuals for all of my properties. For first-time home buyers this manual would include warranty information on anything I installed new (roof, appliances, windows, etc.), and a contact list of anyone who worked on the house (plumbers, electricians, air-conditioning system installers/manufacturers, etc.), to call should there be problems. Make it clear to the new owners that as the house is now theirs, they need to take care of any repairs themselves.

For our high-end buyers, we provide a more elaborate version of the warranty manual, which includes warranties, contact lists, and an extensive quality review maintenance checklist, covering the things that need to be done weekly, monthly, quarterly, and yearly, to keep the house in the same immaculate condition as when they bought it. Sometimes we will help the client find a house manager to oversee the property. But our reputation does not extend to property management, and neither should yours.

At some point to maintain your brand you may find yourself moving out of one strength and into another. Before I purchased the 8.78-acre parcel, the scarcity of oceanfront land here in my little corner of South Florida was causing me to look at other opportunities in different parts of the country. Transferring your brand from one kind of real estate or location to another can be difficult at first, but as we've said repeatedly, the Maverick approach will work anywhere and at any price point. You can continue to be a Maverick whether you're developing townhouses, condos, apartment buildings, or $50,000 or $100 million homes. Rather than trying to change your brand, build upon it. Demonstrate the same consistency of approach and you'll find your reputation and results will continue to be excellent.

SHARE YOUR BLESSINGS: THE TRUE DEFINITION OF SUCCEEDING IN THE "BUSINESS OF LIFE"

A few years ago, Nilsa and I took a TV crew down to Haiti, where we were building a village for more than 1,000 desperately homeless people. The cluster of small, neat, brightly colored concrete houses would be deeded, at no cost, to homeless families chosen by local churches as the most in need and deserving. Through our Caring House Project Foundation, we provided the funds, chose the site, and offered some supervisory and design assistance. We partnered with international relief organizations that already had established a presence in the area, and used only local labor and materials for the construction. For just $4,000 per house, around 1,000 men, women, and children were going to have permanent, sturdy shelters—homes they would own. Nilsa was sitting on the porch of one of those little houses when she spread her arms wide and said, "You know why we do the big houses? So we can build the little ones."

One of my life lessons is, "Each one of us is blessed with the ability to succeed not for our own sole benefit but to assist others." A passage in the Bible says: "To whom much has been given, much will be asked." If you want to experience true joy while achieving success as a Maverick, you've got to share what God has blessed you with. I began helping the homeless well before I ever built my first oceanfront home. Every Monday night I would go with an organization called Caring Kitchen to feed homeless people from the back of a beat-up old minivan. That was where I met Buster, an 80-year-old gentleman who was going to be evicted from the ratty apartment he'd been paying half his Social Security check to rent every month. I bought a small house in Palm Beach County, fixed it up, and rented it to Buster for $1 a month. That was the first Caring House. Since then the Caring House Project Foundation, a nonprofit organization that I founded, has provided housing for more than 2,500 homeless in different countries all over the world while contributing to a wide range of worthy causes here at home.

I don't think that you can create a lasting, memorable, recognizable professional brand without outside charitable involvement. When you're spending time to better the world community, you're developing relationships while adding dimensions to your brand that most others won't even consider. What better way to establish a name for yourself in your community than by making a difference in someone else's life? Now, I am in no way suggesting that brand creation should be your reason for sharing your blessings. I didn't get involved in caring for the homeless to enhance my professional career. I did it because of my conviction that contributing to others was an important part of any worthwhile life. I did it because no one expected me to be out on a truck feeding the homeless. I did it because it reminded me of the blessings I had even when, in material terms, I myself was struggling. I did it because I liked the way I felt when I gave of my time to others. I did it because it's what God expects of me. It made going to the job site that much easier, and it made me a better person in the process.

When I speak to groups, I always talk about the Caring House Project Foundation, and people are inevitably touched. They come up to me afterward and say, "I really relate to what you said about sharing your blessings. I'll be so happy when I've made it and I can do that, too." There's a great temptation to believe that you should wait to make a difference until you've achieved enough success to make it worthwhile. But you can share your blessings *right now*—by offering either your (1) time, (2) talent, and/or (3) treasure. Can you spend an hour a week visiting someone in a nursing home, laying sod or painting siding for Habitat for Humanity, or volunteering at your local school? Do you have a talent you can contribute—building, or organizing, or cooking, or networking? And how much of your treasure could you share with those who have nothing? Even if you don't have a lot of spare cash, could you do something to help raise funds for a good cause? Perhaps you could host a fundraiser in one of your renovated properties. (This can bring you some great exposure and also bring potential buyers through your doors.)

You may not have a lot of treasure to start with, or a lot of time or talent to donate, but with a little bit of the fourth T—thought—you can devise some way of sharing your blessings. For example, our church has a yearly collection for the hungry on Super Bowl Sunday. On a day when most Americans are focused on football and food, they ask we remember those who have nothing to eat. (They call it Souper Bowl Sunday.) So my six-year-old daughter, Laura, and I decided to set up a drink stand at the end of our driveway. We used all the marketing principles from the Maverick approach—it was a great combination of free enterprise and contribution. We had a big sign, LAURA'S SUPER BOWL DRINK STAND—A PORTION OF THE PROCEEDS GO TO THE CARING KITCHEN, and lots of balloons. Laura dressed up in her Junior Miami Dolphins cheerleader outfit, complete with Mylar pom-poms. We sold water, sports drinks, sodas, juice boxes, Pop Tarts, and Flintstone vitamins (the kids loved those). We had a bowl of candy on the table, and we gave away a piece with each purchase. Laura stood by the stand, shaking the pom-poms and waving at the cars driving by. Laura and I thought we'd make around $10 to $12; well, over the course of three hours we cleared $57. Laura got to keep $10, and the rest we took back to church and put in the "soup bowl." That's a small example of sharing time, talent, and treasure. It was a great lesson for my daughter in free enterprise, in the necessity of hard work (for a six-year-old, three hours outside in the hot sun is a long day), and most important, how good it feels to share your blessings.

It's very easy in the early days to focus only on what you need to accomplish for yourself. But remember one of the fundamental lessons of the Maverick approach: The only way to achieve the highest levels of success is to start small and be consistent. In the same way that building a net worth takes sustained effort based on habits developed from day one, building personal net worth requires that you develop the habit of sharing your blessings from the start. We all need to learn to share our blessings early rather than waiting until we feel we have enough time, talent, or treasure. That way, when the treasure comes around, we're responsible stewards, understanding what we need to do with our abundance. People like Rich DeVos, the co-founder of Amway, or Bill Gates, who contributes billions of dollars through the Bill & Melinda Gates Foundation, are high-profile examples of this. If you do well with the Maverick approach and you want to sustain your success, you must follow their example.

I firmly believe that sharing your blessings needs to be a part of your business plan as well as your brand. Anytime I look at a project, in the back of my mind is, "How will the success of this project benefit those less fortunate?" I donate all the revenue from my speaking appearances and all book royalties to CHPF. (If you purchased this book, you've just made a small contribution to help people who've been homeless for years finally put a roof over their heads. To find out more about the work of the Caring House Project Foundation, go to www.frank-mckinney.com/caring_house.html.)

The focus of the Maverick approach is always to find undervalued assets and add value where little or none has existed before. That's the foundation of a Maverick's success. When you share your blessings, you are finding the areas, groups, people, or aspects of our world that are undervalued, underappreciated, undersupported, underloved and underfunded, and adding your time, talent, and treasure to create new value. When you do this, you will become wealthy and successful— not just in terms of your bottom line, but with the kind of spiritual wealth you will be proud to view from your rocking chair at the end of your life.

Crossing the finish line of the Badwater 135 Ultramarathon.

Photo credit Chris Kostman/Badwater.com

11

The Upward Spiral of the Maverick Approach

true Maverick knows he or she can never stand still. It is not my desire to maintain the level of past achievements. Maintenance is never the goal of a Maverick; maintenance usually means falling behind because the world is constantly moving, growing, and changing. You should always look to do better, to reach the next level, and to grow inner worth along with net worth. By continually applying the principles of the Maverick approach, you can expand personally, spiritually, and financially, creating a constant upward spiral as you create both your real estate and personal legacy.

There are four keys to ensure that you will continue to make progress along the upward spiral of the Maverick approach.

BE DISCIPLINED

The approaches and techniques described in this book may go against what you've learned about real estate, but they aren't necessarily brand-new or earth shattering. What sets the Maverick brand apart is the disciplined application of these techniques conscientiously and consistently over time. Discipline is one of the primary strains in a Maverick's character and career. The only way you can keep moving upward is to follow the Maverick approach in a disciplined way, not deviating from its primary tenets especially at the beginning, and continuing to apply its four steps as you produce the results you desire.

I encourage you to give the Maverick approach a fair trial. Undertake at least two to three deals and a year's application of this approach to evaluate your success. Be patient and realize that your first six months of applying the Maverick approach will be spent learning, so you may not see quantifiable results initially. But believe me, you are laying the groundwork for explosive, legacy-type results. I hope that, like me and many other investors, you'll come to enjoy being a Maverick, creating value, and being paid well for it. If ultimately you decide it's not for you, that's fine—as long as you've put in the effort and time to make a qualified decision.

The Maverick approach to real estate is not like stock trading, where you can buy a stock one hour and realize a profit the next. It's also not built around "flipping" properties (reselling quickly at wholesale value), although occasionally you may find it's possible to make a quick if smaller profit on a deal. The Maverick approach takes time, and you must have the discipline not to pull the trigger too early. For instance, when I started building the $17 million house in Manalapan, a lot of zoning and permit issues came up. I was increasingly frustrated trying to work with the then-current town commission. I could have simply sold the land for a moderate profit and moved on to another deal, but instead I decided to revamp my plans to build a smaller house and include more outdoor elements on the property. I also started lobbying the local government for changes in regulations to allow me more flexibility in building. Because I was disciplined and took a long-term approach, I was able to build a great house, sell at an excellent profit, and create a new market high once again for that size of property. We were able to change our own fate through the application of diligent effort, patience, and keeping to our long-term vision.

In looking back over my career, the only regrets I have (and they're not really regrets, just a sense of missed opportunities, and I learned from them) occurred when I went for the easier deal/profit and didn't take a long-term approach, thereby missing out on a much bigger win. Recently I acquired a property right across A1A from my home in Delray Beach. It was an oceanfront house that had been built 10 years ago, and it just didn't have the kinds of architecture and finishes that properties do nowadays. I was heavy with inventory when we bought it, so I decided to clean it up and sell it as-is. We bought for $2.3 million, sold for $3.3 million, and made a quick million-dollar profit, but just the other day I said to Nilsa, "Do you realize that if we'd done the million-dollar renovations in that house like we planned, we could have gotten $7 to $8 million for that property in today's market?" While there is nothing wrong in making a profit, you must be disciplined enough to evaluate the opportunities in front of you, and be willing to wait for your profits while you continue to apply the Maverick approach. Believe in yourself, have the discipline to stick with your long-term plan, and eventually you will be able to make a market. Remember, doubts are natural, but you must keep your focus on the new standards you are creating.

At the same time, you must be flexible enough to act if the deal is obviously too good to pass up or if conditions change radically. After September 11, 2001, the real estate market (along with most other businesses in the United States) took a significant pause, and after the hurricanes blew through Florida in 2004, it became extremely difficult to get subcontractors for renovations. In either of those situations, if I had been a beginning investor with a couple of properties, I definitely would have reevaluated the market as well as my own plans to see (1) if I needed to cut my expenses and sell as-is or with fewer improvements, or (2) if I could wait until the markets recovered to sell at my target price. Remember the law of impermanence. Conditions change. Markets change. Your assumptions may or may not prove to be correct. You must be disciplined enough to stick with your long-term plan while being flexible enough to change if necessary to accomplish your ultimate goal of building a significant net worth.

LOVE WHAT YOU DO AND HAVE FUN DOING IT

A few years ago, I visited Donald Trump in his offices at Trump Tower in New York City. Throughout our meeting, I noticed there was a recurring theme in his answers to my questions.

> "Donald, why do you continue to do what you do?"
> "Because it's fun."
> "What about the golf course project on the ocean in California?"
> "Oh, that's just for fun."

He must have used the word "fun" at least a dozen times.

It's clear Donald Trump loves what he does, and I believe that's a key component of the upward spiral. Success requires the disciplined application of effort through time, and that only happens when you love what you're doing or you love the results you will produce.

You also have to enjoy the character and brand you've devised. There's nothing wrong, unhumble, or overly egotistical about loving what you've created, whether it be the character you put on to do your job or the products you build/improve. Donald Trump is certainly in love with his persona, and for good reason. I truly enjoy putting on the "Frank McKinney, real estate rock czar" costume and going out to make deals, create masterpieces, and set new market levels. As a Maverick, you must love your products, but you also must love what remains even after the products are sold, that is, the brand and character you've created in the process.

One of the ways I have had fun with what I do is to put my office in a tree house. I never had a tree house when I was a little boy, so a few years ago I decided to build one in the large strangler fig tree with a direct ocean view in the front yard of my property. (The little boy in me got carried away and built an enclosed, air-conditioned tree house with electricity, DSL, a king-sized bed, hardwood floors, a custom desk made of bamboo, a shower, toilet, refrigerator, and sink.) One branch of the tree literally grows through the floor of the tree house, and another goes through the shower. There are 12 custom-built windows that let in ample light and give me an unobstructed view of the azure blue waters of the

Atlantic Ocean. I engineered the structure very carefully so it was completely safe and able to be permitted. You reach the tree house platform either with a ladder and trap door from the driveway, or via a suspended gangplank, built by a shipbuilder and held up with marine-grade hardware and antique-looking rope, that runs to the tree house from our second-floor bedroom. My commute to work is navigating the 40 feet along this suspended bridge. The tree house is where I have written this book and where I design all of our oceanfront masterpieces. For me it represents everything I love about the Maverick approach. It expresses my personality, allows the little kid to come out and play, and contains the kind of big and little touches that are the Frank McKinney hallmark. (As a window in the shower, I put in one of the same 85-pound brass portholes salvaged from a yacht that sank off the coast of Maine that I used in the door to our $17 million mansion).

There are many aspects of the Maverick approach that I truly love. I love the acquisition day—the day we buy the opportunity—because it represents potential in terms of artistic creativity, new market creation, and the profits at the end of the deal. I love the creative process of putting the design on paper, and I love choosing finishes, stones, fabrics for our mansions. I love planning and holding the grand unveilings and showings; they allow me to express the theatrical side of my personality while I showcase our exquisite masterpieces. I like the planning of our marketing campaigns and creating the vision and passion statements. Surprisingly, I don't like closings that much because they are so routine. The excitement of the chase is over. The rainbow is more enjoyable than the pot of gold at the end. Making sure the deal closes completes the circle, and in between these times there is the lunchpail approach of doing the job, day in and day out. Instead of happiness, those days bring a satisfaction, a kind of joy that you feel deep inside your soul. But that kind of "daily bread" quiet pleasure allows us to reach those fleeting moments of euphoria.

I also have discovered there are things that are part of the process that I don't love and never will. I don't like the failure of human nature when it comes to subcontractors. I get frustrated and will show it when I feel people aren't following the Frank McKinney Way and striving to produce the best. While I try to get employees and sub-contractors to live up to my high standards, there's no way they're going to be as invested in the deal as I am. I've learned to deal with these frustrations as best I can, and know that they are part of the process that I will never enjoy. There is no system in the world that will produce enjoyment 24/7. As a Maverick, you must be realistic and identify the parts of the approach that you don't enjoy or have limited control over, and do your best to overcome them, mitigate them, or delegate them.

You, too, need to discover the parts of the Maverick approach that you can enjoy. If you have to wait until you get the sale check in your hand to feel happy, then you're spending 97 percent of your life waiting for the 3 percent of good feelings, and no one is going to stick with that. If the Maverick approach doesn't give you the level of satisfaction to keep you putting in the day-to-day effort required for success, then you'd better find something else, because you're not going to be that good at it. Whether you choose to use the Maverick approach or something else, you must find ways to enjoy the process in addition to the end result.

LEARN FROM EVERYTHING, AND NEVER STOP

At that meeting with Donald Trump, I had a long list of questions I wanted to ask. "How is it that you continue to do what you do after you've done it for so long? Where do you find your motivation now that you've reached the top?" Was I ever surprised; when I got into his office, the first 25 minutes of the meeting was him asking *me* questions! He wanted to learn everything I knew about ultra-high-end speculative residential (single-family in particular) investing and construction. He asked rapid-fire, one-after-the-next questions that I found easy to answer. Then I remembered: Donald Trump was constructing multimillion-dollar homes at a couple of golf course projects in California and New Jersey. I thought, "Here's a guy that just never stops learning." (Not too long afterward, Trump and I were bidding against each other for a Palm

Beach property. He bought it, and now he's renovating the existing home and will market it for approximately $125 million. I look forward to the competition.)

A Maverick must never stop learning. I learn from every single real estate meeting, transaction, negotiation, and deal I do, and you should do the same. Even if you're buying and selling identical townhouses or condominiums, each client is going to be able to teach you something about your marketplace, what it takes to close a deal, and so on. Especially when you're first getting started, you must become a sponge, learning everything you can. Go to classes and seminars if that's helpful; but more than that, I suggest you learn (1) one-on-one from others, and (2) from just getting out there, trying things, and seeing what happens.

Remember, however, that the most meaningful lessons come from doing something yourself. Do something no one's ever done at a showing in your area. Go into a neighborhood others aren't willing to enter. Make sure you can handle the consequences of your actions. Will all of your risks turn out the way you want? Of course not. You'll undoubtedly do a deal that won't return you the profits you desire. You're going to make decisions that won't pan out. Your responsibility is to regard each temporary failure as an investment in future success, and a challenge to change the mind of fate itself—as long as you learn from your mistakes and avoid making the same ones in the future. Some of the lessons may be painful, but others will help you jump ahead of your competition.

You also must learn not to be too hard on yourself. There's a great temptation to look at even the smallest setbacks or learning experiences as failures. Yes, you must always recognize your failures and shortcomings and try to correct them, but you must appreciate your successes as much if not more. The upward spiral of the Maverick approach requires you to replicate and then outdo past successes. Spend at least 50 percent of your time appreciating and learning from your successes, and the other 50 percent focusing on correcting your less-than-perfect results, and you'll be more likely to make a long-term fulfilling career.

ALWAYS BE AWARE OF THE NEXT CHALLENGE; IT'S NOT ABOUT THE END GAME

At the end of the movie, *Willy Wonka and the Chocolate Factory*, Willy says to the little boy, "Charlie, whatever happened to the little boy who got everything he ever wanted?" And with a twinkle in his eye, Wonka answered his own question: "He lived happily ever after." In 2004 for a short while that's how I felt. We had completed a very intense run of about two years, where we had built three spectacular houses and bought back another. When those four properties sold within a period of six weeks, for the first time in almost 20 years of following the Maverick approach—buying a piece of real estate, adding value, selling the property, retiring some debt from that sale, using some of the equity to create another opportunity, and doing that over and over again—I had no inventory and nothing on the horizon. Everything was paid off, including all the taxes and fees, and I had a net worth that could have allowed me to do something else for the remaining years of my life.

I recall that when the wire for the $50 million sale hit my bank, I literally fell to my knees, then all the way flat on the floor of my treehouse as I cried, "It's over, it's over." I thought that the high I experienced at that point was happiness, but in truth it was relief. That was when I truly learned the difference between happiness and euphoria. Reaching the pot of gold felt great for a short while, but happiness, real joy, was what I felt while I was riding the rainbow, in the middle of following the Maverick approach, facing and overcoming challenges. I discovered that never being quite satisfied was also part of that happiness. Yes, I loved the projects I was doing; yes, I enjoyed finding a new level every time. But satisfied would mean I had done everything I was on the earth to do. Satisfied would mean perfection. Satisfied would ultimately mean no more mountains to climb.

In some ways I've found that end goals can be a dead-end. When you achieve an end goal—the sale of a property, a certain net worth, retiring all your debt—no matter how ambitious that goal was and how hard you worked to achieve it, there can be an emotional let-down. Unless you have something else to pull you forward that is equal to the goal that you've just accomplished, you can lose your edge. My father was an example of this. As a young man Dad won gold, silver, and bronze Olympic medals in swimming, then he came home to Indiana and became a banker. I saw my dad stretching and reaching in different directions when I was growing up, but he never seemed to be completely happy. He certainly never found something that drove him as much as the Olympic swimming had. Sadly, he died in a plane crash in 1992.

The philosopher Anthony de Mello once wrote something about the perils of standing still, that human beings would cease to live if we didn't continually seek out some sense of uncertainty and challenge. Far too many people cease to live long before they stop breathing, simply because they stop seeking the next challenge, the next step in their growth. The Maverick approach is built upon the premise that you will always be looking for the next step up: the next property that's a little better than the one before, the next way you can stretch your own boundaries and achieve greater success by doing so. Following the Maverick approach will help you develop a set of risk muscles, evaluation muscles, work muscles, brand muscles, and selling muscles that will itch to be used. Every success, from your first fixer-upper to your multimillion-dollar properties, can produce a high that you'll crave the next time. But more important, you'll develop the desire for the joy that comes from the journey and the growth you experience in pursuit of each deal.

FACING THE ULTIMATE TEST: BADWATER, DEATH VALLEY

In the previous chapter I talked about building your risk tolerance both in your business and by seeking out challenges in other areas. In July 2004, when I was getting ready to sell the $7 million and $17 million properties, and to buy the property that we would ask $50 million for, my next great challenge showed up on a family vacation—an old-fashioned 2,000-mile road trip in my 1991 pickup truck, going from Colorado through Arizona, Nevada, and California. I've always been fascinated by extreme experiences and the intensity of living one feels at those times. I had looked up the hottest spot in the country and, sure enough, in July that was Death Valley. That's where I wanted to go! So, after spending two nights at the Grand Canyon and another two in Las Vegas, Nilsa, Laura, my mom, and I drove into Death Valley at around noon. As soon as we got out of the car, I felt the most beautiful sensation of furnace-type heat caressing my body. It was intoxicating. I told Nilsa, Laura, and my mom, "You go eat lunch, I'm going for a run; I've got to experience this."

I had already gone for a run in Las Vegas early that morning, but out I went and hit the road. Blow-dryer-type heat slapped me in the face. I'm used to running in Florida's 80 percent humidity; Death Valley averages between 3 percent and 5 percent. I was unaware that water was being sucked from my every pore. I ran for about three miles, then turned around and headed back. I was in pretty bad shape when I got to the hotel, probably on the verge of a heat stroke, but the run was an awesome experience. Once I had cooled down and gotten rehydrated, I went to the little general store to buy some Gatorade, bananas, and water so I could recover and run again the next day. The checkout clerk, who looked like an old miner, noticed I was flushed and asked if I was okay.

"Yeah, I was out running and got a little overheated," I told him.

"You know, you must be in last place in the race," he said.

"What race?" I asked.

"The Badwater 135," he told me. "Starts at Badwater, the lowest place in the United States, 282 feet below sea level. About 80 people run 135 miles nonstop, across Death Valley and up the side of Mount Whitney, the tallest mountain in the continental United States, to about 9,000 feet. According to *National Geographic* it's the toughest footrace in the world."

After that, I couldn't get Badwater out of my mind. I came back to Florida and started learning everything I could about the race and the cultlike sport of ultramarathoning. Only a very few athletes run these races, which can be anywhere from 32 miles, 50 miles, 100 kilometers, 100 miles, and a few over the 100-mile mark. Badwater is an invitation-only race. You must qualify to apply by having already run other ultramarathons. Of the hundreds who apply, only 90 people are invited, about 75 to 80 actually run, and only 60 percent of those complete the race. You must finish the race in less than 60 hours of nonstop running in 120- to 130-degree heat. There are no aid stations en route; you have to provide your own support crew and van. I looked at the information about Badwater for more than two months, while I had three mansions on the market. I'm not going to make a commitment and not see it through to the end, so I thought, "If my properties sell and all the stars line up, I'll go for it." Now, that was highly unlikely. But by the grace of God, by September 13 all of our inventory had sold, so I sent an e-mail to Lisa Smith Batchen, a top running coach who has finished Badwater seven times, asking her to take me on.

The next step was to qualify before the application deadline at the end of the year. I signed up for a 100-mile race in Ohio on November 6. I had six weeks to prepare. Now, I was a tennis pro and I've been a runner for years, but the longest run I'd ever done at that point was 13 miles. I'd never even run a marathon, and here I was getting ready to run the equivalent of four marathons in a row, with the goal of qualifying for Badwater, which clocked in at more than five marathons in length in average temperatures of 125 degrees!

That 100-mile race was the hardest thing I'd done in my life to that point. The race was on a nine-mile loop around a lake in the middle of Amish country. At mile 30 I broke down. I thought, "What am I doing this for? I could be semiretired. I should be sitting on a beach in Tahiti. I don't need to be putting myself through this." At that point one of the aid workers, a 76-year-old little guy by the name of Leo, saw past the sunglasses that shielded my true feelings and noticed the tears streaming down my cheeks. He stepped out on the course and said, "Hey, I need to train for my next marathon. Do you mind if I run with you for a while?" I wasn't very nice to him; in fact, I was pretty negative: "Yeah, whatever, but I'm not going very fast." For the next 18 miles that 76-year-old took my mind off my frailty, my failures, and my breakdown, and helped me get past the wall that every ultramarathoner faces. At mile 48 he said, "Okay, Frank, I'm done now—good luck," and he peeled off. What a great soul!

At mile 70 I hit the wall again, and this time it was Nilsa who was there at every aid station, telling me, "You're going to make it," giving me water, electrolytes, supplements, and different kinds of liquid nutrition. I finished that race in 23 hours, 23 minutes, 3 seconds; it's unheard-of to finish your first 100-mile race in less than 24 hours, especially with six weeks of training. My body collapsed after that race and I had to ride to the airport in an ambulance. It was two weeks before I could even run a mile, and a month before I could get back to decent training. In that unforgettable day I learned about the necessity of relentless forward motion, to keep moving no matter what.

That lesson would stand me in good stead over the next few months as I prepared for Badwater. I sent my application in January 15, 2005. In it, I wrote, "For me the competition will be against myself, not other racers. I deeply desire to experience the most challenging and toughest footrace in the world, and triumph against the inner demons that will try to prevent me from finishing." I got my acceptance notification on January 28, 2005.

I knew, however, that I wasn't going to be satisfied with doing this race for myself; I wanted to use the race to invite people to share their blessings. I decided to turn Badwater into a fundraiser for the Caring House Project Foundation and Badwater's official charity, the Challenged Athletes Foundation. Our press release read, "Frank McKinney Challenges Death! (Death Valley, that is) in the Ultimate Foot Race!" (Thanks to my brother Bob for that headline.) I invited people to sponsor my run at various levels. My goal was to raise $300,000 in pledges. I put it in very simple terms: For $30 a mile, someone could build a whole house; for $10 a mile, the foundation; $4 a mile would buy the walls; $2 a mile the roofing materials; and a dollar a mile the windows.

At the same time, I was preparing for the race itself. I brought to bear every lesson I've ever learned from real estate. I knew I would need incredible discipline over the months of preparation and training required for the race. Instead of a "progression to closing" plan, I created a detailed "progression to the finish line" plan. I brought together a superb crew for my support team. (One of the greatest lessons of Badwater was the importance of topnotch support. I gathered the best people from all over the world—Lisa, my coach, Jay Batchen, Mary Kashurba, Joe Kashurba, and Mike Magistein—along with Nilsa and Mark Bernardi, my assistant, to help prepare me and crew the race. At the same time, I knew that it was my race to run, so I was actively involved in the choice of the team, assigning roles, designing the preparation, and so on.) I made sure to crank up the marketing and selling of the race because I believed Badwater could add another dimension to the Frank McKinney brand, by branching out into uncharted territory of conquering, challenging, and succeeding at a higher level. And of course, I tied the entire race to my commitment to share my blessings with others.

Lisa set up a rigorous training schedule for me, which included running nearly 100 miles every week, using a treadmill in a 175-degree dry sauna with huge fans (to accustom my body to the desiccation of the dry desert winds), and undergoing a grueling cross-training regimen to strengthen every system of my body. I also ran one other marathon in Miami as a short tune-up race (I did it in 3:43, in the top 20 percent of finishers). I didn't even let an emergency appendectomy in February slow me down; the day after I left the hospital I walked four miles. (I also learned how quickly you can lose muscle mass when you stop your relentless forward motion. What with running the Miami marathon, a stomach virus, and the hospital stay, I lost 15 pounds.) We had a planning retreat for the entire team in Florida in March. Then in April and May we went out to the Badwater site, to test the terrain and get used to the heat, lack of humidity, and altitude, to run different parts of the course, and see what kinds of fluids and supplements would work best.

At six o'clock in the morning on July 11, 2005, in the middle of Death Valley, I took my first step on the Badwater course. With me were 80 other racers from 23 states and 12 countries. Forty or so of us were first-timers. The youngest racer was 28, the oldest 70; I just about split the difference at age 42. At 6 A.M. it was fairly cool, under 100 degrees. By the end of the race, we had experienced a high of 131 degrees on the course. Others measured temperatures of 137; one German team took a reading just above the newly paved asphalt and it read an astounding 203 degrees.

Badwater seemed less like a race than a timeless, pure experi-ence. Many times it was absolute agony; waves of nausea and dizziness overtook me, and my team covered me with cold towels and iced me down until I could continue. I suffered from sleep deprivation; I'd never stayed awake that long at one stretch. I sank to the depths of physical, mental, and emotional debilitation only to roll out of the van and run a few more miles. "Relentless forward motion" was my mantra. My support crew were astound-ing: Jay, Mary, and Mike paced me as I ran; Mary also aided with medical; Mark and Joe prepared drinks and supplements and did anything and everything that was needed. Lisa, my coach, talked me through my lowest points via satellite phone. And al-ways there was Nilsa; it was her pretty face I would try to focus on as I ran or pulled myself up from the floor of the van to get out on the course again.

One very special moment came at mile 105. I'd been through my worst point yet at mile 98, and it had taken my entire crew to coax me out on the course again. That's when my mother, Katie, and my daughter Laura came driving up behind me as I was struggling down a straightaway that seemed like it terminated beyond the horizon. They both walked a few blocks with me, giving my spirits a lift just when I needed it most.

One of my goals for the race was to enjoy the moment and not focus only upon the finish line. In this, the desert was both my foe and my ally. My focus always had to be "the next step—take the next step—keep moving." I couldn't focus on my body because I would have quit instantly. Yet again and again the extreme beauty of nature burst into my awareness. I looked forward to the sunsets for the beauty and the coming drop in temperature. I saw night skies that were more white than black, with countless stars and distant galaxies. Every time I looked up I saw shooting stars by the dozens.

As the sun rose and the canyons and mountains reappeared, my spirits and my energy level would rise. The majestic colors of the sunrise served as my morning cup of coffee and kept me going just a little longer.

The last 13 miles of the course climbed from 3,500 to 8,500 feet, up a steep grade with multiple switchbacks to slow my progress. I started the climb at 3 A.M. walking, not running. When the sun rose at 5 A.M. (our third sunrise of the race) I could see the long, snaking highway disappearing behind me over another range of hills—the road I had run the day before. The entire crew came out on the course with me and, joined by my mom and daughter, we crossed the finish line as a team 48 hours, 49 minutes, and 20 seconds since my first step. That moment I was overwhelmed with crystalline pure jubilation. We all joined hands and thanked God for the strength, courage, patience, and enlightenment that had gotten us to that point. In total I took more than 200,000 steps, drank 13 gallons of liquid, went through 3 pairs of shoes (we had to cut the sides out of one pair due to the extreme swelling of my feet), and took more than 100 electrolyte replacement tablets. I hit lower points than I ever have in my life, and achieved heights that I never dreamed were possible.

My coach, Lisa, told me that after Badwater my life would be forever changed, and she was right. I discovered new characteristics within my body and soul; some I was happy about, others I resolved to improve. I learned the vital importance of health—without it we are nothing. I learned anew the need for a strong support crew. I treasure my family, especially Nilsa and Laura, even more deeply. But the real rewards of Badwater have come from sharing these critical success lessons with the people I know, with those less fortunate, with those in the audience at my appearances, and now with you. Every lesson, every aspect of the Maverick approach has been magnified and enhanced through my experience. That truly is the reason for my own quest for the upward spiral. I put myself through life tests like Badwater and building $100-million-plus spec houses because they make me stronger as a man and as an example. Only when I can say, "I've done it," do I feel I can ask others to do the same.

None of this comes naturally to me, and I suspect it doesn't to you. I've created my life, and this Maverick personality, through diligent application and hard work. You can do the same as long as you're willing to put in the effort. My hope is that because I'm passing along 20 years of life lessons that your journey will be a little shorter and easier—but not too much. The last few miles of Badwater were uphill, not down; they made the finish line all the sweeter. Part of the requirement and the joy of the upward spiral is the effort of overcoming the odds. Never stand still or rest upon your laurels. True Mavericks are always looking for the next turn in the upward spiral of their development, whether it be the next deal or the next goal or the next challenge. With each challenge that you meet, your opportunities will expand along with your capacity. Remember the mantra, "relentless forward motion," and apply it to every part of your life.

CREATING AN ENDURING LEGACY

In my first book, *Make It BIG!*, I talked about the rocking chair test. Imagine you're eighty or ninety years old, sitting in a rocking chair on a porch somewhere, reviewing your life. What will be important to you? What do you think you'll be remembered for? What will you be proud of when you look back over your life? What legacy do you want to leave? When you're first getting started, this is a test you should take on a regular basis, as it will help direct the course of your career.

"Legacy" is a big word, and it represents a lot of time put into developing and nurturing a career and a brand. I certainly remember wanting to leave some kind of legacy in the world. But even after 20 years, I'm still not thinking in terms of legacy because I don't spend a lot of time looking back. I have a tray in my office that holds many recent press clippings about my projects, books, and appearances, but I read everything only once. I never reread to look back and relive; there will be plenty of time for that with my grandchildren. I also feel there's so much more I have to do. But I can look around the little part of South Florida where I've concentrated my efforts, see how the parts of Palm Beach County where I bought my first fixer-uppers have improved, and feel proud of being part of that transformation. I can look around at the magnificent estates I've created, and know that I've set new standards for this part of the world. More important to me, I can look at the scores of houses the Caring House Project Foundation has built in Florida, Haiti, Honduras, Nicaragua, and Indonesia, and be grateful that my brand and hard work, combined with the generosity of our donors and board members, caused that to happen.

You create a legacy through the upward spiral, seeking greater and greater challenges, learning bigger lessons, and reaping larger rewards. When you continue on the upward spiral, after a time it becomes like the vortex of a tornado, spinning ever quicker as you get to the center. But for the upward spiral to kick in, you must put what you have learned in this book to use. Remember the day you were online or in a bookstore looking through 25 different real estate books, and you chose this one? You've come a long way since that moment of choice. If you've read through the book, you have your road map to become a Maverick real estate investor. Now you must take action. Jump in, just do it, take the risks that set the Mavericks apart from the herd. I've done everything I can to lay out a path for you to follow. The course is laid out and I'm happy to be part of your support crew, but your feet are the ones that must run the long road that disappears over the horizon of the Maverick approach. Then one day you'll have enough material for your own book, and I'll be happy to have played a small role in your success.

One final word: When I was running through the Death Valley desert, in so much pain that every step felt like my last on earth, the one thing that kept me going was the images of the people who would be helped by my efforts and the contributions of hundreds of others. My thoughts turned into a prayer:

I can suffer for a few more hours for those who spend a lifetime suffering.
I can stomach another saltine or gel for those who have nothing to eat.
I can shelter myself in this van for a few more minutes only to get going for those who have no shelter.
I can be sick once more for those who are so often due to malnutrition.

It was the thought of the homeless in Haiti, Indonesia, Honduras, Nicaragua, and here at home that kept me going. I believe that your most important legacy won't be the houses you build or even the financial net worth you accumulate, but the contributions you make to others. The world should be a better place for your having walked upon it. That's the real legacy of every human being, famous or unknown, successful or just getting by. My goal is for you to feel truly wealthy—emotionally, financially, and spiritually—because you've lived life as a Maverick on your own terms and done well in the process. May God bless you as you start on your journey with the Maverick approach.

INDEX

OTHER OFFERINGS
by Frank McKinney

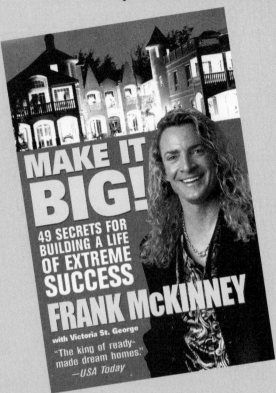

MAKE IT BIG!

49 Secrets for Building a Life of Extreme Success

John Wiley & Sons, Inc.
$27.95 USA; Cloth;
ISBN:0-471-44399-9
wiley.com

FRANK MCKINNEY'S SUCCEEDING IN THE BUSINESS OF LIFE—THE SERIES™

12 hour audio/video series
frank-mckinney.com

FRANK MCKINNEY'S MAVERICK APPROACH TO REAL ESTATE SUCCESS—THE SERIES™

10 hour audio/video series
frank-mckinney.com

THE FRANK MCKINNEY EXPERIENCE—CARING HOUSE PROJECT FOUNDATION

One-on-One or group Experience
frank-mckinney.com

Other offerings

frank-mckinney.com
benefiting the Caring House Project Foundation (CHPF.org)